# 100 CLASSIC HIKES
# ARIZONA

## 100 CLASSIC HIKES

# ARIZONA

**4th Edition**

### SCOTT S. WARREN

Grand Canyon | Colorado Plateau | San Francisco Peaks
Mogollon Rim | Sedona | Sky Islands | Sonoran Desert

MOUNTAINEERS
BOOKS

**MOUNTAINEERS BOOKS**

Mountaineers Books is the publishing division of The Mountaineers, an organization founded in 1906 and dedicated to the exploration, preservation, and enjoyment of outdoor and wilderness areas.

1001 SW Klickitat Way, Suite 201, Seattle, WA 98134
800.553.4453, www.mountaineersbooks.org

Printed in China
Distributed in the United Kingdom by Cordee, www.cordee.co.uk
First edition: 1994. Second edition: 2000. Third edition: 2007. Fourth edition: 2015.

Copy Editor: Heath Lynn Silberfeld/enough said
Book Design: Kate Basart
Layout: Jennifer Shontz, www.redshoedesign.com
Cartographer: Scott S. Warren
All photographs by the author.
Cover photograph: *Sunrise in Sunset Crater Volcano National Monument*
Frontispiece: *A backpacker in the Narrows of Paria River Canyon*

*Library of Congress Cataloging-in-Publication Data*
Warren, Scott S.
    100 classic hikes in Arizona : grand Canyon, Colorado Plateau, San Francisco Peaks,
Mogollon Rim, Sedona, Sky Islands, Sonoran Desert / Scott S. Warren. – 4th edition.
        pages    cm
    ISBN 978-1-59485-907-6 (trade paper)—ISBN 978-1-59485-908-3 (ebook)
1. Hiking—Arizona—Guidebooks. 2. Trails—Arizona—Guidebooks. 3. Arizona—
Guidebooks. I. Title. II. Title: One hundred classic hikes in Arizona.
    GV199.42.A7W37 2015
    796.5109791—dc23

                                                    2015007257

Mountaineers Books titles may be purchased for corporate, educational, or other promotional sales, and our authors are available for a wide range of events. For information on special discounts or booking an author, contact our customer service at 800-553-4453 or mbooks@mountaineersbooks.org.

ISBN (paper): 978-1-59485-907-6
ISBN (ebook): 978-1-59485-908-3

# Contents

Hikes at a Glance . . . . . . . . . . . . . . . . . . . . . . . 7
Locator Map . . . . . . . . . . . . . . . . . . . . . . . . . 10
Introduction . . . . . . . . . . . . . . . . . . . . . . . . . 11

## *Colorado Plateau*

1. Bright Angel Trail . . . . . . . . . . . . . . . . . 24
2. Tonto Trail . . . . . . . . . . . . . . . . . . . . . . . 27
3. Dripping Springs . . . . . . . . . . . . . . . . . . 30
4. Clear Creek . . . . . . . . . . . . . . . . . . . . . . 32
5. North Kaibab Trail . . . . . . . . . . . . . . . . . 35
6. Widforss Trail . . . . . . . . . . . . . . . . . . . . 37
7. Uncle Jim Trail . . . . . . . . . . . . . . . . . . . 38
8. Kanab Creek . . . . . . . . . . . . . . . . . . . . . 40
9. Mount Trumbull . . . . . . . . . . . . . . . . . . 43
10. Havasu Canyon . . . . . . . . . . . . . . . . . . . 44
11. Paria River Canyon . . . . . . . . . . . . . . . . 47
12. Spencer Trail . . . . . . . . . . . . . . . . . . . . . 50
13. Soap Creek . . . . . . . . . . . . . . . . . . . . . . 52
14. Onyx Bridge . . . . . . . . . . . . . . . . . . . . . 54
15. Keet Seel . . . . . . . . . . . . . . . . . . . . . . . 56
16. White House Ruin . . . . . . . . . . . . . . . . . 58
17. Mount Elden Lookout . . . . . . . . . . . . . . 60
18. Abineau/Bear Jaw Loop . . . . . . . . . . . . 62
19. Humphreys Peak . . . . . . . . . . . . . . . . . 64
20. Kachina Trail . . . . . . . . . . . . . . . . . . . . 66
21. Inner Basin . . . . . . . . . . . . . . . . . . . . . . 68
22. Lenox Crater . . . . . . . . . . . . . . . . . . . . 70
23. Walnut Canyon . . . . . . . . . . . . . . . . . . . 71
24. Red Mountain . . . . . . . . . . . . . . . . . . . 73
25. Kendrick Mountain . . . . . . . . . . . . . . . . 75
26. Bill Williams Mountain . . . . . . . . . . . . . 77
27. Sycamore Rim . . . . . . . . . . . . . . . . . . . 79

## *Central Highlands*

28. West Fork Oak Creek . . . . . . . . . . . . . . 82
29. Wilson Mountain . . . . . . . . . . . . . . . . . 84
30. Vultee Arch . . . . . . . . . . . . . . . . . . . . . 87
31. Airport Loop . . . . . . . . . . . . . . . . . . . . 89
32. Boynton Canyon . . . . . . . . . . . . . . . . . 91
33. Courthouse Butte Loop . . . . . . . . . . . . 93
34. Secret Mountain . . . . . . . . . . . . . . . . . 95
35. Jacks Canyon . . . . . . . . . . . . . . . . . . . 97
36. Parsons Spring . . . . . . . . . . . . . . . . . . 99
37. Wet Beaver Creek . . . . . . . . . . . . . . . 101
38. West Clear Creek . . . . . . . . . . . . . . . . 103
39. Woodchute Mountain . . . . . . . . . . . . . 105
40. Granite Mountain . . . . . . . . . . . . . . . . 107
41. Thumb Butte Loop . . . . . . . . . . . . . . . 109
42. Groom Creek Loop . . . . . . . . . . . . . . . 111
43. Pine Mountain . . . . . . . . . . . . . . . . . . 113
44. Fossil Springs . . . . . . . . . . . . . . . . . . 115
45. Horton Creek . . . . . . . . . . . . . . . . . . . 118
46. Indian Spring Trail . . . . . . . . . . . . . . . 120
47. Mount Baldy . . . . . . . . . . . . . . . . . . . 122
48. Escudilla Mountain . . . . . . . . . . . . . . . 125
49. P-Bar Lake . . . . . . . . . . . . . . . . . . . . . 127
50. Bonanza Bill–Tige Rim Loop . . . . . . . . 129
51. Bear Wallow . . . . . . . . . . . . . . . . . . . . 132
52. Painted Bluff . . . . . . . . . . . . . . . . . . . 134

## Central Deserts

53. Piestewa Peak . . . . . . . . . . . . . . . . . . . . 138
54. Hidden Valley . . . . . . . . . . . . . . . . . . . 140
55. Badger Springs Trail. . . . . . . . . . . . . . 141
56. Black Canyon Trail . . . . . . . . . . . . . . 144
57. Cave Creek. . . . . . . . . . . . . . . . . . . . . 146
58. Pass Mountain Loop . . . . . . . . . . . . . 148
59. Treasure Loop . . . . . . . . . . . . . . . . . . 151
60. Butcher Jones . . . . . . . . . . . . . . . . . . 153
61. McDowell Mountain Park . . . . . . . . . 155
62. The Boulders . . . . . . . . . . . . . . . . . . . 157
63. Browns Saddle. . . . . . . . . . . . . . . . . . 159
64. Mazatzal Peak Loop. . . . . . . . . . . . . . 161
65. Upper Cliff Dwelling. . . . . . . . . . . . . 163
66. Hieroglyphic Canyon . . . . . . . . . . . . . 165
67. Peralta Trail . . . . . . . . . . . . . . . . . . . 167
68. Dutchman's Trail . . . . . . . . . . . . . . . . 169
69. Oak Flat. . . . . . . . . . . . . . . . . . . . . . . 172
70. Icehouse Canyon . . . . . . . . . . . . . . . .174
71. Picacho Peak . . . . . . . . . . . . . . . . . . . 177

## Southeastern Basin and Range

72. Wasson Peak . . . . . . . . . . . . . . . . . . . 180
73. Brown Mountain. . . . . . . . . . . . . . . . . 182
74. Bridal Wreath Falls . . . . . . . . . . . . . 185
75. Seven Falls . . . . . . . . . . . . . . . . . . . . 187

76. Sabino Canyon . . . . . . . . . . . . . . . . . . 189
77. Finger Rock Canyon . . . . . . . . . . . . . 191
78. Romero Canyon . . . . . . . . . . . . . . . . . 193
79. Green Mountain. . . . . . . . . . . . . . . . . 196
80. Aspen Loop . . . . . . . . . . . . . . . . . . . . 198
81. Bog Springs . . . . . . . . . . . . . . . . . . . 200
82. Mount Wrightson . . . . . . . . . . . . . . . 203
83. Cochise Trail . . . . . . . . . . . . . . . . . . . 206
84. Heart of Rocks . . . . . . . . . . . . . . . . . . 207
85. Echo Canyon . . . . . . . . . . . . . . . . . . . 210
86. Chiricahua Peak. . . . . . . . . . . . . . . . . 212
87. South Fork Cave Creek . . . . . . . . . . . 215
88. Rucker Canyon . . . . . . . . . . . . . . . . . 216
89. Pole Bridge Canyon. . . . . . . . . . . . . . 218
90. Fort Bowie. . . . . . . . . . . . . . . . . . . . . 220
91. Arcadia National Recreation Trail . . . 222
92. Powers Garden . . . . . . . . . . . . . . . . . 224

## Western Deserts

93. Vulture Peak . . . . . . . . . . . . . . . . . . . 228
94. Margies Cove . . . . . . . . . . . . . . . . . . 230
95. Harquahala Peak . . . . . . . . . . . . . . . 232
96. Ben Avery Trail. . . . . . . . . . . . . . . . . 234
97. Bull Pasture . . . . . . . . . . . . . . . . . . . 236
98. Palm Canyon . . . . . . . . . . . . . . . . . . 238
99. Hualapai Mountain Park . . . . . . . . . . 240
100. Arizona Hot Spring . . . . . . . . . . . . . . 242

Appendix A:
   Land Management Agencies . . . . . . . . 245
Appendix B:
   Further Reading . . . . . . . . . . . . . . . . 249
Index. . . . . . . . . . . . . . . . . . . . . . . . . . . . . . 251

# Hikes at a Glance

| NO. | NAME | DIFFICULTY | SEASON | HIGHLIGHTS |
|---|---|---|---|---|
| **HALF–DAY HIKES** | | | | |
| 3 | Dripping Springs | moderate | All year | deep canyon |
| 7 | Uncle Jim Trail | easy | May–Oct | plateau top, canyons |
| 9 | Mount Trumbull | moderate | Apr–Nov | forested mountain |
| 12 | Spencer Trail | strenuous | All year | viewpoint, desert |
| 14 | Onyx Bridge | easy | All year | desert, petrified wood |
| 16 | White House Ruin | moderate | All year | canyon, prehistoric ruins |
| 21 | Inner Basin | moderate | Jun–Oct | forests, mountain vistas |
| 22 | Lenox Crater | easy | May–Nov | geology, mountain scenery |
| 23 | Walnut Canyon | easy | Apr–Nov | shallow canyon |
| 24 | Red Mountain | easy | Apr–Nov | geology |
| 30 | Vultee Arch | easy | All year | natural arch |
| 31 | Airport Loop | easy | All year | redrock scenery |
| 32 | Boynton Canyon | easy | All year | canyon scenery |
| 33 | Courthouse Butte Loop | easy | All year | redrock scenery |
| 37 | Wet Beaver Creek | easy | All year | canyon, riparian life |
| 41 | Thumb Butte Loop | moderate | All year | geology, scenery |
| 49 | P-Bar Lake | easy | Jun–Oct | forests, small riparian area |
| 53 | Piestewa Peak | strenuous | Oct–May | desert mountains, scenery |
| 54 | Hidden Valley | easy | Oct–May | desert valley, cactus |
| 55 | Badger Springs Trail | easy | Oct–May | desert canyons, riparian life |
| 56 | Black Canyon Trail | easy | Oct–May | desert canyon, riparian life |
| 59 | Treasure Loop | easy | Oct–May | desert scenery, cactus |
| 60 | Butcher Jones | easy | Oct–May | desert scenery, lake views |
| 61 | McDowell Mountain Park | easy | Oct–May | desert scenery, burn area |
| 63 | Browns Saddle | moderate | Apr–Nov | mountain scenery |
| 65 | Upper Cliff Dwelling | moderate | Nov–May | desert scenery, cliff dwellings |
| 66 | Hieroglyphic Canyon | easy | Oct–May | desert scenery, petroglyphs |
| 67 | Peralta Trail | moderate | Oct–May | desert scenery, history |
| 69 | Oak Flat | easy | All year | canyon sceneray, riparian life |
| 73 | Brown Mountain | moderate | Oct–May | desert scenery, cactus |
| 74 | Bridal Wreath Falls | moderate | Oct–May | desert scenery, cactus, waterfall |
| 75 | Seven Falls | moderate | Oct–May | desert canyon, riparian |
| 80 | Aspen Loop | easy | May–Nov | forested mountain terrain |

| NO. | NAME | DIFFICULTY | SEASON | HIGHLIGHTS |
|---|---|---|---|---|
| 85 | Echo Canyon | moderate | All year | geology, vistas |
| 87 | South Fork Cave Creek | easy | All year | riparian area, forests |
| 89 | Pole Bridge Canyon | strenuous | May–Nov | forested mountains |
| 90 | Fort Bowie | easy | All year | upland desert, history |
| 93 | Vulture Peak | strenuous | Oct–May | desert mountains. cactus |
| 96 | Ben Avery Trail | easy | Oct–Apr | desert scenery, rock art |
| 97 | Bull Pasture | moderate | Oct–Apr | desert mountain. cactus |
| 98 | Palm Canyon | easy | Oct–Apr | desert mountains, botany |
| 99 | Hualapai Mountain Park | moderate | May–Oct | mountain scenery |

## SHORT DAY HIKES

| NO. | NAME | DIFFICULTY | SEASON | HIGHLIGHTS |
|---|---|---|---|---|
| 6 | Widforss Trail | easy | May–Oct | plateau top, canyons |
| 17 | Mount Elden Lookout | strenuous | May–Oct | fire tower, vistas |
| 18 | Abineau/Bear Jaw Loop | strenuous | Jun–Sep | forests, mountain vistas |
| 25 | Kendrick Mountain | strenuous | May–Sep | forests, fire tower |
| 26 | Bill Williams Mountain | strenuous | May–Sep | forests, fire tower |
| 28 | West Fork Oak Creek | easy | All year | deep, sinuous canyon |
| 36 | Parsons Spring | easy | All year | riparian community |
| 39 | Woodchute Mountain | moderate | Apr–Nov | forests, vistas |
| 40 | Granite Mountain | moderate | Apr–Nov | geology, scenery |
| 48 | Escudilla Mountain | moderate | Jun–Oct | forests, scenery, burn area |
| 58 | Pass Mountain Loop | moderate | Oct–May | desert scenery, cactus |
| 62 | The Boulders | moderate | Oct–May | desert scenery, cactus |
| 71 | Picacho Peak | strenuous | Oct–May | rugged desert peak |
| 72 | Wasson Peak | strenuous | Oct–May | desert mountains, cactus |
| 76 | Sabino Canyon | moderate | Oct–May | desert canyon, riparian life |
| 79 | Green Mountain | moderate | Apr–Nov | forested mountain terrain |
| 81 | Bog Springs | moderate | All year | forests, riparian areas |
| 83 | Cochise Trail | moderate | All year | mountains, history |
| 84 | Heart of Rocks | moderate | All year | geology, canyons |
| 88 | Rucker Canyon | strenuous | May–Nov | riparian, forests, scenery |
| 100 | Arizona Hot Spring | moderate | Oct–May | desert canyon, hot spring |

## LONG DAY HIKES

| NO. | NAME | DIFFICULTY | SEASON | HIGHLIGHTS |
|---|---|---|---|---|
| 13 | Soap Creek | strenuous | All year | sinuous canyon |
| 19 | Humphreys Peak | strenuous | Jun–Sep | forests, alpine tundra, scenery |
| 20 | Kachina Trail | moderate | Jun–Oct | forests. mountain vistas |
| 27 | Sycamore Rim | moderate | Apr–Nov | plateau top, nice meadows |

| NO. | NAME | DIFFICULTY | SEASON | HIGHLIGHTS |
|---|---|---|---|---|
| 29 | Wilson Mountain | strenuous | Mar–Nov | redrock scenery |
| 35 | Jacks Canyon | strenuous | Mar–Nov | canyon country, vistas |
| 38 | West Clear Creek | moderate | All year | canyon bottom |
| 42 | Groom Creek Loop | moderate | May–Nov | forests, fire tower |
| 43 | Pine Mountain | moderate | All year | forests, vistas |
| 44 | Fossil Springs | moderate | All year | canyon scenery, riparian life |
| 45 | Horton Creek | strenuous | May–Nov | riparian life, forests |
| 46 | Indian Spring Trail | easy | May–Oct | forests, meadows |
| 47 | Mount Baldy | strenuous | Jun–Oct | subalpine forests, meadows |
| 50 | Bonanza Bill–Tige Rim Loop | strenuous | May–Nov | forests, scenic vistas |
| 52 | Painted Bluff | strenuous | All year | rugged scenery, forests |
| 57 | Cave Creek | moderate | Oct–May | riparian and desert life |
| 70 | Icehouse Canyon | strenuous | Mar–Nov | forests, vistas |
| 77 | Finger Rock Canyon | strenuous | All year | desert canyon, cactus |
| 78 | Romero Canyon | strenuous | All year | desert canyons, vistas |
| 82 | Mount Wrightson | strenuous | Apr–Nov | forests, vistas, summit |
| 86 | Chiricahua Peak | moderate | May–Oct | forests, mountain vistas |
| 91 | Arcadia National Recreation Trail | strenuous | May–Oct | forests, vistas |
| 94 | Margies Cove | easy | Oct–May | desert basins, cactus |
| 95 | Harquahala Peak | strenuous | Oct–May | desert mountains, history |

## SHORT BACKPACKS

| NO. | NAME | DIFFICULTY | SEASON | HIGHLIGHTS |
|---|---|---|---|---|
| 1 | Bright Angel Trail | strenuous | All year | deep canyon |
| 10 | Havasu Canyon | strenuous | All year | deep canyon |
| 15 | Keet Seel | strenuous | May–Sep | canyon, prehistoric ruins |
| 34 | Secret Mountain | strenuous | Apr–Nov | redrock vistas, forests |
| 51 | Bear Wallow | moderate | May–Oct | forests, riparian areas |
| 64 | Mazatzal Peak Loop | strenuous | Mar–Nov | desert mountains, vistas |
| 92 | Powers Garden | strenuous | All year | mountains, history |

## EXTENDED BACKPACKS

| NO. | NAME | DIFFICULTY | SEASON | HIGHLIGHTS |
|---|---|---|---|---|
| 2 | Tonto Trail | strenuous | All year | deep canyon |
| 4 | Clear Creek | strenuous | All year | deep canyon |
| 5 | North Kaibab Trail | strenuous | May–Oct | deep canyon |
| 8 | Kanab Creek | strenuous | All year | deep canyon, desert |
| 11 | Paria River Canyon | moderate | Apr–Nov | deep canyon, desert |
| 68 | Dutchman's Trail | strenuous | Oct–May | desert scenery, history |

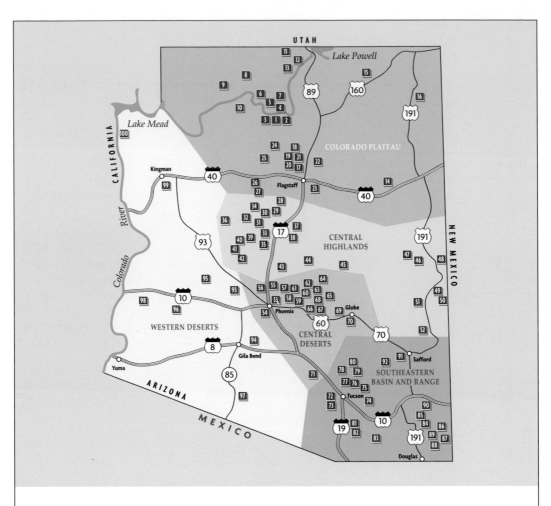

## LEGEND

| | | | | |
|---|---|---|---|---|
| Paved Road | (40) | Interstate | ← | Direction of Travel |
| Gravel Road | (191) | US Highway | ] [ | Bridge |
| 4WD Road | (39) | State Highway | ∿º | Spring |
| Featured Trail | [503] | Forest Road | ■ | Building |
| Cross-Country Route | ) ( | Pass/Saddle | ⚒ | Mining Camp / Mine |
| Other Trail | 🅣 | Trailhead | ⊼ | Picnic Area |
| Wilderness Boundary | ▲ | Campground | ▲ | Peak |

# Introduction

*Few, if any, states can match the variety of backcountry terrain that Arizona has* to offer. From arid deserts and lush riverside thickets to tall stands of conifer and alpine tundra, Arizona has it all. For the hiker and backpacker, this diversity, combined with the many trails that have been established in Arizona's outback over many years, translates into a vast and interesting array of backcountry excursions from which to choose.

## TOPOGRAPHY

Undoubtedly, it is Arizona's topography that accounts for its greatly varied terrain. Geographers identify two primary provinces in Arizona: the Colorado Plateau Province and the Basin and Range Province. Stretching across the northern and northeastern third of the state, the *Colorado Plateau Province* is an expansive uplift that extends into Utah, Colorado, and New Mexico.

This is a land sliced by deep canyons and spiked by red rock mesas and scattered mountain ranges. Carved over millions of years by the Colorado River, the Grand Canyon cuts across the northwestern quarter of the state; the San Francisco Peaks reach dramatic heights near the city of Flagstaff. The more expansive White Mountains rise along the Arizona–New Mexico border to the east, and a grand escarpment known as

Saguaro cactus at dusk along the Ben Avery Trail

the Mogollon Rim borders the Colorado Plateau for hundreds of miles along its southern end. Elevations in the Colorado Plateau Province range from 1200 feet in the bottom of the Grand Canyon to 12,633 feet in the San Francisco Peaks.

South and west of the Mogollon Rim is the *Basin and Range Province* which features expansive desert basins that are repeatedly interrupted by sharply rising mountain ranges. Changes in topography are rather sudden here. Climatic variations are equally impressive, as some of the continent's most arid deserts quickly give way to cool, tree-topped summits. Known as "sky islands," these mountain ranges often feature a biological profile typical of more moderate latitudes to the north. Among the most notable of these ranges are the Mazatzals and the Superstitions near Phoenix, the Santa Catalinas and the Rincons near Tucson, and the Chiricahuas and the Pinaleños in the southeastern portion of the state. Elevations in the Basin and Range Province extend from 70 feet in the southwest corner of the state to nearly 11,000 feet in the Pinaleño Mountains.

## CLIMATE

Because Arizona's topography extends from nearly sea level to above 12,000 feet, the state features an incredible diversity of climates. Throughout the year, temperatures can range from below zero degrees Fahrenheit in the mountains to well above the century mark in the lower basins. The highest temperature ever recorded in Arizona was 128 degrees, reached in 1994 at Lake Havasu. Similarly, precipitation may be a scant few inches of rain a year on the desert floors to more than 25 inches of moisture in the higher mountains. Typically, most of this precipitation falls at two different times of the year. Winter brings periodic snowfall in the higher terrain and gentle rains in the desert, and summers feature frequent afternoon thunderstorms throughout the state.

## FLORA AND FAUNA

Because of Arizona's wide range of climate conditions, the state is home to an impressive number of plants and animals. These species of flora and fauna typically find niches within certain

Wet winters bring on an explosion of color as Mexican poppies grow at the foot of the Ajo Mountains.

parameters of temperature and moisture, which are, in turn, dictated by elevation and latitude. Saguaro cactus, for instance, mostly grows below 3000 feet, where temperatures rarely drop below freezing, whereas Engelmann spruce prefer a much cooler climate found above 9000 feet. Similarly, elk live mostly in the cooler forests north of the Mogollon Rim, and javelina inhabit desert regions to the south. Having recognized entire groups of plants and animals that share similar climate needs, scientists have identified specific biological communities or life zones. Corresponding to elevation levels, these life zones can be identified in the field by the dominant plants that grow there.

Extending from nearly sea level to about 4500 feet is the *Lower Sonoran Zone*. Covering roughly one-third of the state, the Lower Sonoran Zone is home to Arizona's famed saguaro cactus. Other plants include cholla and barrel cactus, ocotillo, palo verde, creosote bush, saltbush, and mesquite. Wildlife within these arid lands includes javelinas, desert bighorn sheep, ringtail cats, coatimundis, coyotes, jackrabbits, rattlesnakes, Gila monsters, and a variety of birds.

The *Upper Sonoran Zone*, which extends from 4500 feet to 6500 feet, often features stunted forests of pinyon pine and juniper but may also include manzanita and a variety of oaks. Unlike oaks of the eastern woodlands, Arizona's various species of oaks (about a dozen in all) range in size from shrubs to small trees. Identifying these species is sometimes made difficult by the fact that they often interbreed. Animals that inhabit the Upper Sonoran Zone include mule and white-tailed deer, black bears, coyotes, and pronghorn antelopes.

Reaching to elevations around 8000 feet, the *Transition Zone* includes the impressive forests of ponderosa pine found in many parts of the state. The largest stand of ponderosa pine in the country, in fact, stretches from the Williams area to the New Mexico border. Other tree species include Douglas fir, Gambel oak, and juniper. Mule deer favor this zone, as do elk, black bears, tassel-eared squirrels, and wild turkeys.

Sumac in autumn along the Sandys Canyon Trail

The *Canadian Zone*, which extends from 8000 feet to 9500 feet, is next, with its cool, wet timberlands of Engelmann spruce, Colorado blue spruce, white fir, subalpine fir, and aspen. Fauna that live here include elk, mule deer, black bears, and a variety of squirrels.

Stretching from 9500 feet to timberline, which in Arizona is around 11,500 feet, is the *Hudsonian Zone*. In this harsh environment, dominant plant species include bristlecone pine, spruce, and fir. Weather conditions are harsh at this elevation; strong winds and snow are quite common. Close to timberline these trees often become stunted and twisted and are collectively called krummholz forests.

Extending above the 11,500-foot mark, the *Alpine Zone* is found in only one location in Arizona: the San Francisco Peaks near Flagstaff. Because conditions are so harsh at these lofty elevations, no trees grow here. Instead, these areas support meadows of flowering annuals and perennials, many of which are found in other alpine areas of the world as well.

Although elevation plays an important role in plant and animal distribution in Arizona, so too does the presence of water. Perennial streams and rivers, and even those that flow intermittently but with some regularity, are the foundation of what are called riparian ecosystems. In

A prehistoric petroglyph depicts what looks like a mountain lion in Hieroglyphic Canyon.

an arid state like Arizona, riparian ecosystems are incredibly important in maintaining ecological diversity. They are also wonderful places to explore. Characterized by thick and leafy canopies formed by cottonwoods, ashes, alders, Arizona sycamores, and other deciduous trees, riparian areas usually include thickets of shrubs, vines, and ground cover as well. In comparison to the surrounding desert or arid forestlands, these jungle-like environments can be quite refreshing. Adding to their allure is the presence of a great variety of insects, mammals, and birds. Especially in southern Arizona, riparian areas constitute some of the best birding areas around. Several of the hikes in this book visit riparian areas around the state.

One additional factor that adds to Arizona's great variety of flora and fauna is the state's proximity to Mexico. As bird-watchers will tell you, a number of Mexican bird species regularly fly north of the border to nest or just escape the heat. Trees such as the Chihuahua pine grow in the mountains of southern Arizona, and some species of mammals have filtered north too. In 2013 a jaguar was photographed on several occasions with remote sensor cameras in the Santa Rita Mountains. In May 2014, the same set of cameras photographed an ocelot roaming the area.

## USING THIS BOOK

This book sets out to describe in detail one hundred of the best hikes in Arizona. All of these hikes follow either designated trails or, at the very least, established routes of travel. Cross-country excursions, or off-trail travel, are avoided to lessen impact on the environment. Most of these hikes either access a particular point of interest or follow a loop route. Attention has also been paid to representing the variety of terrains and ecosystems found in Arizona and to providing as wide a geographical representation as possible. This is why some urban-area hikes have been included in this book, along with classic wilderness walks. Two regions of the state that are underrepresented here include the expansive Navajo Indian Nation in the northeastern corner of the state and the Basin and Range deserts to the west. This is because both areas are lacking in established backcountry trails. Some of the hikes presented here are quite popular and are best avoided on weekends and holidays, but a great many others are not as heavily visited.

Snaking through the state, and connecting some of the trails discussed in this book along the way, the Arizona Trail runs from the Mexico border to Utah. This trans-state route is some 800 miles long, and it links together an array of topographies from cactus-studded deserts to montane stands of aspen, spruce, and fir. In so doing, it provides a long-distance journey unrivaled in beauty and diversity. Among the many hikes in this book that include a portion of the Arizona Trail are Tonto Trail (Hike 2), Clear Creek (Hike 4), North Kaibab Trail (Hike 5), Walnut Canyon (Hike 23), Mazatzal Peak Loop (Hike 64), Sabino Canyon (Hike 76), and Aspen Loop (Hike 80). For more information about the Arizona Trail, including volunteer opportunities, go to the Arizona Association website at www.aztrail.org.

## Information Block

Each hike begins with an information block designed to provide pertinent facts and figures at a glance. By scanning these headings, you should know right away what to expect during each hike.

In all but a few cases the *Distance* figure refers to the hike's roundtrip distance. If a particular trail is 3.2 miles long, the distance figure will indicate "6.4 miles roundtrip" to let you know the total number of miles to be hiked. In a few cases where it may be impractical to retrace the entire route, the distance figure will read "one-way." For these hikes a shuttle is required.

The *Difficulty* of each hike is calculated mostly by the trail's elevation gain, length, and overall trail condition, and each is rated as easy, moderate, or strenuous. One short steep pitch may not necessarily bump a hike into the strenuous category, but continuous steep grades would. Hiking conditions such as the presence of deadfall, loose rock, and so on are also considered. Some routes that are not too steep may still be rated as strenuous because of obstacles along the way. For the most part, the hiking terrain involves established trails, although some short stretches may require scrambling skills.

The *Hiking time* for each hike is calculated for persons of moderate hiking ability and strength who enjoy stopping occasionally to rest and take in the scenery. Each takes into account such factors as distance, elevation changes, and trail conditions. These times will not fit every hiker's purposes and are provided simply as a guide.

The *Elevation* entry gives the range in elevation that the hike covers. The first figure indicates the trailhead elevation, and the second is that of either the high or low point of the hike. In many cases, this is also the destination of the hike. If this second entry is lower than the first, the hike descends in elevation (typical of many canyon hikes). If the second figure is greater, the hike climbs in elevation. In some instances, additional climbing may be required in the course of the hike. This added elevation gain is usually discussed in the hike descriptions.

The *Management* entry indicates which government agency holds title to portions or all of the route. Entities include lands managed by the Bureau of Land Management (BLM), national forest (NF), national park (NP), national monument (NM), national historic site (NHS), national recreation area (NRA), national wildlife refuge (NWR), state park (SP), county park, and city park. Additional information about a particular hike, such as maps, may be available from the managing agencies. For contact information, see Appendix A: Recommended Resources.

The *Wilderness status* entry indicates whether or not the hike enters an established wilderness area (WA) or a primitive area (PA). Such information is helpful in determining what rules and regulations apply (see the "Wilderness Etiquette" section of this chapter).

The *Season* entry points out the best times of the year to attempt the hike. Where high mountain hikes are concerned, that means the months when the trail is free of snow. In lower-elevation deserts, the optimal months for hiking are when the danger of heat exposure is not too great.

Many of the hikes in this book can be completed year-round. Before setting out, however, you should check with the managing agency about the road conditions leading to the trailhead and the trail conditions beyond. During certain times of the year rainy conditions may, in fact, preclude access.

The *USGS maps* entries indicate which 7.5-minute topographic map or maps cover the hike. Keep in mind that these maps are sometimes outdated in terms of trail delineation. Some routes may not have been in existence when the maps were drafted, whereas other trails have since been rerouted. Nevertheless, topo maps come in handy, especially in combination with updated management-agency maps.

The final entry in the information block is the *GPS coordinate* for the trailhead of each hike. By entering this coordinate in Google Maps, it is possible to obtain directions for reaching each trailhead.

The information block is followed by driving directions to the start of the hike. This paragraph also mentions possible fees charged to visitors. Some of these fees, such as the Tonto Pass and Red Rock Pass, cover trailhead parking, whereas others are actually entry fees to parks, monuments, or roadways. Annual passes may also be purchased. These include the America the Beautiful Pass for national parks and monuments and the Arizona State Parks Annual Pass. Contact information concerning agencies that charge a fee can be found in Appendix A.

### Maps

Although each hike in this book is illustrated on a topographic map, you may also want to bring along the actual topographic map(s) that show more details of the surrounding area. In addition, various GPS applications are available for smartphones that allow the user to download topographic maps and then follow along with GPS services. Often, these map services indicate updated trail routes.

### Hike Description

The main body of the text begins with an introductory paragraph, followed by a running narrative of the route itself, which includes a description of grades, cardinal directions, possible hazards, and general trail conditions. Major trail junctions and vegetation found along the way are noted. Possible wildlife sightings are sometimes discussed, as is the geology of an area. A historical perspective is also included on occasion. These discussions of the natural and human history of each hike are short, and

additional research will only enhance your hiking experience. Each description ends with a summation, entitled "Be Prepared," of such technicalities as water availability, specific hazards, and regulations.

## WILDERNESS ETIQUETTE

Fortunately, much of Arizona's backcountry is now protected as wilderness. There are currently ninety-two designated wilderness areas across the state. These are included on National Forest Service, Bureau of Land Management, National Park Service, and National Wildlife Refuge lands.

As established by the Wilderness Act of 1964, a variety of regulations apply so as to preserve the natural character of the land and provide visitors with a true wilderness experience. Paramount among these regulations is that all means of mechanized travel are prohibited. This includes motorized vehicles, hang gliders, and all-terrain bicycles (ATBs). In Arizona, as in other states, ATBs, or mountain bikes as they are more commonly known, present land managers with a particularly pressing problem. A few bicyclists either do not know that bicycles are prohibited or they choose to ignore the law. Although most users of this book will be traveling on foot, keep in mind that mountain bikes are strictly prohibited from all trails within wilderness areas. They are not allowed on most national park and monument trails either.

Aspen leaves brighten the Inner Basin Trail.

Of course, the Wilderness Act also prohibits such mechanized equipment as chainsaws and generators. Commercial enterprises such as livestock grazing and outfitting are allowed under a permit system. Restrictions on fires and campsite location are imposed in some areas. Because dogs are disruptive to wildlife, some backcountry areas are off-limits to pets. In all other locations, pets should be strictly controlled. Fishing and hunting regulations fall under the auspices of the Arizona Department of Game and Fish.

In addition to the regulations dictated by the Wilderness Act, all visitors should follow a number of commonsense rules having to do with leave-no-trace camping and hiking. These rules should be applied not just to designated wilderness lands but to all backcountry areas:

- Do not build campfires—use a stove instead.
- Avoid camping in sensitive areas such as mountain meadows and around fragile desert plants.
- Camp at least 100 feet from the trail and use existing sites when possible.
- Camp at least a quarter mile from any spring or watering hole—state law actually dictates this to benefit wildlife that comes to drink at night.
- Never cut standing trees, dead or alive.
- Do not leave behind structures or nails of any sort.
- Do not dig holes and trenches, or level tent areas.
- Bury human waste and use biodegradable soap at least 200 feet from water sources. Pack out or safely burn used toilet paper.
- Travel in small groups.
- Never cut across switchbacks or walk over sensitive ground such as microbiotic (cryptogamic) soil.
- Pack out all litter.

Although these leave-no-trace rules certainly apply to the backcountry, they also make good sense when camping at or near a trailhead. Far too often, backcountry travelers forget to exhibit care for the environment once they are

A Superstition Wilderness sign along the Hieroglyphic Trail

back at their cars. The end result is trailhead areas that are trashed out and overused. In such areas, practice low-impact camping just as you would in any wilderness setting, and be sure to keep your vehicles on established roadways and parking areas.

Of course, all plants, animals, rocks, and historical relics should not be removed, destroyed, or disturbed in any way. All natural objects and historical artifacts are protected by law in national parks, monuments, recreation areas, and wildlife refuges. Similarly, many species of cactus are protected by state laws, passed in response to an increase in cactus rustling in recent years. Antiquities of prehistoric or historic origin are protected by federal law. Artifacts, especially those of the prehistoric Native Americans, have been looted at an alarming rate. Prehistoric structures are also threatened by careless treatment. The simplest rule is also the best: Look, but don't touch.

## BACKCOUNTRY SAFETY

Backcountry hazards are numerous in Arizona, but if you take a few precautions, the possibility of problems becomes quite small. This book outlines some of those hazards, but it does not presume to represent the final word on treatment or prevention. The best prevention is knowledge and experience. Listed in Appendix B: Further Reading are a few books that may be helpful in giving you a deeper understanding of outdoor travel, the dangers you may encounter on the trail, and what you can do to make your outings as safe and enjoyable as possible.

### Heat and Sun

Perhaps the most prevalent danger to hikers in Arizona is the heat, especially in the low deserts. Temperatures regularly top the 100 degrees Fahrenheit mark in the summer months, and sometimes reach 120 degrees. Under such conditions the body can quickly become dehydrated. This, in turn, leads to fatigue, exhaustion, heat-stroke, and even death. The best course of action is to avoid hiking during these hot periods. If you do choose to hike during hot weather, however, it is extremely important to carry plenty of drinking water: A gallon per person per day is the recommended amount. It is also important to remember to drink often. Surprisingly, many people fail to drink the water they carry at frequent enough intervals. To detect heat exhaustion, watch for cool and pale skin, headaches, dizziness, and lack of energy. Heat exhaustion may lead to heatstroke, which is very serious. Immediate treatment for both of these conditions includes having the victim rest in a cool, shady area. Give him or her plenty of water and seek medical attention as soon as possible.

In addition to the possibility of heat exhaustion and heatstroke, exposure to the sun can also result in severe sunburn. In addition to being uncomfortable, the severest cases can present specific medical problems, including third-degree burns. To prevent sunburn, wear a

A reflective pool in a stream near Cochise Spring

hat to protect your head and neck. Wearing light-colored clothing is also helpful. Use plenty of sunblock (SPF 30 or above) on all exposed areas, and remember to reapply it frequently.

## Hypothermia

Hypothermia is a common hazard in many of Arizona's backcountry areas. Sudden changes in weather can bring on cold rain or even snow, especially in the high country. This combination of cold and wet can cause the body's core temperature to drop to dangerous levels. Symptoms include uncontrollable shivering, impaired judgment, deteriorating speech, drowsiness, and weakness.

Hypothermia can be an efficient killer, but it is treatable. As soon as possible, replace wet clothing with dry and place the victim in a pre-warmed sleeping bag. It may also be necessary to warm any victims by huddling them. Give warm liquids and high-energy food, and get the victim to a doctor as soon as possible. As with any backcountry hazard, prevention is the best course of action. It is always best to avoid getting wet and cold, to carry spare clothing and raingear, and to eat plenty of high-energy foods.

## Lightning

Lightning is a killer in Arizona, and not just in the higher terrain. The Mogollon Rim, in fact, holds the dubious honor of having one of the highest rates of lightning strikes in the country. It is certainly best to avoid open terrain during electrical storms. This means keeping a watchful eye on the weather. Watch for clouds building up, especially in the afternoon, although lightning can occur at any time. If you should happen to be caught, retreat to a flat area or depression. Stay away from tall trees. Caves and deep alcoves are safe, as are cars, but shallow rock overhangs, ravines, and tents are not.

## Flash Floods

Flash floods are a common hazard in Arizona, especially in desert areas where bare ground tends to shed runoff rather than absorb it. If storm clouds are building, avoid washes, canyon bottoms, and creekbeds. Also, do not attempt to drive across flooded roadways. Typically, such floods will recede within an hour or two.

## Wildlife

As one might expect, the deserts of Arizona are home to a variety of venomous creatures: scorpions, black widow spiders, Gila monsters, and rattlesnakes, to name four. Although the bite of any of these creatures can cause medical problems (and even death in some cases), the chance of your being bitten is actually quite remote. Rattlesnakes, for instance, try to avoid people just as much as people avoid them. To lessen the chance of unwanted encounters with venomous creatures, stay away from rocky areas where such species might be hiding. If bitten, seek medical attention immediately.

Other creatures in the forests and deserts of Arizona may also pose a threat, although the possibilities are, again, quite remote. In recent years a handful of black bear attacks on campers have been reported, especially in the southeastern mountains. These conflicts have mostly arisen, however, because people have not taken the proper precautions. Be sure to store all food, trash, toiletries, and other scented items in bear-resistant food containers. Many campgrounds are now equipped with bear-proof trash containers, and signs have been posted warning visitors that they are in bear country. It is conceivable that mountain lions might pose a threat, although the chance of seeing one is extremely rare.

A danger recently discovered in the American Southwest is hantavirus, a deadly disease that strikes its victims swiftly. Hantavirus is thought to be transmitted through contact with rodents, particularly deer mice, or their droppings. Hikers and campers should avoid contact with rodents and rodent burrows, stay out of rodent-infested structures such as abandoned cabins and shelters, sleep in a tent (not on open ground), and store food in rodent-proof containers.

One additional hazard is important to mention: Africanized, or "killer," bees. Spreading north following their accidental introduction

Setting up camp along the Dutchman's Trail

in Brazil some years ago, these overly aggressive bees have reached the American Southwest. There have been reports of people being attacked in the Phoenix and Tucson areas, and some have been killed. Their sting is no worse than that of an ordinary bee, but these bees will defend their hives with incredible ferocity. The best defense against Africanized bees is to avoid their hives altogether. If you do find yourself near a beehive, move away slowly. If you are attacked, your best bet is to run away as fast as you can, but keep in mind that they may follow you for up to half a mile. Seek medical assistance as quickly as possible.

## Giardia

Although not deadly, *Giardia lamblia* is a real hazard that plagues most parts of Arizona. A microorganism that is now found in most open water sources (streams, pools, ponds, and lakes, for example), Giardia can cause digestive tract problems if ingested. Symptoms of giardiasis include severe diarrhea, which may not appear until a week or two later, and treatment requires a doctor's attention.

Prevention is the best means of dealing with Giardia. Essentially, you should not drink any surface water without first treating it properly. Either filter the water with a specially designed filter system (Giardia cysts are very small) or bring water to a rolling boil for at least 1 minute. For day hikes, simply bring along all the water you need.

## Getting Lost and Found

For even the most experienced hiker, the possibility of becoming hurt or lost is real. First-time hikers should not travel alone, and seasoned veterans should consider taking a companion on more difficult hikes. Regardless of your ability, however, you should always let someone know where you are going. If you do become injured or disoriented, above all remain calm. Hopefully, another hiker or a backcountry ranger will happen along. While cell phones do not work everywhere in Arizona, they do work in a surprising number of wild places, especially from higher ridges and mountain slopes. Bring a cell phone, keeping it turned off to save the battery and ready to use in case of emergency—provided you're in an area with reception.

## BEFORE YOU GO

When planning a hike, a little preparation goes a long way to help make the trip fun and successful, but it is also necessary to ensure that you return safely.

A good place to begin is with your selection of clothes. Sturdy hiking shoes with good soles are important, as is comfortable clothing. Weather conditions may warrant short pants and a short-sleeved shirt when you start out, but always come prepared with warmer clothing, especially when hiking Arizona's higher terrain. In the desert areas, light-colored, long clothing is helpful in preventing sunburn. A wide-brimmed hat is also a necessity. For hikes of any length, bring along raingear—either a poncho or rain parka and pants—in your pack. Two pairs of socks are a good idea, but experienced hikers have no doubt worked out their own best solution for footwear long ago.

In addition to proper clothing, experts have put together a list of Ten Essentials that they deem necessary for a safe and rewarding adventure.

1. Navigation (map and compass)—be sure your map is the right one for the trip and be sure to know the declination, east or west.
2. Sun protection (sunglasses and sunscreen)—especially important for alpine and snow travel, and in desert lands
3. Insulation (extra clothing)—more than is needed in good weather
4. Illumination (headlamp or flashlight)—with extra bulb and batteries
5. First-aid supplies
6. Fire (firestarter and matches/lighter)—bring matches in a weatherproof container and a candle or chemical fuel for wet wood.
7. Repair kit and tools, including knife (for first aid and emergency firebuilding)
8. Nutrition (extra food)—so that something is left over at the end of the trip
9. Hydration (extra water)—in Arizona's generally arid climate, a gallon of water per person per day should command room in your pack.
10. Emergency shelter

Interior detail of a re-created Apache wickiup

## CAMPING EXCURSIONS

When planning an overnight trip, you cannot go wrong by investing in (or renting) good camping equipment. First, take a look at your shoes—with added weight on your back, it is important that your ankles are supported with higher boots. To carry that extra weight in the most comfortable manner possible, a good backpack is a must. Packs have become quite sophisticated, especially in harness systems. Be sure that you bring extra clothing, including a change of socks for each day. A good lightweight sleeping bag will be a friend for years to come if properly cared for, and a sleeping pad is well worth the weight for added warmth and comfort.

Shelter is an important consideration. Some hapless backpackers may assume that it is not going to rain, or that they can find natural shelter along the way. It is far better, however, to pack along a good, lightweight tent to ensure your comfort and safety.

You will want to bring extra water, especially if none is available along the route. Checking beforehand with the managing agency on water availability is extremely important, as is carrying a good water filter. Plan your meals carefully so that you do not either go hungry or wind up carrying too much food.

You will need a cook kit, spoon, fork, cup, and lightweight stove for preparing meals. In this day and age, a stove is not only convenient but a real godsend for the environment. Let's face it: Campfires may be romantic, but they are messy eyesores once they are extinguished. If you really need something to curl up with at night, bring a good book.

*A Note about Safety:* Safety is an important concern in all outdoor activities. No guidebook can alert you to every hazard or anticipate the limitations of every reader. Therefore, the descriptions of roads, trails, routes, and natural features in this book are not representations that a particular place or excursion will be safe for your party. When you follow any of the routes described in this book, you assume responsibility for your own safety. Under normal conditions, such excursions require the usual attention to traffic, road and trail conditions, weather, terrain, the capabilities of your party, and other factors. Keeping informed on current conditions and exercising common sense are the keys to a safe, enjoyable outing.

—*Mountaineers Books*

Opposite, top: Petroglyphs near Lithodendren Wash in Petrified Forest National Park

Opposite, bottom: Aspen forest along the Inner Basin Trail

# Colorado Plateau

1. Bright Angel Trail . . . . . . . . . . . .24
2. Tonto Trail . . . . . . . . . . . . . . . . . .27
3. Dripping Springs . . . . . . . . . . . . 30
4. Clear Creek . . . . . . . . . . . . . . . . . .32
5. North Kaibab Trail . . . . . . . . . . . 35
6. Widforss Trail . . . . . . . . . . . . . . .37
7. Uncle Jim Trail . . . . . . . . . . . . . . 38
8. Kanab Creek . . . . . . . . . . . . . . . . 40
9. Mount Trumbull . . . . . . . . . . . . . .43
10. Havasu Canyon . . . . . . . . . . . . . . .44
11. Paria River Canyon . . . . . . . . . . . .47
12. Spencer Trail . . . . . . . . . . . . . . . 50
13. Soap Creek . . . . . . . . . . . . . . . . . .52
14. Onyx Bridge . . . . . . . . . . . . . . . . .54
15. Keet Seel . . . . . . . . . . . . . . . . . . 56
16. White House Ruin . . . . . . . . . . . 58
17. Mount Elden Lookout . . . . . . . . 60
18. Abineau/Bear Jaw Loop . . . . . . .62
19. Humphreys Peak . . . . . . . . . . . . . .64
20. Kachina Trail . . . . . . . . . . . . . . . 66
21. Inner Basin . . . . . . . . . . . . . . . . . 68
22. Lenox Crater . . . . . . . . . . . . . . . . .70
23. Walnut Canyon . . . . . . . . . . . . . . .71
24. Red Mountain . . . . . . . . . . . . . . . .73
25. Kendrick Mountain . . . . . . . . . . .75
26. Bill Williams Mountain . . . . . . . .77
27. Sycamore Rim . . . . . . . . . . . . . . . .79

*Arizona's share of the Colorado Plateau, highlighted by one of America's premier* national parks (Grand Canyon National Park), is a wonderland of colorful canyons, plateaus, and mesas. The Grand Canyon is not to be missed, for its depths promise hidden corridors, waterfalls, and impressive vistas to all who venture within. Beyond this great abyss are lesser "gulches," each alluring in its own right. Other units of the national park system in this sector of Arizona offer prehistoric ruins and petrified forests. Near Flagstaff, the remnants of an ancient volcano—the San Francisco Peaks—boast the state's only true taste of alpine tundra and its highest elevation, Humphreys Peak. From shadowed riverways and slickrock passages to old-growth forests and treeless summits, backcountry explorations within Arizona's Colorado Plateau region are unmatched in diversity and color. Keep in mind that substantial elevation changes characterize many of these hikes. Be prepared.

## 1  Bright Angel Trail

**Distance:** 19.2 miles roundtrip
**Difficulty:** strenuous
**Hiking time:** 2 days
**Elevation:** 6840 to 2400 feet
**Management:** Grand Canyon NP
**Wilderness status:** none

**Season:** year-round
**USGS maps:** Bright Angel, Grand Canyon, Phantom Ranch
**GPS coordinates:** 36.057142 N, 112.143636 W

**Getting there:** The Bright Angel trailhead is located at the west end of Grand Canyon Village, just past the Bright Angel Lodge. To reach the Bright Angel Lodge from Flagstaff, drive northwest on US Highway 180 to Arizona Highway 64. Continue north, drive about 30 miles to the Grand Canyon Village, and turn left on Hermit Road.

In addition to offering the most convenient access to the bottom of the Grand Canyon, the Bright Angel Trail is also one of the most popular hiking routes in the park. Wide enough to allow safe passage for tourist-toting mules, this is a virtual highway among backcountry trails. Although the Bright Angel Trail ends at the Colorado River, this description continues on to the Silver Bridge and Phantom Ranch a short distance beyond.

From the start, the route wastes no time snaking its way down Garden Creek as it drops 3000 feet in the first 3.1 miles. Along this stretch are two rest shelters that offer emergency phones and drinking water from mid-May to October. Beyond the second rest house, the trail enters a relatively level stretch of canyon bottom.

At about 4.5 miles from its start, the Bright Angel Trail reaches Indian Garden. A popular destination for day hikers, Indian Garden features a campground, a toilet, and a reliable source of drinking water. In addition, a 1.5-mile side trail leads from here to Plateau Point on the rim of the Inner Gorge. The verdant Indian Garden enjoys a rich past. The Ancestral Puebloans raised crops here, as did the Havasupai during more recent times. Miners frequented it in the late 1800s. By the turn of the century, the area's

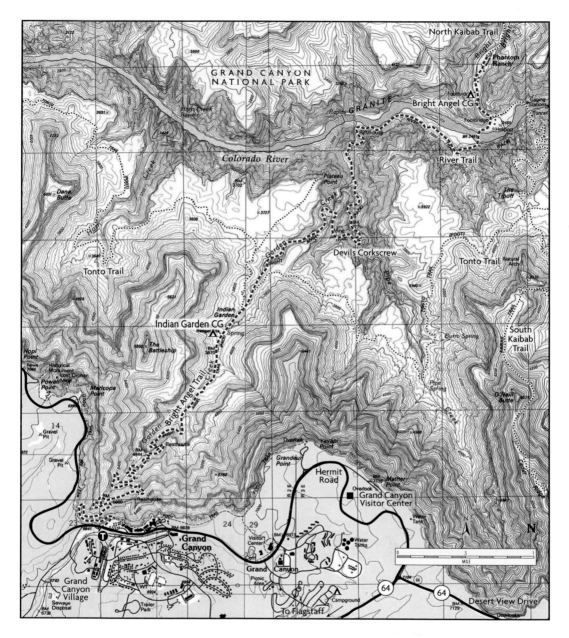

potential for tourism was being realized. In 1903 Ralph Cameron gained control of the Bright Angel Trail and turned it into a toll route.

Although it marks the halfway point for this hike in terms of distance, Indian Garden is about two-thirds of the way down in elevation. By this point, the trail has encountered several layers of geologic history. First to be traversed is Kaibab Limestone. Light in color, this formation was deposited in a shallow sea about 270 million years ago. Next in line is the Toroweap Formation, a layer of tan-colored sandstones and limestones. It is followed by Coconino Sandstone, a heavily cross-bedded rock that consists

Tourist-toting mules on the Bright Angel Trail

of deposits by ancient sand dunes. Hermit Shale—a deposit that collected in swamps and lagoons—is next, followed by the Supai Group. Near the Three-mile Resthouse is the top end of the imposing Redwall Limestone. Below that are layers of Temple Butte and Muav Limestones. Forming the gently sloping Tonto Plateau below is Bright Angel Shale. Dating back about 515 million years, Bright Angel Shale originated from mud deposited in a shallow sea. Beyond Indian Garden, the Bright Angel Trail encounters two additional formations before reaching the Colorado River: First is a layer of Tapeats Sandstone, and then comes the very impressive Vishnu Schist; dropping into the Inner Gorge, this dark rock dates back some 1.7 billion years.

From Indian Garden the Bright Angel Trail passes through Tapeats Narrows before reaching the Devils Corkscrew—a lengthy set of switchbacks that cascades down the Vishnu Schist.

At the bottom the trail heads down Pipe Creek before finally reaching the river. At this point, 7.8 miles from the trailhead, the Bright Angel Trail ends and the River Trail begins. A rest house here is equipped with an emergency phone and a chemical toilet. For the next 1.4 miles the River Trail parallels the Colorado River to the Silver Bridge, across which lie a ranger station, the Bright Angel Campground, and Phantom Ranch.

Because of the Bright Angel Trail's popularity, camping is restricted to the established Indian Garden and Bright Angel Campgrounds. Needless to say, reservations for sites at both facilities must be made well in advance. Similarly, an overnight stay at Phantom Ranch, in either dorms or private cabins, should be planned months ahead of time. Constructed in 1922, Phantom Ranch includes a snack bar and restaurant. There is even a pay phone.

**Be prepared:** No matter the time of year, expect to see a lot of other hikers on the Bright Angel Trail. When encountering mules it is best to step off the trail and let them by. Water in Garden and Pipe Creeks is not potable, but you can count on finding reliable sources at the upper rest houses between May and October, and at Indian Garden and Bright Angel Campgrounds year-round. Summer temperatures regularly climb above 100 degrees Fahrenheit in the Inner Canyon, so plan accordingly. Most important, keep in mind that the hike back out involves nearly a vertical mile of climbing. Many unprepared hikers have found themselves in a lot of trouble because they were fooled by the easy descent to the bottom. Although the hike down to the river takes about five hours, the walk back out may take twice as long. Don't attempt to do it all in just one day. Backcountry permits are available up to four months in advance.

## 2  *Tonto Trail*

*Distance:* 28.4 miles one-way
*Difficulty:* strenuous
*Hiking time:* 4 days
*Elevation:* 7400 to 3800 feet
*Management:* Grand Canyon NP
*Wilderness status:* none

*Season:* year-round
*USGS maps:* Bright Angel, Cape Royal, Phantom Ranch, Grandview Point
*GPS coordinates:* 35.998021 N, 111.987724 W

*Getting there:* Begin this hike at Grandview Point, which is east of the Grand Canyon Village on Desert View Drive (Arizona Highway 64). To reach Desert View Drive, drive north from Flagstaff on US Highway 180 to the junction with Highway 64. Turn north and drive 30 miles north to the Grand Canyon Village. Turn right and drive about 11 miles to the turnoff for the Grandview trailhead, on the left. (From March to November you cannot drive on Desert View Drive; instead, you will need to take a free shuttle bus from the Grand Canyon Village.) The trailhead is well marked, and ample parking is provided.

Visitors to the South Rim get a wonderful bird's-eye view of the Grand Canyon, but a walk along part of the 92-mile Tonto Trail provides a very different, yet equally spectacular, look at this scenic wonder. There are several possible hikes to choose from on the Tonto; this description follows a 20-mile segment from the Grandview Trail west to the South Kaibab Trail.

Dropping convincingly, the Grandview Trail descends 2600 feet in 3 miles to reach Horseshoe Mesa below. Within the first mile, the trail descends through a moderately steep series of switchbacks. After passing a small saddle it then begins dropping at a steeper rate along the upper reaches of the Cottonwood Creek drainage. Leveling out a bit after the second

mile, the route traverses north toward Horseshoe Mesa. Although the trail is never hard to follow, it features loose rocks in many sections and care should be taken.

Horseshoe Mesa, an aptly named tableland at an elevation of 4800 feet, has long been a source of copper. It is believed that prehistoric Indians used the blue copper ore as an ingredient for paint. In 1892, Pete Berry, Niles Cameron, and Ralph Cameron began extracting high-grade ore from underground mines on the mesa. The operation ceased in 1907, but not before several structures were built. The remains of one building, along with some antiquated mining machinery, are still visible today. Keep in mind that these old mines are unsafe and should not be entered.

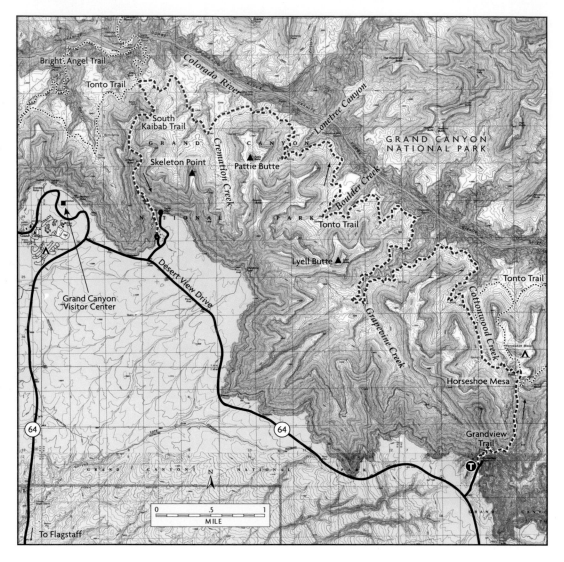

When securing a backcountry permit (required for overnight hikes in the canyon; see Grand Canyon National Park in Appendix A, under "National Parks and Monuments"), keep in mind that the Horseshoe Mesa area is very popular. Camping on Horseshoe Mesa is confined to designated backcountry campsites that fill up quickly. Alternate sites exist along Cottonwood Creek, although staying there would make for a long first day of hiking. Water is sometimes available at an intermittent spring here, but it is always advisable to check with the National Park Service's Backcountry Office about the availability of water all along the Tonto Trail before setting out.

To reach the Tonto Trail from Horseshoe Mesa, turn west onto a trail located in the vicinity of the old cabin foundation and head into the Cottonwood Creek drainage. Within a mile this route reaches the canyon bottom 800 feet below, and at about 1.5 miles from the turnoff it joins the Tonto Trail.

The grade of the Tonto Trail changes surprisingly little as the route follows the relatively flat Tonto Plateau. Formed by a layer of Tapeats Sandstone, the Tonto Plateau appears as a benchland from the rim above. Although easy enough to follow, the route does run dangerously close to the edge of the Inner Gorge in places. In addition, very little shade exists because plant life here includes relatively low-growing blackbrush, saltbush, prickly pear cactus, and century plants.

Continuing west from the Cottonwood Creek drainage, the Tonto Trail soon runs into the imposing Grapevine Creek. In a place like the Grand Canyon, even side drainages can prove impassable. Once it encounters Grapevine Creek, the trail must skirt several miles to the southwest before getting around to the other side. After rounding Lyell Butte, the route arrives at the smaller Boulder Creek drainage. Part-time springs and suitable camping spots are located along both Grapevine and Boulder Creeks.

From Boulder Creek, the Tonto Trail continues on to Lonetree Canyon, the site of the last spring along the hike. Suitable camping is available here, as well as in Cremation Creek, the next drainage over. Fanning out between Pattie Butte and Skeleton Point, the Cremation Creek basin is comparatively broad as the trail crosses three tributaries. You may find evidence of prehistoric people in this desolate area of the canyon. Be sure you do not disturb any of these archaeological sites, and you should not expect to find any water.

A mile beyond Cremation Creek is the South Kaibab Trail. From this junction it is a 4.4-mile, 3000-foot climb up to the South Rim and the end of this hike. Because the South Kaibab

The last rays of sun bathe the Inner Gorge at sunset as seen from the remote Tonto Trail.

Trail is one of two major routes into the canyon, expect to see a lot of hikers along the way. Like the Bright Angel Trail, the South Kaibab Trail challenges hikers with its near-constant climb in elevation.

**Be prepared:** Because summer brings extremely high temperatures to the lower canyon, late fall, winter, and spring are the best times to hike the Tonto Trail. The availability of water can also be a factor in determining when to go. It is not advisable to hike the Tonto Trail alone because it is remote and rugged in places. Backcountry permits are available up to four months in advance.

## 3  *Dripping Springs*

*Distance:* 6 miles roundtrip
*Difficulty:* moderate
*Hiking time:* 4 hours
*Elevation:* 6700 to 5200 feet
*Management:* Grand Canyon NP

*Wilderness status:* none
*Season:* year-round
*USGS maps:* Bright Angel, Grand Canyon
*GPS coordinates:* 36.060572 N,
112.212344 W

*Getting there:* Arrive at the Grand Canyon Village by driving northwest on US Highway 180 from Flagstaff. Turn north on Arizona Highway 64 and continue 30 miles to the village. This hike begins at Hermits Rest, which is located at the end of Hermit Road. Between the months of March and November, day hikers must park at the Grand Canyon Village and ride the free shuttle out to Hermits Rest. Buses run at 15-minute intervals beginning an hour before sunrise and continuing until an hour after sunset. From Hermits Rest, walk west to the road's end (less than 0.25 mile) and find the start of the Hermit Trail, a popular route to the river below.

For a moderately easy introduction to the world below the rim of the Grand Canyon, take this 3-mile trail to Dripping Springs offers both spectacular views and a perennial source of cool spring water.

The Hermit Trail begins by making a moderately steep descent into Hermit Basin, a broad, gently sloping expanse covered by arid pinyon-juniper forests. The trail is rocky in many parts, although some stretches were riprapped with sandstone slabs in the early part of the 20th century. The result is an unusual tread that is both easy to walk and visually interesting. A little more than a mile into the hike, the Hermit Trail connects with the Waldron Trail, a 2-mile route that climbs back up to the rim. Keep right at this junction. A short distance farther, approximately 1.5 miles from the trailhead, take the

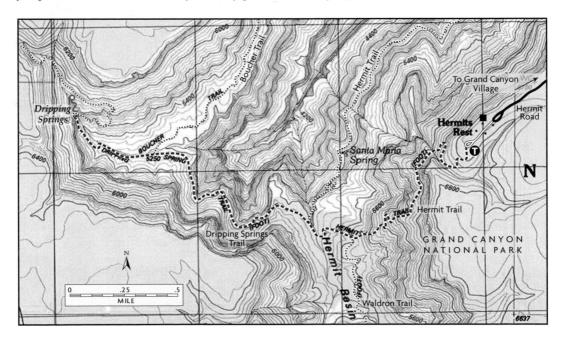

Hermit Gorge as seen from the Dripping Springs Trail

signed left-hand turn for Dripping Springs. From this junction, the Hermit Trail continues down Hermit Gorge, and the Dripping Springs Trail traverses west along the head of the gorge. Skirting along the top of the deep red Supai Group Formation, this segment of the hike opens up to awesome views of the canyon below.

Within a mile of the Dripping Springs–Hermit Trail junction is the start of the Boucher Trail, a route that eventually connects with the Tonto Trail (Hike 2). The Dripping Springs Trail stays left here and climbs a few hundred feet before reaching its namesake in another 0.5

mile. Nestled in a protective alcove at the base of the Toroweap Formation, Dripping Springs is a relatively small flow that drops from the rock wall above. The National Park Service recommends that you treat the water from the springs before you drink it.

Louis Boucher, the hermit of Hermits Rest, maintained a camp at the springs around the turn of the 20th century, and reportedly kept goldfish in a trough here. He also planted fruit trees along nearby Boucher Creek. Although this hike ends at the springs, a much-faded trail does climb steeply to gain the rim above.

**Be prepared:** Carry plenty of water on this hike, even if you plan on filling up at the springs. Camping is prohibited along the entire route.

# 4 Clear Creek

| | |
|---|---|
| **Distance:** 32.6 miles roundtrip | **Wilderness status:** none |
| **Difficulty:** strenuous | **Season:** year-round |
| **Hiking time:** 4 days | **USGS maps:** Bright Angel, Phantom Ranch |
| **Elevation:** 7200 to 2400 feet | **GPS coordinates:** 36.052816 N, |
| **Management:** Grand Canyon NP | 112.083908 W |

**Getting there:** Although the Clear Creek Trail starts at Phantom Ranch, this hike begins at the South Kaibab trailhead, which is on the road to Yaki Point. From Flagstaff, drive northwest on US Highway 180. Turn north on Arizona Highway 64 and drive 30 miles to the Grand Canyon Village. Turn right onto Desert View Drive and follow it for a little over 1 mile to the turnoff for Yaki Point. From March to November you cannot drive the Desert View Drive; instead, you will need to take a free shuttle bus from the Grand Canyon Village. The trailhead is on the left side of the road about a half mile from the turnoff to Yaki Point.

Just as the Tonto Trail follows its namesake plateau below the South Rim, the Clear Creek Trail travels across the same landform on the north side of the river. Climbing east from Phantom Ranch, the Clear Creek Trail eventually reaches a major drainage of the North Rim. Rewards of this lengthy hike are spectacular views of the Inner Gorge, a clear running creek, and access to the Colorado River.

Providing the quickest access to Phantom Ranch, the South Kaibab Trail is a well-developed and heavily used corridor to the canyon bottom. The geology along the South Kaibab route is easily identifiable as it descends through layer upon layer of Earth's history. Of particular interest are the rose-colored bands of Zoroaster Granite that slice through dark walls of Vishnu Schist in the Inner Gorge. These were formed when molten rock intruded into cracks in the surrounding bedrock. In 6.4 miles the trail drops 4780 feet to the Kaibab Suspension Bridge (itself a marvel of engineering a hundred or so years ago) and the Colorado River. It reaches Phantom Ranch in about another mile.

Campsites are available at the Bright Angel Campground, adjacent to Phantom Ranch. If this facility is full, your only alternative is to climb out of Bright Angel Canyon and find a spot above on the Tonto Plateau. However, this would make for an extremely long day of hiking, and rangers report that many hikers, in fact, have trouble completing it. Make certain you have a permit, which should include a reserved campsite at the Bright Angel Campground.

From Phantom Ranch, the Clear Creek Trail climbs rather steeply (1500 feet in the first 2 miles) to the Tonto Plateau. From the rim of the plateau, it is a 6-mile traverse east to the lip of Clear Creek Canyon. Although this segment is mostly level, some grade changes are encountered as the route crosses smaller drainages. In the last mile to Clear Creek the trail drops about 500 feet to the drainage bottom below. Here, among scattered cottonwoods, are found several suitable camping spots. In all, Clear Creek is 9 miles from Phantom Ranch.

At Clear Creek, two exceptional side trips are possible, both of which take most of a day to complete. The first is an 8-mile hike (round-trip) to Cheyava Falls, the highest falls in the canyon. The falls only flows for a few weeks in the spring after winters with good precipitation. To reach this spectacle, follow the main fork of Clear Creek upstream. The second side trip follows Clear Creek down to the Colorado River. Twisting and bending for about 5 miles, the creek drops through a narrow labyrinth of Vishnu Schist. At one point a 10-foot-high

One of many waterfalls along Clear Creek

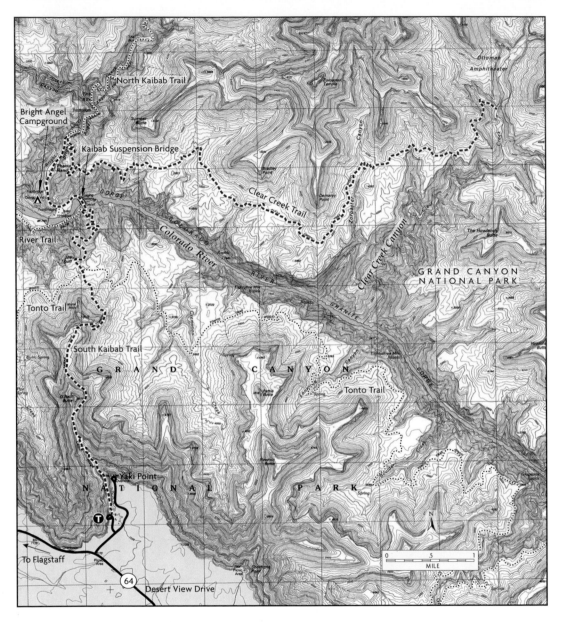

waterfall seems to block passage, but it is possible to scramble around to the right. Hikers with a fear of heights may want to bring a rope for this portion. Within 0.25 mile of the river, watch for schools of spawning trout. Once at the river, you may see a rafting party drifting by.

**Be prepared:** When considering this hike, keep in mind that water is available only at Phantom Ranch and Clear Creek; it is advisable to treat water from the latter. A backcountry permit is required for overnight stays. Be prepared for very hot temperatures in the summer. Backcountry permits are available up to four months in advance.

# 5  *North Kaibab Trail*

**Distance:** 28.4 miles roundtrip
**Difficulty:** strenuous
**Hiking time:** 3 days
**Elevation:** 8240 to 2400 feet
**Management:** Grand Canyon NP
**Wilderness status:** none

**Season:** May to October
**USGS maps:** Bright Angel Point, Phantom Ranch
**GPS coordinates:** 36.052816 N, 112.083908 W

**Getting there:** The North Kaibab trailhead is located about 3 miles north of the Grand Canyon Lodge at North Rim Village. To reach North Rim Village, follow US Highway 89 north from Flagstaff to Alternate US Highway 89. Turn west and drive 55 miles to Jacob Lake. Turn south on Arizona Highway 67 and drive 45 miles to the North Rim. It is a 215-mile drive from the South Rim to the North Rim.

Although separated by only 10 air miles, the South Rim and the North Rim of the Grand Canyon are worlds apart. Only 10 percent of the millions of people who visit the park each year ever make it to the remote North Rim. For hikers that means a less crowded alternative to the popular Bright Angel and South Kaibab Trails. Beginning at the North Rim, the North Kaibab Trail provides a longer, but in many ways more interesting, avenue to the canyon bottom.

Starting out among tall stands of Douglas fir, Engelmann spruce, ponderosa pine, and aspen, the North Kaibab Trail begins descending almost immediately into the upper end of Roaring Springs Canyon. Within the first 0.5 mile, a number of switchbacks are encountered as the route drops at a moderate to steep pace. About 1.7 miles in, the trail encounters the Supai Tunnel, which was cut through a sandstone wall. About 3 miles in, the route reaches the usually dry bottom of upper Roaring Springs Canyon, where it again must switchback to maintain a suitable grade. After crossing a bridge, the trail takes up the southwest wall of the canyon and makes a long traverse high above the canyon floor. Sections of this corridor have been blasted into solid rock. Eventually, the trail drops through a few final switchbacks to reach the mouth of the canyon and a side trail that leads 0.25 mile to Roaring Springs. In the nearly 5 miles between the trailhead and this junction, the trail descends some 3000 feet.

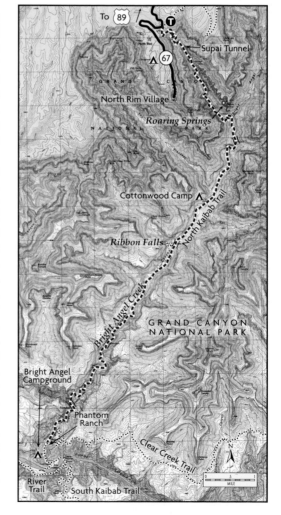

Ribbon Falls is one of the attractions along the North Kaibab Trail.

A popular destination for day hikers, Roaring Springs is quite a sight to behold. From caves at the base of the Redwall Limestone Formation, a massive discharge of water spews noisily out. A picnic area is located near the springs, and a shady mix of cottonwoods and other deciduous trees haunt this riparian environ.

Continuing on from the Roaring Springs turnoff, the North Kaibab Trail turns south to follow the perennial Bright Angel Creek. The trail crosses a bridge about 0.5 mile beyond the junction, then follows the creek downstream, mostly staying in the canyon bottom for the rest of the way. Grades beyond the creek crossing are easy to moderate in difficulty.

Nearly 7 miles from the trailhead (and 2.2 miles from Roaring Springs) is Cottonwood Camp. Featuring picnic tables, toilets, phone, drinking water, shade trees, and a seasonally staffed ranger station, Cottonwood Camp is the first designated camping spot along the North Kaibab Trail. The camp can be hot in the summer, but the fishing is reported to be good.

From Cottonwood Camp the route descends easily for 1.8 miles to a short side trail that leads to Ribbon Falls. Enclosed in a red rock grotto, this 100-foot-high waterfall cascades over a travertine formation below to break up into thin laces of water. Beyond Ribbon Falls, the North Kaibab Trail continues for another 5.5 miles to Phantom Ranch. Much of this stretch follows the bottom of an impressive narrows section formed by ever-deepening walls of Vishnu Schist. Bridges allow for easy crossing of Bright Angel Creek in several locations. Thickets of tamarisk and willows grow in several places. Among the surrounding cliffs and slopes, a scrubby collection of barrel cactus, agaves, and other plants typical of the lower Sonoran life zone stand in stark contrast to the lush forests at the hike's beginning.

**Be prepared:** Phantom Ranch has cabins for rent, but reservations are hard to come by. The Bright Angel Campground, which is 0.3 mile beyond Phantom Ranch, is the only other overnight option, but it too is usually booked up months in advance. Because camping along the North Kaibab Trail is restricted to the Cottonwood and Bright Angel camps, it is important to plan your trip well in advance. Potable water is available at the North Rim, Roaring Springs, Cottonwood Camp, Supai Tunnel, Phantom Ranch, and the Bright Angel Campground. All other sources should be treated first. Watch for mules along the North Kaibab Trail, and take care along the many precipitous sections of the route. Because the North Rim is open only from mid-May through October, hikers are likely to encounter very hot temperatures in the canyon bottom. And keep in mind that the climb out is very long and steep—nearly 6000 feet! Backcountry permits are available up to four months in advance.

## 6  *Widforss Trail*

**Distance:** 10 miles roundtrip
**Difficulty:** easy
**Hiking time:** 5 hours
**Elevation:** 8100 to 7950 feet
**Management:** Grand Canyon NP

**Wilderness status:** none
**Season:** May to October
**USGS map:** Bright Angel Point
**GPS coordinates:** 36.223781 N, 112.065214 W

**Getting there:** Drive about 3 miles north of the Grand Canyon Lodge at North Rim Village to a gravel road signed for the trail. Turn left and follow this road for almost a mile through Harvey Meadow to the trailhead and parking area. To reach the Grand Canyon Lodge from Flagstaff, drive north on US Highway 89 to Alternate US Highway 89. Turn west and drive 55 miles to Jacob Lake. From this junction continue south on Arizona Highway 67 for 45 miles to the lodge. The distance from Flagstaff to North Rim Village is 211 miles.

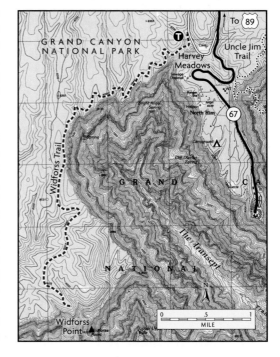

Accessing a highly scenic point on the North Rim of the Grand Canyon, the Widforss Trail is named in honor of Gunnar Widforss, an artist who painted extensively here in the 1920s. This 5-mile route offers one of the most inspiring vistas along the North Rim. It also features some interesting lessons concerning the natural history of the North Rim area.

With the exception of a short climb at the start and a few shallow drainages later on, the Widforss Trail is very level. This, combined with the fact that the entire route is well maintained, makes for an easy hike. A guide pamphlet that corresponds to numbered sites along the first 2.5 miles of the walk is available at the trailhead.

Within the first 0.5 mile the Widforss Trail reveals much of its natural character as hikers encounter various types of timber. Typical of the higher North Rim, these forests include Colorado blue spruce, Engelmann spruce, white fir, Douglas fir, and quaking aspen, plus several nice stands of ponderosa pine growing in the more

A stand of aspen trees along the Widforss Trail

arid areas. Patches of Gambel oak and maple are not uncommon. Many types of wildlife, including mule deer, make their homes here.

Adding to the trail's allure are the many vistas that open up on the first half of the trail. At several places along this segment the route skirts the edge of The Transept. Although this abyss is only an insignificant side drainage of Bright Angel Creek, its size nevertheless hints at the true scale of the Grand Canyon. From some overlooks it is possible to see Bright Angel Point and the Grand Canyon Lodge on the far side of the drainage. On a clear day, you can even see the San Francisco Peaks, which lie 70 miles to the south.

After 2.5 miles the Widforss Trail strays away from the canyon's edge and heads due south through the forest. Dropping ever so slightly, the route passes a couple of picnic tables before breaking out of the trees to reveal a grand panorama. The trail stops short of Widforss Point itself (it is located less than 0.5 mile to the southeast), but the vista at trail's end is nevertheless impressive. From this spot, the view looks into Haunted Canyon directly below and Phantom Creek just beyond. It also takes in such landmarks as Osiris Temple, Tower of Set, Isis Temple, Cheops Pyramid, Buddha Temple, and Manu Temple.

**Be prepared:** Before setting out on the Widforss Trail, be sure to pack some water; none is found along the hike. Watch for lightning, especially during the thunderstorms that often build on summer afternoons. Although this hike takes 4 to 5 hours to complete, you may want to consider an overnight visit to enjoy the views during different times of the day. If so, be sure to obtain a backcountry permit.

## 7  *Uncle Jim Trail*

*Distance:* 5 miles roundtrip
*Difficulty:* easy
*Hiking time:* 3 hours
*Elevation:* 8260 to 8475 feet
*Management:* Grand Canyon NP

*Wilderness status:* none
*Season:* May to October
*USGS map:* Bright Angel Point
*GPS coordinates:* 36.217030 N, 112.056631 W

*Getting there:* The Uncle Jim Trail shares a trailhead with the North Kaibab Trail. To find it, drive about 2 miles north from the Grand Canyon Lodge to the signed right turn. To reach the Grand Canyon Lodge at North Rim Village from Flagstaff, drive north on US Highway 89 to Alternate US Highway 89. Turn west and drive 55 miles to Jacob Lake. Turn south onto Arizona Highway 67 and continue for another 45 miles to the lodge.

The Uncle Jim Trail provides a short introduction to the forests and rim area of the North Rim. A somewhat dubious honor, the route was named for "Uncle Jim" Owens, a game warden who worked in the region in the early part of the 20th century. Following accepted game management practice at the time, Owens reportedly killed more than five hundred mountain lions in order to strengthen the deer population. The slaughter was thought by some ecologists to have had just the opposite effect, however; the deer multiplied and reached numbers too great for the area to support. The resulting starvation of thousands of deer highlighted the importance of predators in maintaining nature's balance.

Like the Widforss Trail, this route leads through a variety of forests typical of the North Rim. Ponderosa pines grow in the drier areas, and a lush mix of white fir, Douglas fir, Engelmann spruce, Colorado blue spruce, and quaking aspen is found in areas that hold more moisture. Many of these trees are quite mature and impressive, to say the least. Mule deer are a common sight along the trail.

From the trailhead, the Uncle Jim Trail follows the canyon rim for a short distance, offering views into Roaring Springs Canyon. In less than 0.5 mile, the trail reaches a junction. The Uncle Jim Trail keeps right, and the Ken Patrick Trail heads left. Shortly thereafter, the route crosses a shallow drainage where the trail makes its only noticeable climb—less than 200 feet—out the other side. It then reaches a second trail junction, with a 1.5-mile loop. Either way is fine: Both routes cut across mostly level terrain before reaching the vicinity of Uncle Jim Point. A hitching post and signs of heavy stock use along the route are evidence that Uncle Jim Point is a favorite destination for mule trains on the North Rim.

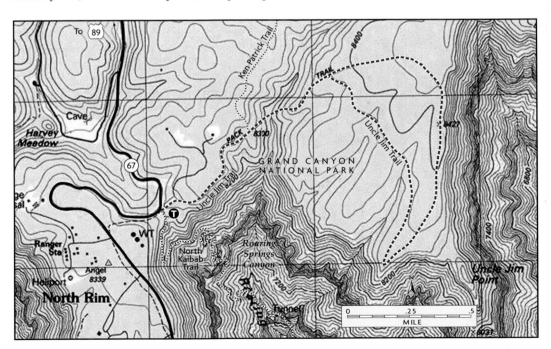

Trail signs offer guidance along the Uncle Jim Trail.

From land's end, you get a good view of both Roaring Springs Canyon and the sinuous North Kaibab Trail, which drops into its depths. It is also possible to peer into the upper end of the Bright Angel Creek drainage. Underfoot, note the variety of fossils embedded in the exposed Kaibab Limestone. This rock was deposited 270 million years ago at the bottom of a warm inland sea, and the accumulated remains of various marine creatures are abundant. The plants along the rim area are strikingly different from those of the forests you just walked through. Because of the rim's southern exposure and steeper topography, it is both drier and warmer. This results in a floral community more typical of lower elevations, one where pinyon pine, juniper, Gambel oak, and manzanita are the dominant species.

**Be prepared:** No water is found along the Uncle Jim Trail, so pack your own. Watch for lightning during stormy periods.

## 8 *Kanab Creek*

*Distance:* 31 miles roundtrip
*Difficulty:* strenuous
*Hiking time:* 4 days
*Elevation:* 3800 to 3050 feet
*Management:* BLM, Kaibab NF
*Wilderness status:* Kanab Creek WA

*Season:* year-round
*USGS maps:* Jumpup Canyon, Kanab Point, Grama Spring
*GPS coordinates:* 36.565547 N, 112.744609 W

***Getting there:*** As one of two main access points for Kanab Creek, Hack Canyon is quite remote in comparison to most trailheads mentioned in this book. From Fredonia, drive 8 miles west on Arizona Highway 389 to County Road 109, a well-maintained gravel road signed for Mount Trumbull. This is also the turnoff for Toroweap Point. Turn south and drive 23 miles to a sign for Hack Reservoir. Turn left onto a secondary dirt road and follow it 9.5 miles to the end. At one time improved to serve a uranium mine nearly 6 miles in, this road is sometimes impassable after heavy rains. Be sure to check with the BLM before driving in. The 4 miles beyond the mine are characteristically rougher. The hike begins at a fence marking the Kanab Creek Wilderness boundary.

Running some 60 miles from the town of Fredonia to the Colorado River, the lower corridor of Kanab Creek offers some of the finest canyon hiking anywhere. With its headwaters deep within Utah, this is the largest drainage system on the North Rim of the Grand Canyon. Within its last 30 miles, Kanab Creek has etched out a spectacular gorge among soaring red rock cliffs. This hike begins near Willow Spring in Hack Canyon and descends to the park boundary at the mouth of Jumpup Canyon.

From the trailhead, the route follows the bottom of Hack Canyon to its confluence with Kanab Creek, 5 miles away. If you should happen to begin the hike on a hot afternoon, don't be discouraged by the desolate nature of the surrounding landscape. About 2.5 miles in, sandstone walls appear and eventually close ranks to give the canyon a more comfortable feel.

Dropping very little in 5 miles, Hack Canyon can be explored via the gently meandering but rocky wash bottom. You can also save time by

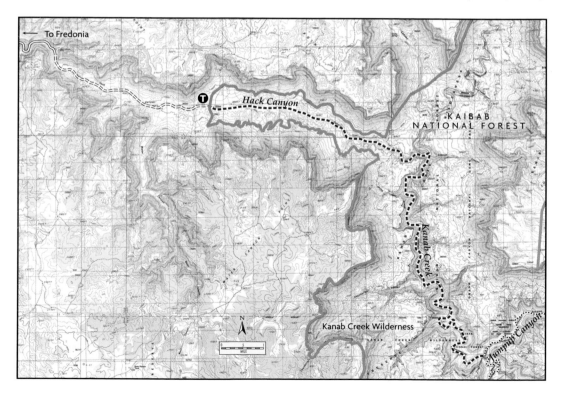

Ferns growing at a spring along Kanab Creek

picking out old cattle trails that cut across the meanders. Watch for shell fossils in the limestone rubble of the creekbed. Within the last mile of Hack Canyon, a fence dividing BLM and Forest Service lands is encountered.

When you reach Kanab Creek, turn downstream to follow the main canyon south. Here again, cow trails that cut across the meanders can save some time and wrangling among thick growths of tamarisk. Kanab Creek is intermittent at this point and the creek itself cannot be counted on as a source of water. About 2.5 miles downstream from the mouth of Hack Canyon is the first of several reliable springs along Kanab Creek. This one, located in a shady grotto in the canyon's east wall, is marked by a hanging garden of maidenhair fern and columbine. Here, steady drips will eventually fill water bottles.

In addition to the canyon's prodigious thickets of tamarisk, some rather ancient cottonwood trees are scattered along the creek bottom. Signifying the light use that the area receives, very few of these inviting trees are accompanied by the hiker-established campsites that plague the more popular canyons of the Colorado Plateau. As long as access remains difficult, Kanab Creek should stay this way.

Defined by cliffs of Supai Formation sandstone, the hike along Kanab Creek is scenic, even in its early stages. Distant cliffs of Kaibab Limestone and the Toroweap Formation add depth and visual interest to the drainage. Beginning at the mouth of Jumpup Canyon, however, the canyon begins to descend through the massive layer of Redwall Limestone that gives the Grand Canyon much of its vertical latitude. From this point to the Colorado River, the route becomes considerably more rugged.

From Hack Canyon it is 10.5 miles to the mouth of Jumpup Canyon, the turnaround point for this hike. With a shuttle, you could continue hiking another 9 miles up Jumpup Canyon to the end of Forest Service Road 423. Because this road drops off from the Kaibab Plateau, it is not passable during the winter months. Several days of hiking may also be added by continuing downstream from Jumpup Canyon to the Colorado River, a one-way trip of 16 miles. Unlike the upper end of Kanab Creek, this route requires a bit of scrambling over boulders and across ledges, and perhaps even a swim or two. Because the national park boundary is crossed at Jumpup, a permit is required for overnight hiking beyond this point. Located about 5 miles downstream from Jumpup Canyon is Shower Bath Spring, an interesting discharge of water that was mentioned by John Wesley Powell. From the end of the road in Hack Canyon, it is a 63-mile roundtrip hike to the Colorado River.

**Be prepared:** Because Hack Canyon and the upper part of the Kanab Creek section of this hike are normally dry, be prepared to pack in two days' worth of water. Willow Spring lies within 0.25 mile of the trailhead, but it has been fouled by cattle. Summertime temperatures can be particularly high in this canyon system, and it is not advisable to travel alone as this is one of the remotest sections of the state. Flash floods may pose a threat, especially in the summer months.

# 9 *Mount Trumbull*

| | |
|---|---|
| **Distance:** 5 miles roundtrip | **Wilderness status:** Mount Trumbull WA |
| **Difficulty:** moderate | **Season:** April to November |
| **Hiking time:** 3 hours | **USGS map:** Mount Trumbull NW |
| **Elevation:** 6500 to 8029 feet | **GPS coordinates:** 36.391837 N, |
| **Management:** BLM, Grand Canyon– | 113.150978 W |
| Parashant NM | |

**Getting there:** Follow Arizona Highway 389 west for 8 miles from Fredonia, and turn south onto County Road 109 at the BLM's Mount Trumbull sign. This long but good gravel road is also the way to Toroweap Point in Grand Canyon National Park. Follow it south for 47 miles to County Road 5, the turnoff for Mount Trumbull. Continue up this winding but maintained gravel road for 7 miles to a BLM administrative site. The signed trailhead is located just beyond on the right.

Rising above the remote Tuweep region of the Arizona Strip, Mount Trumbull offers a wonderful walk through pine forests, plus some nice views. In January 2000 Mount Trumbull became part of the newly established Grand Canyon–Parashant National Monument, which encompasses more than a million acres of the Arizona Strip.

The hike begins by following an old road to the east, but it soon turns to a single-track trail. It also starts to climb at a moderate grade across the south face of Trumbull. Here, among mature stands of pinyon pine and sporadic patches of manzanita, much of the hike's 1500-foot climb is achieved. Views to the south include Mount Logan, which, like Mount Trumbull, is an old basalt flow.

A forest of ponderosa pine dominates the southeastern face of the mountain, and scattered about are many stately old-growth trees, or yellow barks. Inhabitants of this timberland include mule deer and the tassel-eared Kaibab

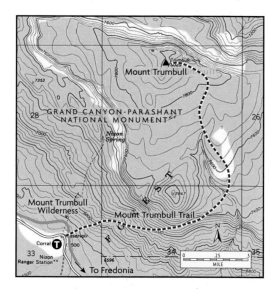

squirrel. Hiking among these tall trees is quite pleasurable.

At approximately 1.5 miles from the trailhead the actual trail disappears, but it is easy to

Ponderosa pines on Mount Trumbull

bushwhack to the summit from this point. The forest understory is open save for a few thickets of Gambel oak, and although some may wish to use a compass and topo map, it is just as easy to follow an uphill grade in a northerly direction until you can climb no farther. In order to protect the pristine condition of the mountain's summit, the BLM has purposely forgone trail construction along this final leg of the hike. Hikers who are uncomfortable about traveling cross-country may want to avoid this route.

The summit is marked by geological survey markers, a pile of rocks, and the remains of an old weather station. A trail register passes along the interesting experiences of previous hikers, and views to the north, south, and east are spectacular. Included in the panorama is the Toroweap section of the Grand Canyon and the wooded Kaibab Plateau.

**Be prepared:** Be sure to fill your canteen at the spring near the parking area; no water exists along the trail.

## 10  *Havasu Canyon*

| | |
|---|---|
| *Distance:* 20 miles roundtrip | *Wilderness status:* none |
| *Difficulty:* strenuous | *Season:* year-round |
| *Hiking time:* 2 days | *USGS maps:* Havasu Falls, Supai |
| *Elevation:* 5200 to 2700 feet | *GPS coordinates:* 36.159824 N, |
| *Management:* Havasupai Indian Tribe | 112.709359 W |

**Getting there:** From Flagstaff, drive 74 miles west on Interstate 40 to the small town of Seligman, where you will find the last services along this drive. Turn onto Arizona Highway 66 and follow it northwest for 28 miles to Tribal Road 18. Turn right and follow this paved road for 68 miles to Hualapai Hilltop at the road's end. Before leaving for this hike, you must make a reservation with the Havasupai Tribe. As of

2015, the price includes an entry fee, an environmental care fee, and a camping fee. Because camping spaces are limited, it is advisable to make reservations well in advance. Reservations may be made by calling or writing the Havasupai Tourist Enterprise (see Appendix A, under "Other Agencies").

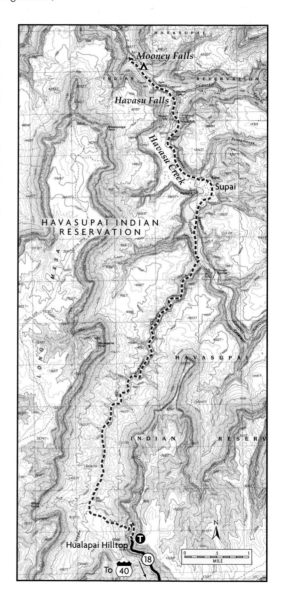

Havasu is one of those places where a spectacular natural setting combines with the fascination of native peoples to create a uniquely memorable backcountry excursion. Living for the past several centuries within this beautiful side canyon of the Grand Canyon, the Havasupai Indians are comfortably isolated from the maddening rush of the outside world. Adding to the Garden of Eden ambience of their home are the clear blue-green waters of Havasu Creek and the incredible waterfalls that are formed as the creek tumbles toward the Colorado River.

With plenty of parking and stable facilities for the tribal horse packers, Hualapai Hilltop is the route's trailhead. For the first mile the trail descends through a series of moderately steep switchbacks. It then continues to drop at a moderate grade for another 0.5 mile before reaching the canyon bottom. For the rest of the way the trail is either level or it descends along easy grade changes. Because the route is utilized by pack animals, it is well maintained and easy to follow.

For the first 6.5 miles from Hualapai Hilltop, the route follows a dry canyon. But 1.5 miles before reaching the village of Supai, it joins Havasu Canyon, in which flow the brilliant blue-green waters of Havasu Creek. Gaining its color from limestone deposits above, this permanent creek supports an inviting riparian ecosystem of cottonwoods, willows, and other water-loving trees, which provide welcome shade, especially on hot summer days.

Upon reaching Supai, 8 miles from the trailhead, the trail passes scattered homes and fields before arriving at the village center. You must stop at the tourist office to pick up your permit and pay your entry fee. A short distance beyond the tourist office is a restaurant that serves breakfast, lunch, and dinner. A store sells various food supplies, and a US Post Office accepts outgoing mail. Because most supplies are brought to the village via horse or mule trains, everything is more expensive, but not unreasonably so.

After registering at the tourist office and stocking up on any extra supplies, continue

Don't miss scenic Mooney Falls along Havasu Creek.

through the village (signs point the way) and hike another 2 miles to Havasu Falls and the campground. The trail skirts left of 100-foot-high Havasu Falls, offering a good view of the spectacle. Navajo and Fiftyfoot Falls, not visible from the trail, are passed on the way. Shortly beyond Havasu Falls you reach the campground, which is scattered along the next 0.5 mile of the creek. A campground host is usually on hand to check your permit. Because ground fires are prohibited, you will need to bring a camp stove, a must for any overnight visitor.

A short distance beyond the last campsite is the largest of the falls: 200-foot-high Mooney Falls. Good views can be had from the rim of the drop-off, but make the climb down to the base to really experience this natural wonder. This is achieved by passing through two tunnels and then descending a steep (and somewhat frightening) series of ladders and steps built by miners more than a hundred years ago. This descent is an adventure in itself.

Although this hike turns around at Mooney Falls, you can continue another 2 miles to smaller Beaver Falls and eventually to the Colorado River, 4 miles beyond. Because of flooding, however, the going can be slow beyond Mooney. Devastating flash floods occasionally sweep down Havasu Creek, altering the creekbed and wiping out natural pools in the process.

**Be prepared:** Be sure to plan your visit to Havasu Canyon well ahead by making reservations early. Temperatures in the canyon can be above the century mark during summer afternoons. Be sure to bring plenty of water for the hike in (water is available at the village and campground), and pack along some sandals for wading and swimming in the creek.

## 1 1  *Paria River Canyon*

*Distance:* 38 miles one-way
*Difficulty:* moderate
*Hiking time:* 4 days
*Elevation:* 4300 to 3200 feet
*Management:* BLM, Vermilion Cliffs NM, Glen Canyon NRA

*Wilderness status:* Paria Canyon–Vermilion Cliffs WA
*Season:* April to November
*USGS maps:* Bridger Point, Wrather Arch, Water Pockets, Ferry Swale, Lees Ferry
*GPS coordinates:* 37.079948 N, 111.890280 W

*Getting there:* From Page, Arizona, drive west on US Highway 89 to the turnoff for the White House trailhead. Turn south and drive 2 miles beyond the Paria Ranger Station to the signed trailhead.

Certainly one of the most impressive abysses of the Colorado Plateau, the Paria River Canyon offers adventurous hikers an exceptional four- or five-day trip. With sandstone walls soaring hundreds of feet above the wash bottom, this drainage offers an unforgettable introduction to the geology of northern Arizona's red rock country. So spectacular is this canyon that it has been highlighted in many national publications over the years. Unfortunately, this publicity has led to an increase in visitation numbers—the end result of which has been the institution of a permit system and additional user regulations.

Before beginning the hike, be sure to obtain and pay for a day- or overnight-use permit from the BLM. This may be done online or by mail (see Arizona Strip Field Office in Appendix A, under "Bureau of Land Management").

Although the canyon may be followed in either direction, it makes the most sense to begin

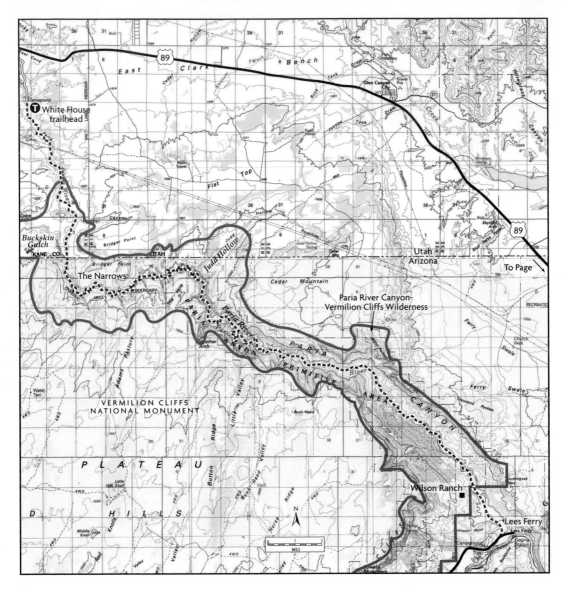

upstream and travel down. Three trailheads (all within Utah) allow access at the upper end of the canyon system—one on the main canyon and two on Buckskin Gulch. This description follows the Paria River Canyon route beginning from the White House trailhead.

Begin the route by following the wash bottom downstream toward the south. Expect to make hundreds of stream crossings through ankle-deep water in all seasons. Upon passing beneath a powerline 2.3 miles from the trailhead, the canyon enters the Paria Canyon–Vermilion Cliffs Wilderness. Arizona's share of the canyon also falls within the 294,000-acre Vermilion Cliffs National Monument.

Nearly 4 miles from the trailhead the river enters The Narrows. Prior to this point, the geologic landscape includes the colorful siltstones of the Carmel Formation. Upon entering The Narrows, however, the scene is dominated by soaring walls of Navajo Sandstone. In places these walls rise hundreds of feet straight up and are only a couple of dozen feet apart.

Because of this restricted canyon bottom, The Narrows is no place to be during a flash flood. Typically, a heavy rain upstream can send a wall of water up to 80 feet high gushing through the canyon, and a lack of high places in The Narrows precludes escape from this danger. For that reason, do not plan on camping within The Narrows. Suitable campsites are found both at the start of The Narrows and 4 miles farther downstream—about 8 miles from the trailhead. To avoid the threat of flooding, keep in mind that the flash flood season includes the months of July, August, and early September (although flash floods can occur at any time of year) and that these summer cloudbursts often occur in the afternoon.

Partway through The Narrows, 7.1 miles from the trailhead, the Paria River reaches Buckskin Gulch. Even narrower than the main canyon, the walls of this abyss are only a few feet apart in places, greatly obstructing the sky and sunshine. Rockjams and logjams, along with stagnant pools of water, must be negotiated along the way, but this stunning slot canyon is well worth the challenges. From the Paria River it is 13.5 miles up Buckskin Gulch to the Wire Pass trailhead and 16.3 miles to the Buckskin trailhead.

A short distance beyond the mouth of Buckskin Gulch, the Paria River enters Arizona. The route still follows the canyon bottom at this point. About 12 miles from the trailhead (5.2 miles below Buckskin Gulch) is the first reliable spring. Although the Paria River flows throughout the year, stream water in this area should not be consumed, even after treating, because it may be tainted with pesticides. Its discoloration is due to bentonite. A second spring is located 22 miles from the trailhead, and a third is found 25.4 miles in. Although these are springs, you should treat the water anyway.

Throughout the hike you may come across evidence of prehistoric inhabitants of this part of the Colorado Plateau. Petroglyphs and other artifacts indicate the area's onetime occupation by

Vibrant box elder tree leaves add color to the confines of the Narrows in spring.

the Ancestral Puebloans (formerly known as the Anasazi). Archaeologists believe that the Ancestral Puebloans utilized the Paria River Canyon as a travel route and for hunting and gathering. Use of the canyon during historic times is also evident. At 17.6 miles, at the mouth of Judd Hollow, are the remains of a pumping station installed by ranchers in the 1940s. The ambitious plan was to irrigate grazing lands hundreds of feet above. Nearly 33 miles from the trailhead is the old Wilson Ranch site. And at trail's end, the antiquated John D. Lee homestead welcomes hikers back to civilization. Sent to this spot on the Colorado River to establish a ferry crossing in 1871 (Lees Ferry), Lee and three others drove Lee's cattle downstream from the Mormon town of Pahreah, making them the first white men to traverse the entire length of the canyon.

After following the canyon bottom for 28 miles, the route begins following a trail that leaves the wash to skirt around a boulder slide. Accessing a low benchland to the right of the river, this trail provides the most sensible route for the remainder of the hike.

**Be prepared:** When traversing the lower portion of the canyon, the terrain opens up considerably, so heat exposure can be a problem. Be sure to carry plenty of water through this last stretch. Campfires are prohibited in the Paria River Canyon, and group size is restricted to ten or fewer. Other regulations also apply. Drinking water is at a premium, as is shade in many parts of the canyon. Flash floods occur frequently, especially during the summer months. Peak visitation months include April, May, June, September, and October, and crowds are especially heavy during university spring breaks and on holiday weekends. The BLM can provide information on commercial shuttle services, as well as a detailed map and guide to the canyon for a nominal fee. This one-way hike takes four days or longer to complete and requires a shuttle back to the upper trailhead.

## 12  *Spencer Trail*

| | |
|---|---|
| *Distance:* 3 miles roundtrip | *Wilderness status:* none |
| *Difficulty:* strenuous | *Season:* year-round |
| *Hiking time:* 3 hours | *USGS map:* Lees Ferry |
| *Elevation:* 3180 to 4740 feet | *GPS coordinates:* 36.866411 N, |
| *Management:* Glen Canyon NRA | 111.586971 W |

*Getting there:* The trailhead is located at Lees Ferry—the put-in for rafters headed down the Grand Canyon. To reach Lees Ferry, turn north from Alternate US Highway 89 at Marble Canyon and drive 5.9 miles to the boat ramp at the end of the paved road. Park here and walk upstream past a scattered collection of old stone structures.

Although a short hike distance-wise, the historic Spencer Trail climbs 1500 feet in only 1.5 miles. This effort is not without its rewards, however, as the top offers spectacular views of the Colorado River and the surrounding red rock desert.

The trail actually begins at the far end of the Lees Ferry Historic District. Sent to this spot in 1871 by the Mormon Church, John D. Lee established a ferry to transport travelers across the Colorado River. This is also the place where part of the Spanish expedition led by Silvestre Vélez de Escalante crossed in 1776. Because the Grand Canyon runs downstream from this point and Glen Canyon stretches upstream, this is the only suitable crossing for many, many miles. Among the antiquities still found there today are the remains of the Lees Ferry Fort, built in 1874, a post office constructed in 1911, and an old boiler

dating back to the early part of the 20th century. The boiler recalls Charles Spencer's time spent at Lees Ferry. Convinced that there was gold in the local Chinle Shale, Spencer imported a lot of machinery to extract the precious metal. To supply the fuel needed to keep his equipment running, he built the Spencer Trail in 1910 so that mules could pack coal in from Warm Creek 28 miles to the north.

Just beyond the boiler, the Spencer Trail takes off up the rocky slope at trail marker 6. Not regularly maintained, the route is somewhat faint at this point, so follow it carefully. Very shortly, the trail begins a steep, 1500-foot climb to the top of the cliffs directly in front. Conditions along the way include lots of loose rocks, a heavily eroded tread, and exposure to severe drop-offs. The trail also climbs through several switchbacks. The upside to these difficult hiking conditions is

The window of an old stone building at Lees Ferry frames a colorful landscape.

twofold, however. First is the fact that the route receives little use; second is the nonstop scenery afforded along the way. Almost immediately, the view of the river flowing through the Lees Ferry area opens up into a sweeping panorama. The Echo Cliffs rise along the river's left bank, and the Vermilion Cliffs march southward to the right.

Also of interest along the Spencer Trail is the local geology. The Spencer Trail begins by climbing up the dark brown rock of the Moenkopi Formation. This is followed by the lighter

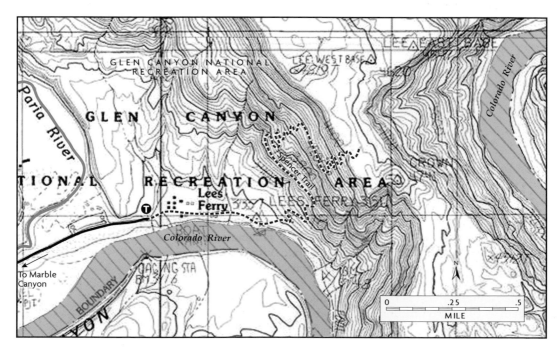

brown Shinarump Formation and then the bluish shale of the Chinle Formation. Above it are the vertical cliffs of the Moenave and Kayenta Formations, and finally an impressive rimrock of Navajo Sandstone.

At trail's end you will find yourself on top of a narrow plateau that separates two meanders in the Colorado River. In addition to the previously mentioned landforms that lie south of Lees Ferry, this high point also affords views of Lake Powell, Navajo Mountain, and the Navajo Power Plant near Page to the north. In addition, you will get a feel for just how sinuous the Colorado River can be.

On the return hike you may notice the hull of a boat lurking in the shallow water near the bank directly below. This is the remains of the *Charles H. Spencer,* an 85-foot-long steamboat. Upon completing his trail, Spencer learned that mules could not haul enough coal to run his mining operation. Determined as ever, he brought in a boat, piece by piece, from San Francisco on which to float the coal down the river. After making five trips, however, he realized that the boat required all of the coal it could carry just to complete the trip. In the end, tests concluded that there was not enough gold in these sedimentary rocks to turn a profit, anyway.

**Be prepared:** Because the trail is steep and rugged, watch your footing. No water exists along the route, so be sure to bring plenty. And, because temperatures can top 100 degrees Fahrenheit from late spring to early fall, you may want to save this hike for cooler seasons.

# 13 *Soap Creek*

| | |
|---|---|
| **Distance:** 9 miles roundtrip | **Wilderness status:** none |
| **Difficulty:** strenuous | **Season:** year-round |
| **Hiking time:** 6 hours | **USGS maps:** Emmett Wash, Bitter Springs |
| **Elevation:** 4200 to 3000 feet | **GPS coordinates:** 36.727666 N, |
| **Management:** BLM, Grand Canyon NP | 111.758609 W |

**Getting there:** This hike begins at a developed trailhead on BLM land. Drive about 8 miles southwest of Marble Canyon on Alternate US Highway 89 to the Cliff Dwellers Lodge. Drive another 1.1 miles past the lodge to a good dirt road that takes off to the left. A small sign is located near a gate (be sure to close it behind you) in the highway fence. At an old corral and cow camp the road veers left to reach the trailhead, which is 0.4 mile from the highway.

Providing an appropriate prelude for boaters heading down the Grand Canyon, Marble Canyon is itself a spectacular abyss worthy of investigation. For those on foot, one of the most interesting approaches is to hike down Soap Creek, which drains into the Colorado River a few miles downstream from the Marble Canyon Bridge.

Generally speaking, the hiking route follows the canyon bottom downstream, but there are some variables along the way. From the parking area, a faded trail heads east into a wash. As you follow this small side drainage for a ways, you will see how this canyon develops as it drops in elevation. The canyon walls become more pronounced, and pour-offs that are at first insignificant eventually become more difficult to pass. At about 0.7 mile from the trailhead, the route reaches the South Fork of Soap Creek. Keep left here and continue downstream.

After reaching the South Fork of Soap Creek, the hike becomes more interesting. At one point

Soap Creek Rapids in Marble Canyon

the canyon is blocked by a massive rockslide. To get through, simply pick whichever way looks best—there is no one route. Within 0.5 mile of this boulder choke, a more ominous obstacle looms as an enormous pour-off drops 100 feet or so to the canyon bottom. Marked by cairns, a precarious trail climbs up and around to the right of the pour-off. Caution should be taken in this stretch because dangerous heights are encountered. The bypass ends by dropping down a stable boulder fall. Upon reaching the canyon bottom, the route continues through house-size rocks

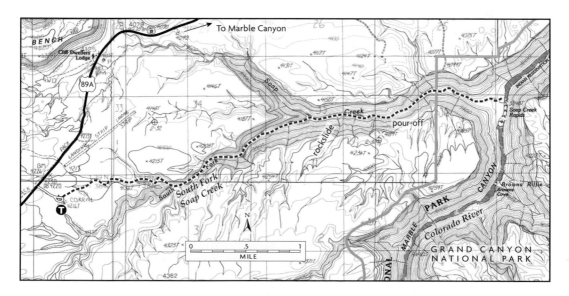

that require some basic bouldering skills to get through. Beyond this difficulty the hike becomes relatively tame, with only minor obstacles.

About 2 miles from the trailhead, the South Fork reaches a major canyon junction at which the route continues downstream to the right. A left turn accesses the North Fork of Soap Creek, which is impassable without ropes. Beyond here, Soap Creek Canyon continues due east for another 2.5 miles to the Colorado River, the turnaround for this hike. A popular camp spot for boaters, the mouth of Soap Creek is also the site of Soap Creek Rapids. Although a mere ripple compared to the big drops of the Grand Canyon, it is still exciting to watch rafters and kayakers run through. This is also a good place to take note of the local geology. The vertical walls of Marble Canyon, like those of Soap Creek Canyon, consist mostly of Coconino Sandstone, but there are exposed faces of Hermit Shale as well.

**Be prepared:** Because some of this hike lies within Grand Canyon National Park, you will need to obtain a backcountry permit for any overnight trips. Where water is concerned, it is either feast or famine in Soap Creek Canyon. Normally the canyon is dry, so be sure to pack a few quarts for drinking. On occasion, however, this drainage witnesses some horrendous flash floods, which should be taken into account when planning a hike. Typically, summer thunderstorms pose the biggest threat, but early fall and spring rain showers may also produce dangerous levels of runoff. Because summers can be unbearably hot, the best seasons for hiking down Soap Creek are spring and fall.

# 14  *Onyx Bridge*

**Distance:** 4 miles roundtrip
**Difficulty:** easy
**Hiking time:** 3 hours
**Elevation:** 5800 to 5500 feet
**Management:** Petrified Forest NP

**Wilderness status:** Petrified Forest WA
**Season:** year-round
**USGS map:** Kachina Point
**GPS coordinates:** 35.083640 N, 109.789036 W

**Getting there:** From the park's north entrance off Interstate 40, drive 2.4 miles to the Southwest-style Painted Desert Inn Museum at Kachina Point. Completed in 1924, this structure was remodeled by the Civilian Conservation Corps (CCC) in the 1930s. It is now a National Historic Landmark. The hike begins behind the museum. Before you start, be sure to check with the ranger inside for complete directions. He or she may be able to point out the location of Onyx Bridge in the distance and offer directions.

Situated in the starkly beautiful northern region of Petrified Forest National Park, Onyx Bridge is one of many petrified logs strewn across this desolate reach of Arizona. It earned its name because it spans a small wash. Nearly as interesting are the countless other pieces of fossilized wood found along the hike. Most of this hike falls within an established wilderness area, and the hike mostly cuts across open terrain rather than following an actual trail.

Dropping down the mesa from Kachina Point, a well-established trail accesses the flats below but fades after 0.5 mile, leaving you to follow small streambeds for the next 0.5 mile north to Lithodendron Wash. (Because no trail exists beyond the 0.5-mile mark, it is important to keep a close eye on the surrounding terrain at all times.) Upon crossing the wash bottom, the unmarked route cuts across a broad meander before reconnecting with the usually dry

You will find plenty of petrified wood in Petrified Forest National Park.

waterway. Follow the wash for another 0.25 mile to where it begins bending to the right, or east. A large tree growing in the middle of the wash marks this point in the wash. A small side canyon or arroyo cutting into a hillside on the left comes into view near there. Follow this arroyo upstream a short distance to where it splits. Keep to the right and follow the main channel past a scattered pile of petrified logs. Less than 100 yards beyond, a 15-foot-high pour-off is reached. Climb the steep bank to the left to find the bridge just above.

Like the countless other mineralized logs in the park, Onyx Bridge was washed to this former flood plain during the Triassic Period—about 225 million years ago. After being covered by mud, volcanic ash, and silt, the original wood fiber was slowly petrified by silicon-enriched groundwater. It is interesting to keep in mind that these trees, now jettisoned in a parched and desolate landscape, are a product of an era when early dinosaurs roamed lush forests. Just as fascinating, though, is the fact that the entire region was subsequently inundated by a vast freshwater lake (about 8 million years ago) and that enough time has since passed to allow erosion to expose this geologic story.

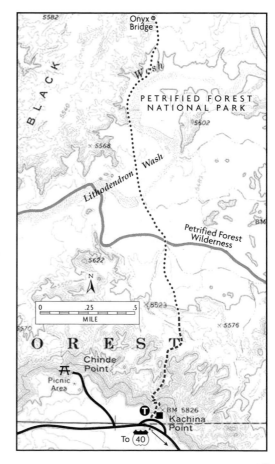

**Be prepared:** Although finding the bridge may prove difficult, you are not likely to get lost, because the Painted Desert Inn Museum at Kachina Point is plainly visible at all times. Because water is not available along the hike, it is important to bring plenty, especially in the summer when temperatures can top 100 degrees Fahrenheit. A hat and plenty of sunscreen are also advisable. Watch for lightning during afternoon storms in the summer months, and flash floods after heavy rain showers. Also keep an eye out for the rattlesnakes that inhabit the area.

You don't need a permit for day hiking, but one is required for overnight stays. The park typically closes around sunset, though budget constraints may shorten the hours. Of course, removing pieces of petrified wood or any other natural material is strictly prohibited. Prehistoric artifacts are protected by law as well.

## 15 Keet Seel

| | |
|---|---|
| **Distance:** 17 miles roundtrip | **Season:** May to September |
| **Difficulty:** strenuous | **USGS maps:** Betatakin Ruin, Keet Seel |
| **Hiking time:** 2 days | Ruin, Marsh Pass |
| **Elevation:** 7220 to 6300 feet | **GPS coordinates:** 36.683008 N, |
| **Management:** Navajo NM, Navajo Nation | 110.542049 W |
| **Wilderness status:** none | |

**Getting there:** Drive 20 miles southwest from Kayenta on US Highway 160. Turn right on Arizona Highway 564 at the sign for Navajo National Monument. Follow this road for 10 miles to the end of the pavement and the monument's headquarters.

Often billed as the largest cliff dwelling in the state, Keet Seel offers one of Arizona's best-preserved glimpses into the prehistoric past. Tucked inside a beautiful alcove in a remote canyon of the Navajo Indian Nation, the ruins provide the perfect reward for a long day's hike. The stunning red rock scenery found throughout the journey is equally rewarding.

Although it lies within the Navajo Indian Nation, Keet Seel is part of Navajo National Monument and is administered by the National Park Service. Before you begin the hike, you must first obtain a permit (see Navajo National Monument in Appendix A, under "National Parks and Monuments"). Because the Park Service limits the number of visitors to Keet Seel to twenty people per day, it is a good idea to get the permit well in advance (the Park Service allows up to sixty days for advance reservations). The cliff dwelling is only open between Memorial Day and Labor Day weekends.

Upon picking up your permit, be sure to obtain complete directions to Keet Seel from the park staff. The hike begins by following the same route that accesses the Betatakin Cliff Dwelling. Because the 5-mile roundtrip hike to Betatakin is ranger-guided, it can be very informative. After paralleling an old dirt road for 1.5 miles, the route reaches Tsegi Point. From Tsegi Point the trail drops 700 feet through a series of switchbacks. The route to Betatakin heads to the right up a side canyon, and the Keet Seel Trail breaks off to the left toward Keet Seel Canyon. From this point, the hike is mostly along sandy wash bottoms; the walking is easy, save for occasional soft ground. Numbered trail markers every 0.5 mile correspond to a trail guide published by the Southwest Parks and Monuments Association.

After entering Keet Seel Canyon, the route comes to a junction of two canyons. To the right is Dowozhiebito and to the left Keet Seel. Just upstream in Keet Seel Canyon is a small

Part of the Keet Seel cliff dwelling in Navajo National Monument

waterfall formed by a resistant layer of Wingate Sandstone. Formed some 200 million years ago, the Wingate Formation resulted from giant sand dunes. The canyon walls above this layer consist of Kayenta and Navajo Sandstones. Like the Wingate, the Navajo Formation once consisted of sand dunes. Shortly ahead, Battleship Rock rises to the right; beyond that a pinnacle known as Kachina Mother marks the halfway point of the hike. Between here and the ruins, three additional falls are encountered. All three are easily negotiated.

In different segments of the hike, you may notice old hogans or wooden corrals in the distance. Navajo families occupy these isolated homes at different times of the year. Unrelated to the prehistoric Ancestral Puebloans, the Navajo are thought to have migrated to the Colorado Plateau soon after the Ancestral Puebloans left, perhaps during the 15th century. Traditionally nomadic, the Navajos acquired sheep from the Spanish hundreds of years ago and made them an integral part of their lives. Even today, many Navajos make a living raising sheep for wool in remote areas such as the Tsegi Canyon system. Because these camps are home to Navajo people, it is imperative to observe them only from a distance.

Prior to the arrival of the Navajos, this region was occupied by the Ancestral Puebloans. Keet Seel, as one of the best-preserved ruins in the Southwest, offers an exquisite view of this past. With 160 rooms, this well-protected cliff dwelling was built between 1250 and 1286 A.D. Some walls are of masonry construction; others are wattle and daub, or vertical sticks with mud packed around them. Due to the fragile nature of Keet Seel, visitors to the ruin must be accompanied by a ranger. Stationed in quarters nearby, rangers conduct regular tours, but each group is limited to five people.

**Be prepared:** A primitive campground is located nearby for anyone who wants to stay overnight at Keet Seel. A backcountry permit is required, however. Water is not available and woodcutting is prohibited, so bring your own water and a stove. Because this is Navajo tribal land, exploring beyond the designated route to Keet Seel is strictly prohibited. In addition, driving beyond designated roadways is also prohibited.

Temperatures in the canyon bottoms can approach 100 degrees Fahrenheit on summer afternoons, so carry plenty of water. Watch for flash floods during the rainy months of July and August. In addition, the Park Service warns of falling rocks near cliff bottoms and areas of quicksand. Disturbing or removing any artifact is strictly prohibited. The best rule is to look but not touch. Although it is possible to complete this hike in a long day, an overnight stay would make the trip more pleasurable.

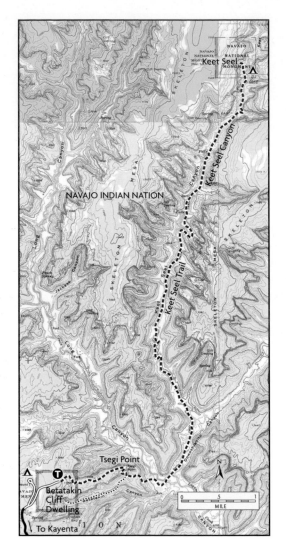

## 16 *White House Ruin*

*Distance:* 2.5 miles roundtrip
*Difficulty:* moderate
*Hiking time:* 2 hours
*Elevation:* 6200 to 5675 feet
*Management:* Canyon de Chelly NM, Navajo Nation

*Wilderness status:* none
*Season:* year-round
*USGS map:* Del Muerto
*GPS coordinates:* 36.130361 N, 109.477611 W

White House Ruin in Canyon de Chelly National Monument

*Getting there:* From US Highway 191, drive 2.7 miles east on Navajo Nation Route 7 through the town of Chinle to reach the headquarters of Canyon de Chelly National Monument. Continue 6.4 miles from the monument's headquarters on the South Rim Drive to the White House Overlook.

L ike Navajo National Monument, Canyon de Chelly National Monument includes some well-preserved Ancestral Puebloans cliff dwellings found within the Navajo Indian Nation. Because of the fragile nature of the ruins, and to protect the privacy of the Navajo families who live here, hiking in Canyon de Chelly is permitted only when in the company of a ranger or authorized Navajo guide. An exception to this rule, however, is the short and pleasant hike to the White House Ruin.

From the White House Overlook, the hiking route follows the canyon rim to the right for a short distance before passing through a tunnel. From here the trail switchbacks about 500 vertical feet down to the canyon bottom, where it enters a second tunnel. A picturesque Navajo farm nearby is strictly off-limits to hikers. The cliff dwellings are located across the canyon, on the canyon floor and in an alcove just above.

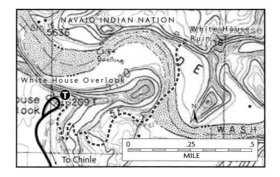

Some wading may be required. Don't be surprised if you meet up with large four-wheel-drive vehicles packed with tourists; this is how many visitors see the canyon—on guided tours that motor along the stream bottom.

A fence surrounds the actual ruins to protect them from the impact of visitors. Named for a section of white-plastered wall, the White House cliff dwelling was begun in 1040 A.D. and was occupied until the late 13th century. Much like the Navajos today, the Ancestral Puebloans grew corn and other crops on the canyon bottom. For reasons not fully understood by archaeologists, the Ancestral Puebloans abandoned this and other reaches of their homeland for areas to the south and east. Hypotheses include a prolonged drought, harassment by warring neighbors, and environmental degradation that resulted from overpopulation.

As for the species of plants encountered along the way, pinyon pine, juniper, prickly pear, and cholla cactus are common as the trail drops into the canyon. On the canyon bottom, look for large cottonwoods, willows, Russian olives, and tamarisk. Like the Russian olive, tamarisk is not native to the Southwest. It was introduced as an erosion control agent in the early part of the 20th century. Unfortunately, it has spread so rapidly that it now chokes canyon bottoms throughout the Southwest.

**Be prepared:** Bring plenty of drinking water, as stream water is not safe for consumption. Summer ushers in bright sun and high temperatures in the canyon, so plan accordingly. Take extra care along the precipitous canyon edge.

## 17 *Mount Elden Lookout*

*Distance:* 6 miles roundtrip
*Difficulty:* strenuous
*Hiking time:* 4 hours
*Elevation:* 6880 to 9280 feet
*Management:* Coconino NF

*Wilderness status:* none
*Season:* May to October
*USGS map:* Flagstaff East
*GPS coordinates:* 35.230186 N, 111.579383 W

*Getting there:* The Mount Elden trailhead is located just north of the Peaks Ranger District office of the Coconino National Forest on US Highway 89, not far from the Flagstaff Mall. Ample parking is provided for this locally popular trail.

Climbing some 2400 feet above the east end of Flagstaff, the Elden Lookout Trail rewards hikers in more ways than one. Not only does the summit afford a great bird's-eye view of the city and the surrounding Coconino Plateau—it also provides insight into how nature mends itself after a large forest fire.

The first 0.5 mile of the trail follows an easy grade through stands of pinyon pine, juniper, and ponderosa pine. Signs in this lower section point out the 1.8-mile Fat Mans Loop to the north and the 2.8-mile Pipeline Trail, which circles south along the base of Mount Elden. Watch for mountain bikers on these lower trails.

Upon reaching the toe of the mountain, the trail begins climbing at a moderate to steep

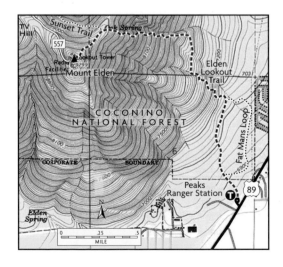

A trail sign near the summit of Mount Elden

pace. Several switchbacks are included in this section, and areas of loose rock can be expected. As the trail climbs the east face of Mount Elden, it encounters some features of the local geology. Volcanic in origin, Mount Elden is characterized in places by interesting rock formations that resulted from the cooling and shrinking of lava flows. Growing in this rocky terrain are alligator juniper, mountain mahogany, Gambel oak, cliff rose, and ponderosa pine, with Douglas fir higher up.

From the ridgetop, 2.8 miles from the trailhead, a different perspective on the area's natural history opens up. Devastated by the expansive Radio Fire in 1977, most of the timberland in the upper reaches of the mountain became a skeleton forest of blackened tree trunks. But growing back with vigor have been thickets of aspen which have begun to mature. Taller aspen trees will, over time, provide shade for evergreen saplings. These will in turn crowd out the aspens and return the area to its original mixed conifer forest. From a signed trail junction on the ridge, take a left turn to go 0.2 mile to the lookout. A right turn would start you down the 4.3-mile-long Sunset Trail which leads to Schultz Pass.

Although surrounded by radio towers, the lookout is still high enough to afford a spectacular 360-degree view. To the north are the San Francisco Peaks, and spreading out just below is the city of Flagstaff. Oak Creek Canyon and Mingus Mountain are visible to the southwest. The heavily forested Mogollon Rim spreads south to a low horizon, and dark cinder hills dot the landscape to the east.

**Be prepared:** Bring water, as none is found along the way. Leave early in the morning during the summer months to avoid lightning.

# 18 *Abineau/Bear Jaw Loop*

*Distance:* 6.8-mile loop
*Difficulty:* strenuous
*Hiking time:* 4 hours
*Elevation:* 8500 to 10,400 feet
*Management:* Coconino NF
*Wilderness status:* Kachina Peaks WA

*Season:* June to September
*USGS maps:* Humphreys Peak, White Horse Hills
*GPS coordinates:* 35.388693 N, 111.670985 W

*Getting there:* From Flagstaff drive about 20 miles north on US Highway 180 to the second signed turnoff for Forest Road 151. Turn right and drive 1.5 miles to Forest Road 418. Turn left and drive 3 miles to the signed right turn for the trailhead. Continue on this high-clearance two-wheel-drive road about 0.5 mile to its end.

Exploring the north slope of the San Francisco Peaks, the Abineau and Bear Jaw Trails combine to form a great loop hike that reveals nice subalpine forests and some great views.

From the trailhead, the route heads east along a mostly level grade for about 0.3 mile to where the Abineau and Bear Jaw Trails divide. Because

this hike description follows the loop counterclockwise, turn right at the signed junction and continue up the Abineau Trail. Climbing at a mostly moderate grade up its namesake canyon, the Abineau Trail begins in a forested mix of ponderosa pine and aspen but eventually encounters more Douglas fir, some of which are quite large. As it climbs, grades become more noticeable and the trail becomes a bit more rocky. After climbing for nearly 2 miles from the trail junction, the Abineau Trail reaches Waterline Road. Servicing a water collection system that supplies Flagstaff with drinking water, Waterline Road is excluded from the Kachina Peaks Wilderness so that service vehicles can occasionally drive the road to various springs and wells. Mountain bicycles occasionally utilize this road as well.

At the junction of the Abineau Trail and Waterline Road, avalanche paths have cleared away the timber and allow for views of Humphreys Peak above and the expanse of forest and grasslands that fall away to the north. Once on Waterline Road, follow it north and east for about 2 miles to the signed turnoff for the Bear Jaw Trail, which drops to the north down the slope of the mountain. This turnoff is about 0.25 mile beyond the actual Bear Jaw Canyon drainage.

From Waterline Road the Bear Jaw Trail descends along varying grades, accessing long abandoned sheep camps along the way.

A cluster of pine cones along the Abineau Trail

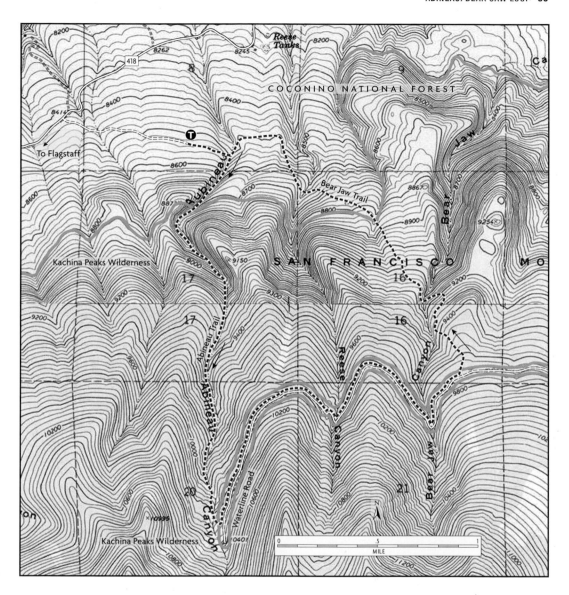

These former camps often include old carvings in the trunks of aspen trees, some of which may still be discernible. The trail also encounters some rather nice yellow-bark ponderosa pine that are quite impressive in their girth. As the trail descends, it first crosses the Bear Jaw Canyon drainage and then the Reese Canyon drainage before returning to the Abineau/Bear Jaw trail junction. From Waterline Road to the trail junction the Bear Jaw Trail covers roughly 2 miles. To return to the trailhead bear right and continue west for a short distance.

**Be prepared:** Although most of this hike falls within forests, lightning can still pose a threat during storms. Water is not typically found along this hike, so pack plenty.

## 19  *Humphreys Peak*

*Distance:* 9.6 miles roundtrip
*Difficulty:* strenuous
*Hiking time:* 6 hours
*Elevation:* 9266 to 12,633 feet
*Management:* Coconino NF

*Wilderness status:* Kachina Peaks WA
*Season:* June to September
*USGS map:* Humphreys Peak
*GPS coordinates:* 35.331144 N,
111.711566 W

*Getting there:* The Humphreys Peak Trail begins in the lower parking lot of the Arizona Snowbowl, Flagstaff's local ski area. Drive north on US Highway 180 for 7 miles to Forest Road 516, the road to the Snowbowl ski area. Turn north and follow this paved route about 7.4 miles to the first parking lot on the left. The trailhead is located at the far end.

The highest summit in the state, Humphreys Peak (12,633 feet) is more reminiscent of Colorado than Arizona. Reaching above timberline, the tallest of the San Francisco Peaks features the only true alpine environment in Arizona. Needless to say, the views from the top are awesome.

Because it stands virtually alone (nearby Agassiz and Fremont Peaks excepted), Humphreys offers hikers a real "top of the world" feeling.

The route begins by traversing a large meadow that is filled with wildflowers in the summer. Ski lifts hang empty overhead, and Agassiz Peak

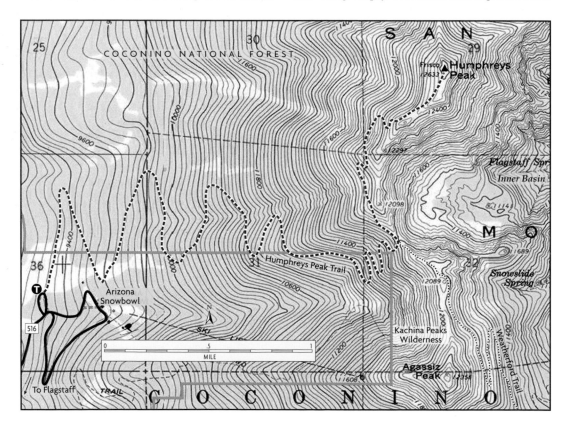

towers above to the east. Shortly, the route crosses into the Kachina Peaks Wilderness and enters a thick forest cover that typifies much of the hike to the top. Species of trees here include Engelmann spruce, cork-bark fir, and occasional aspen. Well maintained and easy to follow, the trail climbs along a mostly moderate grade to a saddle that connects Humphreys and Agassiz Peaks. Here, the tall timber is replaced by a stunted forest of bristlecone pine.

Situated at 11,800 feet, the saddle is a fine place to take in views that were for the most part blocked by the forest cover below. Timberline is not far beyond this point. Because of the fragility of the alpine environment, camping is not permitted anywhere above 11,400 feet. More specifically, because a very rare plant, *Senecio franciscanus*, grows here and nowhere else in the world, hikers are restricted to the established trail. From the saddle, the trail roughly parallels a rocky ridge that runs north for another mile to the summit of Humphreys Peak. Climbing steeply in some sections and often quite rocky, this segment of the hike is strenuous.

From the summit, incredible views stretch out in all directions. The Grand Canyon, Painted Desert, Oak Creek Canyon, Mogollon Rim, Mingus Mountain, Bill Williams Mountain, and Kendrick Mountain are but a few of the landmarks that are visible. Equally inspiring is the surrounding mountain terrain. Agassiz (12,356 feet) and Fremont (11,969 feet) Peaks rise along the ridgeline running south and southeast, and the Inner Basin drops immediately away to the south and east. Collectively, these peaks were once part of a large volcano and the Inner Basin was its crater.

A hiker walks along the summit of Humphreys Peak.

**Be prepared:** As this is wilderness, bicycles are not permitted and dogs must be on a leash at all times. Because no water is available along the Humphreys Peak Trail, be sure to bring plenty. Be prepared for rapidly deteriorating weather conditions, even in the summer months, and watch for lightning. Because thunderstorms of dangerous intensity often develop with very short notice, it is best to get an early start so that you will be off the mountain by midafternoon.

# 20 *Kachina Trail*

**Distance:** 7.2 miles one-way
**Difficulty:** moderate
**Hiking time:** 5 hours
**Elevation:** 9360 to 8620 feet
**Management:** Coconino NF

**Wilderness status:** Kachina Peaks WA
**Season:** June to October
**USGS map:** Humphreys Peak
**GPS coordinates:** 35.326775 N, 111.711330 W

**Getting there:** From Flagstaff, drive north on US Highway 180 for 7 miles to Forest Road 516, the road into the Arizona Snowbowl. Follow this paved route north for 7.4 miles to the first parking lot on the right. The Kachina Trail begins at a signed trailhead at the lot's far end. As this is a one-way hike, you will need to leave a shuttle vehicle at Schultz Pass along Forest Road 420.

Foregoing the high alpine terrain of the San Francisco Peaks in favor of old-growth forests that typify the range's middle elevations, the Kachina Trail descends easily from the Snowbowl ski area to a trailhead north of Schultz Pass. Because this trailhead is accessed by a rough road, however, this hike description tacks on a couple of extra miles by following the

Weatherford Trail to Schultz Pass itself, which is accessed by a much better forest road.

For the first few miles, the Kachina Trail passes among mature aspen groves that are interspersed with small openings thick with ferns and other lush undergrowth. Stands of old-growth Douglas fir—some with diameters of 5 feet or more—add to the forest's allure, as does

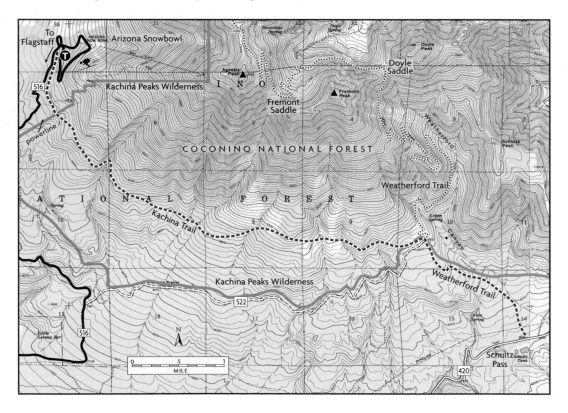

the possibility of spotting mule deer or elk. Only two annoyances detract from the beauty and tranquility of this end of the trail: it parallels the road (a source of traffic noise) for the first 0.5 mile, and it passes under a powerline about 1 mile in. Because the Kachina Trail enters the Kachina Peaks Wilderness just beyond the powerline, however, hikers are assured of eventually finding peace and solitude.

After 1.5 miles the Kachina Trail drops into a small drainage where it then skirts small cliffs and scattered house-size boulders. A trailside cave offers protection in the event of rain. Beyond this drainage the trail slowly winds its way around to the south-facing slopes of Agassiz and Fremont Peaks. As it does, it is easy to see how important slope aspect is in determining forest composition. Although aspens still grow in great numbers along these drier slopes, the firs have mostly been replaced by ponderosa pines. In addition, meadow areas that were previously waist-high with ferns now include lupine, Indian paintbrush, and a number of grasses. Adding variety to the hike is the fact that these aspen-ringed meadows are now broad enough to allow beautiful views of the peaks above.

The Kachina Trail officially ends 5.3 miles from the Snowbowl trailhead on a closed primitive road well short of Schultz Pass. To reach Schultz Pass from this point, turn left on the road and follow it about 0.3 mile uphill to where it connects with the Weatherford Trail. This intersection is just downhill from where the Weatherford Trail enters the Kachina Peaks Wilderness. Turn right onto the Weatherford Trail and follow it 1.7 miles downhill to the Schultz Tank trailhead.

An old-growth Douglas fir stands tall among ferns along the Kachina Trail.

**Be prepared:** No water is found along this hike, so pack all that you will need. Although not a persistent threat, lightning is possible, especially in exposed areas near the trail's southern end.

## 21  *Inner Basin*

**Distance:** 5.4 miles roundtrip
**Difficulty:** moderate
**Hiking time:** 4 hours
**Elevation:** 8600 to 10,000 feet
**Management:** Coconino NF
**Wilderness status:** none

**Season:** June to October
**USGS maps:** Humphreys Peak, Sunset Crater West
**GPS coordinates:** 35.356592 N, 111.623384 W

**Getting there:** Drive about 12 miles north from Flagstaff on US Highway 89. Across from the right turn for Sunset Crater Volcano National Monument, turn left onto Forest Road 420. After 0.5 mile turn right onto Forest Road 552. Drive a little over 4 miles to the far end of the Lockett Meadow Campground. Forest Road 552 is steep and narrow but is passable to high-clearance vehicles.

As its name suggests, the Inner Basin is a sheltered area surrounded by the impressive San Francisco Peaks. In geologic terms, however, it is much more than a beautiful montane landscape. The Inner Basin is actually the inside of an ancient volcano, one that came to a fiery end eons ago.

Because the Inner Basin provides the city of Flagstaff with water, overnight camping in the basin is prohibited. In addition, most Inner Basin trails follow service roads that are occasionally traveled by maintenance vehicles. Springs and wells in the basin have been developed and often include small buildings. Despite these human-made intrusions, this hike is still rewarding.

Within the first 1.5 miles from the trailhead, the Inner Basin Trail climbs along an easy to moderate grade to a junction with Waterline Road. Evidence of the massive Schultz Fire, which burned in 2010, can be seen along the lower portion of this trail. Beyond that the route is mostly surrounded by mature and quite

Aspen forest along the Inner Basin Trail

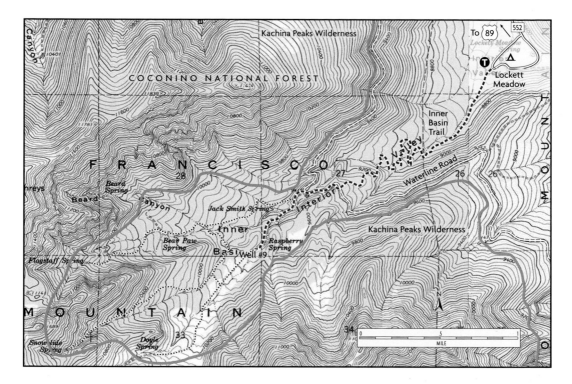

picturesque aspen stands. This would be an ideal hike to make in mid- to late September. A few historic carvings in the aspen trunks can also be seen. Because the trail was reconstructed and rerouted in recent years, it climbs through a series of switchbacks, which help make the ascent more enjoyable. Be sure not to cut across these switchbacks as erosion can result.

Upon reaching Waterline Road, turn right and follow it for 0.5 mile to the first maintenance cabins, which are at the mouth of the Inner Basin itself. From this point Waterline Road continues north to the Abineau and Bear Jaw Trails on the north slope of Humphreys Peak. Marked by a sign, the Inner Basin Trail continues west into the basin itself. After climbing a mostly moderate grade along a service road for another 0.7 mile, this trail reaches Raspberry Spring and Well #9. From here it is possible to take in quite a bit of the surrounding scenery. Forests of aspen, spruce, and fir have receded to make way for large open meadows that are filled with orange sneezeweed, Indian paintbrush, and other wildflowers in the summer. Encircling the Inner Basin are the 12,000-foot summits of Humphreys and Agassiz Peaks, and the slightly lower Fremont and Doyle Peaks. Indeed, it is easy to envision the fact that you are standing inside a long-extinct volcano.

Although this hike description turns back at Raspberry Spring, it is possible to extend your travels for another mile or more to Doyle Spring, which is situated at the foot of the peaks. Eventually the Inner Basin Trail also connects with the Weatherford Trail, which heads south to Schultz Pass. Still other routes access Snowslide and Flagstaff Springs in the far west end of the Inner Basin.

**Be prepared:** Be sure to bring your own drinking water as there are no reliable sources along this hike. Watch for lightning. Because the Inner Basin is a protected watershed, camping is not permitted and dogs must be on a leash.

## 22 Lenox Crater

**Distance:** 1 mile roundtrip
**Difficulty:** easy
**Hiking time:** 1 hour
**Elevation:** 6950 to 7250 feet
**Management:** Sunset Crater Volcano NM

**Wilderness status:** none
**Season:** May to November
**USGS map:** Sunset Crater West
**GPS coordinates:** 35.363664 N, 111.523104 W

**Getting there:** To reach the Lenox Crater Trail from Flagstaff, drive about 12 miles north on US Highway 89 to the signed right turn for Sunset Crater Volcano National Monument. Continue 3.4 miles, through the monument entry gate (pay an entry fee) and past the visitor center, to the signed trailhead. Parking is on the left, and the trail begins on the south side of the road.

In 1064 A.D. the landscape just east of the San Francisco Peaks changed dramatically. Volcanic eruptions took place, spewing ash and debris across the surrounding plateau, and several cinder cones were formed. Today, one of the largest of these cones is 1000-foot-high Sunset Crater, which is the namesake of a small but fascinating national monument. Hiking up Sunset Crater is off-limits, but you can walk to the top of nearby Lenox Crater.

Climbing 300 feet in 0.5 mile, the Lenox Crater Trail is steep along the entire way. The well-delineated route mostly stays among stands of ponderosa pine that have been able to grow in the dark volcanic gravel and sand that make up the monument's topography. As you climb, you will enjoy some nice views of colorful Sunset Crater to the east, and you may look out across the Bonito Lava Flow to the north. Once on top, you will get a nice view southwest into Lenox Crater. Also coming into view are the lofty San Francisco Peaks in the distance.

The geologic lessons posed by the eruptions of Sunset, Lenox, and other volcanoes in the area are quite evident. An interesting side effect of this volcanic activity is that prehistoric peoples found ideal growing conditions in the area after the eruptions quieted. Striking reminders of their

Looking west to the San Francisco Peaks from Lenox Crater

presence are found north of Sunset Cra Volcano National Monument in Wupatki National
Monument.

The return to the trailhead is easy, save for
occasionally slippery footing due to loose gravel.
Be sure to stay on the trail, as these soils are
fragile (it is for this reason that Sunset Crater is
off-limits). Once back at your car, you may want
to explore the Bonito Lava Flow, which spreads
mostly north of the road. Here a jumbled array of
dark volcanic rock offers hours of exploration. A
bit farther up the road, the 1-mile Lava Flow Trail
can also be visited. Use caution when in the lava
flow, as the rock is quite sharp.

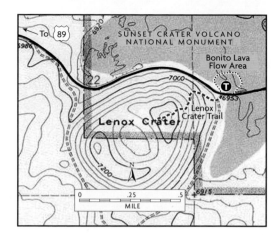

**Be prepared:** No water is available along the Lenox Crater Trail. Watch for lightning during storms. Do not
leave the established trail.

## 23  *Walnut Canyon*

*Distance:* 5.5 miles roundtrip
*Difficulty:* easy
*Hiking time:* 3 hours
*Elevation:* 6800 to 6600 feet
*Management:* Coconino NF

*Wilderness status:* none
*Season:* April to November
*USGS map:* Flagstaff East
*GPS coordinates:* 35.123290 N,
111.598728 W

*Getting there:* From where it turns off US Highway 89 in south Flagstaff, follow Lake
Mary Road 5.5 miles southeast and turn left at the Canyon Vista Campground. The
trailhead is located at the far end of the campground, but parking is only available just
outside of the campground entrance.

Most people know Walnut Canyon, located
south and east of Flagstaff, for the small
national monument that features several Sina-
gua cliff dwellings dating back 700 years. Actually, Walnut Canyon stretches for several miles
across the Coconino Plateau, and a hike into a
section upstream from the monument reveals
the beauty of this small but interesting drainage
without the crowds.

From the trailhead follow Sandys Canyon
Trail north across mostly level terrain along the
canyon's edge. A short distance from the start of
this 1.4-mile trail, the Vista Loop Trail branches
to the right. Keep left and continue less than 0.5

mile to where the trail drops down into Sandys
Canyon and Walnut Canyon. After descending a
couple of hundred feet, the trail levels off at the
bottom of Walnut Canyon, which it then follows
downstream. Geologically speaking, Walnut
Canyon features a cap of dark volcanic rock on
top of a layer of Coconino Sandstone—the same
sedimentary rock found in the upper walls of the
Grand Canyon.

After continuing north in Walnut Canyon for
another 0.5 mile, the Sandys Canyon Trail connects with the Arizona Trail. A right turn at this
intersection would take you up the southbound
portion of the Arizona Trail toward Marshall

The Fisher Point formation features heavy cross-bedding.

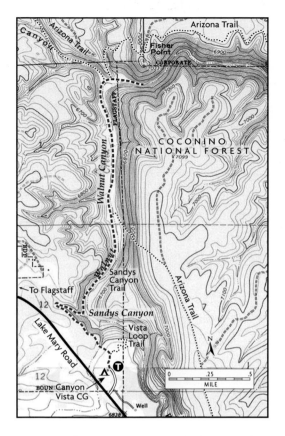

Lake, whereas bearing left you will follow the trans-state route north toward Fisher Point and the city of Flagstaff. Keep left here, and continue north for a little more than a mile to where Walnut Canyon bends to the east. At this turn in the canyon, Fisher Point can be seen rising above a broad meadow that stretches across the canyon bottom. The Arizona Trail actually splits here into two separate trails (one leading to Flagstaff and the other serving as an equestrian bypass to the city). Keep right at both of these junctions and continue a bit farther down canyon to the base of Fisher Point. Rising above the canyon bottom in spectacular fashion, Fisher Point is an impressive chunk of Coconino Sandstone in which it is easy to visualize the cross-bedding formed in what was once a desert sand dune. Although this hike turns around at Fisher Point, it is possible to continue for another mile on a small trail that explores the riparian environment beyond. Narrower and somewhat wetter than the section of the canyon south of Fisher Point, Walnut Canyon features a tangle of box elder, oak, walnut, ash, and poison ivy beyond this point. It is also home to a great variety of wildlife.

**Be prepared:** Water is not available along this hike, so pack plenty. Be prepared to encounter mountain bikers, especially along the Arizona Trail. Watch for poison ivy along much of this hike, especially along the portion of the Sandys Canyon Trail that drops into the bottom of Walnut Canyon.

## 24 *Red Mountain*

**Distance:** 2.5 miles roundtrip
**Difficulty:** easy
**Hiking time:** 2 hours
**Elevation:** 6750 to 7050 feet
**Management:** Coconino NF

**Wilderness status:** none
**Season:** April to November
**USGS map:** Ebert Mountain SE
**GPS coordinates:** 35.536904 N, 111.857815 W

**Getting there:** Drive 33 miles north of Flagstaff on US Highway 180. At mile marker 247, turn left onto a good dirt road and drive about 0.4 mile to the trailhead.

The exceptionally easy nature of this hike aside, it provides one of the most fascinating looks at Arizona geology to be found anywhere.

The trail winds for a pleasant 1.25 miles through pinyon pine and junipers toward a broken rise of cinder and red rock readily visible

Colorful rock formations inside Red Mountain

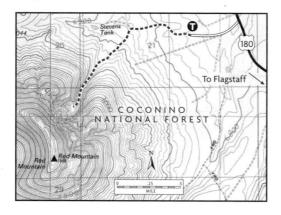

pines, which often grow on barren black cinder slopes. A 6-foot-high stone check dam that must be climbed by way of a wooden ladder marks the entrance into the mountain's interior.

Thought to have erupted over a million years ago, Red Mountain has eroded away over time, and today its inner basin features a fascinating collection of rock pinnacles and formations. It is actually the interior of a cinder cone, and the soft tuff has been sculpted into a variety of well-rounded shapes. Red in color, this geological montage is a great place to spend hours exploring various nooks and crannies. You can access the mountain's 7965-foot summit by following an old road along the south ridgeline and then picking your way through the ponderosa forest on top. A hardened lava flow is located southwest of the summit.

to the west. The route is easy to find, even when it heads up a wash for the last 0.5 mile—a sign points the way. Originating inside Red Mountain, this wash is home to scattered ponderosa

**Be prepared:** Water is not available on this hike. Care should be taken when climbing among the rock formations. Camping, campfires, horses, and bicycles are not permitted along this trail.

## 25 Kendrick Mountain

**Distance:** 9 miles roundtrip
**Difficulty:** strenuous
**Hiking time:** 5 hours
**Elevation:** 7980 to 10,418 feet
**Management:** Kaibab NF

**Wilderness status:** Kendrick Mountain WA
**Season:** May to September
**USGS map:** Kendrick Peak
**GPS coordinates:** 35.386882 N,
111.867698 W

**Getting there:** Drive 18 miles north from Flagstaff via US Highway 180 to Forest Road 193. Follow this gravel road 3.2 miles to the junction with Forest Road 171. Turn right and drive 2 miles. Turn right onto Forest Road 190 and follow it for 0.4 mile to the developed trailhead.

Capping its small namesake wilderness area, Kendrick Mountain (also known as Kendrick Peak) offers some of the finest views in the northern portion of Arizona. Of the three different routes that access the summit, the Kendrick Mountain Trail is the most direct and easiest to follow. Although much of this wilderness was devastated by the 14,760-acre Pumpkin Fire in 2000, some portions of this hike were spared a direct hit. Where the fire did burn more completely, the void in forest cover today opens up to reveal some rather scenic vistas.

For the first 0.5 mile the route climbs along mostly easy grades. Eventually it takes up an old roadbed, which continues north up a drainage. Along this first half of the hike the mountainside was burned over in a mosaic pattern as bands of tall timber alternate with open areas that today sport a plethora of mullein plants. After reaching a ridge just west of the drainage, the Kendrick Mountain Trail then continues to switchback up the south face of Kendrick Mountain. As you climb, you may note a change in vegetation types. Ponderosa pines, which typify the lower elevations, give way to a mix of Douglas fir, white fir, cork-bark fir, and Engelmann spruce. Glades of white-bark aspen are also encountered, along with sloping meadows of ferns. This is ideal habitat for mule deer and elk.

About 0.25 mile before the summit, the trail reaches a saddle where an old cabin is located. This small structure was built around 1912 and was occupied by fire lookout attendants until the 1930s, when the current tower was constructed on the summit. Now listed on the National Register of Historic Places, the cabin was saved from the Pumpkin Fire by firefighters who wrapped the structure with fire-resistant material. The Bull Basin Trail, which climbs up the north side of the mountain, connects with the Kendrick Mountain Trail at this saddle.

Situated on the summit, a lookout that similarly survived the Pumpkin Fire provides some spectacular views of the surrounding country. To the north, the Grand Canyon and the Vermilion Cliffs are plainly visible. Oak Creek Canyon and Mingus Mountain can be spotted to the south. The San Francisco Peaks loom to the east, and Bill Williams and Sitgreaves Mountains rise to the west. Poking above the ubiquitous ponderosa forests that stretch out in all directions from

Lupine growing along the Kendrick Mountain Trail

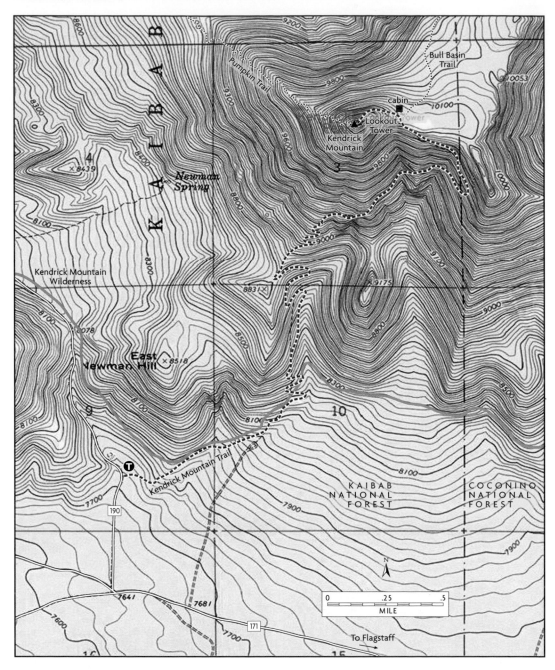

Kendrick Mountain are several small, symmetrically shaped cinder cones. These small remnant volcanoes, like Kendrick Mountain itself, hint at the fiery past of the Coconino Plateau.

**Be prepared:** Water is not available along the hike, so bring plenty. Watch for lightning during the summer season.

## 26 Bill Williams Mountain

**Distance:** 7 miles roundtrip
**Difficulty:** strenuous
**Hiking time:** 4 hours
**Elevation:** 7000 to 9256 feet
**Management:** Kaibab NF

**Wilderness status:** none
**Season:** May to September
**USGS map:** Williams South
**GPS coordinates:** 35.237638 N, 112.214666 W

**Getting there:** From Interstate 40, take Exit 161 and turn south onto Country Club Road. Continue a short distance to the Frontage Road on the south side of the highway. Turn right and drive southwest to a signed left turn for the Williams Ranger Station, about 1 mile west of Williams. The trailhead is a short distance beyond the Forest Service building.

A smaller version of Kendrick Mountain to the northeast, Bill Williams Mountain is a wonderful summit to hike, partly for the views from the top, and partly because of the lush forest encountered along the way. Closing in on this trail are towering aspen and fir, along with a riotous growth of underbrush.

Originally built as a toll trail in 1902, the Bill Williams Mountain Trail accesses the summit via the mountain's north face. Climbing a bit within the first mile, the route levels off some for most of the second mile. Also within the first mile two short side trails head east to Clover Spring. Keep right at both of these junctions to continue to the summit.

Growing along the lower elevations of the Bill Williams Mountain Trail is a mostly low-profile forest of alligator juniper, pinyon pine, and Gambel oak, occasionally spiked by taller ponderosa pines. Eventually, however, the trail encounters stands of large Douglas firs and mature aspens. This change in forest cover becomes especially evident when the trail takes up the bottom of a shady ravine. An undergrowth of ferns, Oregon grape, and Arizona wild rose add to the allure of this section.

After 2 miles the trail steepens as it begins its climb toward the summit in earnest. About 3 miles from the trailhead, the route crosses a gravel road that accesses a fire lookout tower and accompanying radio towers on the summit. The first real vista comes just before you reach the gravel road, from a rock outcrop just to the right

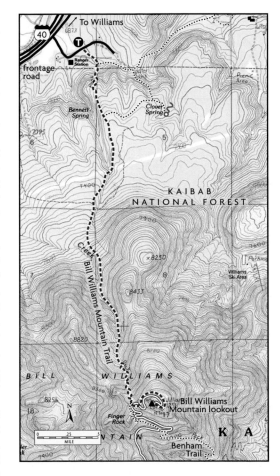

of the trail. Looking west, you can see Interstate 40 dropping off toward the town of Ash Fork.

Despite the dry conditions, a flower blooms along the Bill Williams Mountain Trail.

After crossing the road, the trail cuts up to the next switchback in the road. The trail then follows the road for the remaining 0.5 mile to the top. Built in 1937, the fire lookout on top replaced the original wooden structure, which in turn replaced an even earlier "lookout tree." The 360-degree view from the tower is impressive, although a cluster of radio towers intrudes on all sides.

**Be prepared:** Water is not available on this hike, so bring plenty. You could arrange for a shuttle to pick you up or drop you off on top, thereby cutting the walk in half. Or you could descend the Benham Trail, which drops down the east face of the mountain, and have a shuttle pick you up at the Benham trailhead at the eastern foot of the mountain.

## 27  *Sycamore Rim*

*Distance:* 11-mile loop
*Difficulty:* moderate
*Hiking time:* 7 hours
*Elevation:* 6700 to 7287 feet
*Management:* Kaibab NF

*Wilderness status:* Sycamore Canyon WA
*Season:* April to November
*USGS maps:* Davenport Hill, Garland Prairie
*GPS coordinates:* 35.160036 N, 111.999968 W

*Getting there:* Driving west from Flagstaff on Interstate 40, exit at Garland Prairie Road (Exit 167) which becomes Forest Road 141. Drive 9 miles southeast, turn right on Forest Road 56 and drive 1.9 miles to the trailhead. Because this description follows the trail clockwise, begin by hiking southeast across the meadow.

The Sycamore Rim Trail (also known as the Rim Trail), a beautiful hiking route that runs along a portion of the rim of Sycamore Canyon, offers a wonderful look at the unique ecosystems along the Mogollon Rim.

Established in 1979, the Sycamore Rim Trail was originally marked by frequently placed rock cairns. In 1992, however, tread construction was completed along the entire 11-mile loop. With the exception of a couple of short stretches, the Sycamore Rim Trail is level, and several other trailheads offer convenient access throughout the loop.

After traversing a meadow, the route enters an open ponderosa pine forest. Ponderosa pine is the predominant plant for much of the hike. About 0.5 mile from the start, the trail reaches the rim of a small canyon, which it then follows for the next mile or so. Scattered timbers and an interpretive sign mark the site of an old sawmill dating back to about 1910. After passing beneath a high-tension powerline, the trail accesses views of wonderful pools of water in an increasingly deepening canyon below.

Approximately 3 miles from the trailhead, the Sycamore Rim Trail reaches the rim of Sycamore

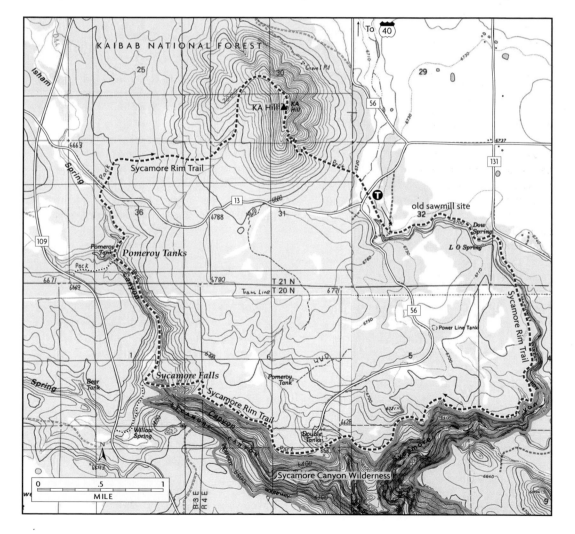

Looking into Sycamore Canyon from the Sycamore Rim Trail

Canyon. For the next several miles this rimrock marks the boundary of the Sycamore Canyon Wilderness. The views along this section are of volcanic cliffs and the verdant canyon bottom. Because the canyon is so wild in its upper reaches, only very rough routes access the bottom.

Although ponderosa pines of all sizes are found along most of the Sycamore Rim Trail, some other interesting ecosystems are also present. A few sunny sections of mesa top harbor small clusters of agaves or century plants. Some opportunistic aspen trees grow in a narrow stretch of canyon near normally dry Sycamore

Falls, about 6 miles from the trailhead. A little more than 7 miles from the trailhead are the Pomeroy Tanks. These perennial pools of clear water support a population of small fish and provide an important source of water for wildlife.

Within the last 2 miles of the hike, the Sycamore Rim Trail climbs some 500 feet to the top of KA Hill (7287 feet). Although the climb is not particularly hard, this change in topography is enough to allow for the addition of alligator junipers and Gambel oaks to the seemingly ubiquitous ponderosa pine forests. From the top of KA Hill you get a nice view of nearby Garland Prairie and the San Francisco Peaks beyond.

**Be prepared:** Although water is present along the trail, it should be treated, so you may want to bring your own. Lightning can be a hazard, especially along the open rimrock. Because four other trailheads (one at Sycamore Falls, one at Pomeroy Tanks, one at the end of Forest Road 56 near the canyon rim, and one at Dow Spring near the first powerline crossing) are situated along the route, you can make the walk shorter by setting up a shuttle.

Opposite, top: The remains of an old stone cabin at Bull Pen Ranch

Opposite, bottom: Some ponderosa pines survived the fire along the Indian Springs Trail.

# Central Highlands

28. West Fork Oak Creek..........82

29. Wilson Mountain .............84

30. Vultee Arch..................87

31. Airport Loop.................89

32. Boynton Canyon ..............91

33. Courthouse Butte Loop........93

34. Secret Mountain .............95

35. Jacks Canyon.................97

36. Parsons Spring...............99

37. Wet Beaver Creek............101

38. West Clear Creek ............103

39. Woodchute Mountain.........105

40. Granite Mountain............107

41. Thumb Butte Loop ...........109

42. Groom Creek Loop...........111

43. Pine Mountain...............113

44. Fossil Springs...............115

45. Horton Creek ...............118

46. Indian Spring Trail...........120

47. Mount Baldy.................122

48. Escudilla Mountain ..........125

49. P-Bar Lake..................127

50. Bonanza Bill–Tige Rim Loop...129

51. Bear Wallow ................132

52. Painted Bluff................134

*Breaking abruptly across much of the state, the Mogollon Rim divides Arizona into* two remarkably different geographies, creating terrain notable for both its scenic wonders and its ecological diversity. Best known is the red rock country surrounding Sedona. Slicing deeply into the tinted underlayers of the Colorado Plateau, canyons in and around Sedona are favored, and often crowded, haunts of many hikers. South and east of Sedona are a number of equally interesting canyons and mountaintops often overlooked by the masses. Farther east are the well-timbered White Mountains and Blue Mountains. Off the beaten path, these subalpine mountainlands offer a sufficiently expansive wilderness to allow for the reintroduction of Mexican gray wolves. Within all reaches of the Central Highlands, hikers can enjoy a fascinating ecological continuity that results from the meshing of two very different regions: the Colorado Plateau to the north and the Sonoran Desert to the south.

## 28 *West Fork Oak Creek*

**Distance:** 6 miles roundtrip
**Difficulty:** easy
**Hiking time:** 4 hours
**Elevation:** 5300 to 5500 feet
**Management:** Coconino NF
**Wilderness status:** Red Rock–Secret Mountain WA

**Season:** year-round
**USGS maps:** Wilson Mountain, Munds Park, Dutton Hill
**GPS coordinates:** 34.990797 N, 111.742846 W

**Getting there:** The hike starts 10.5 miles north of Sedona, near mile marker 385 on Arizona Highway 89A in Oak Creek Canyon. A fee is charged upon entry to the trailhead parking area.

With colorful walls rising hundreds of feet straight up, a picturesque stream, and an interesting collection of flora and fauna, the West Fork of Oak Creek is one of the most spectacular canyon systems in the state. What makes this hike especially wonderful is that it all begins within a few minutes of the trailhead. Although such a combination can make for some crowded hiking, the West Fork is too nice to pass up.

The West Fork Trail is as level and easy to follow as any trail around. Several crossings of the shallow stream are necessary, but with normal runoff these may be completed via stepping stones. Such conditions make it easy for hikers of all ages to enjoy the natural history and beauty of the area.

Besides being included within the Red Rock–Secret Mountain Wilderness, much of West Fork Canyon falls within the Oak Creek Research Natural Area. This designation came about because of the diverse plant life found here. In addition to the enormous ponderosa pines and Douglas firs that shade the canyon bottom, the area also supports box elder, cottonwood, velvet ash, Arizona walnut, bigtooth maple, and Gambel oak. Willows, columbine, Arizona rose, wild grape, Virginia creeper, sumac, asters, lupine, and poison ivy also grow here. Included among

Dramatic sandstone walls rise above the West Fork of Oak Creek.

the canyon's wildlife are the narrow-headed garter snake; mule deer; and Abert's, red, and Arizona gray squirrels.

Encasing this diverse biological community are soaring walls of Coconino Sandstone. Heavily cross-bedded, these impressive cliffs were once wind-drifted sand dunes. At the creek level are deep red façades of the Supai Formation.

Seeps of water, the same agent responsible for cutting this deep abyss, are found in various places along the canyon walls.

For the first 2 miles the hiking remains very easy, but shortly after that the trail becomes overgrown and even climbs out of the canyon bottom at one point. These inconveniences tend to thin out the crowds, but the going is still relatively

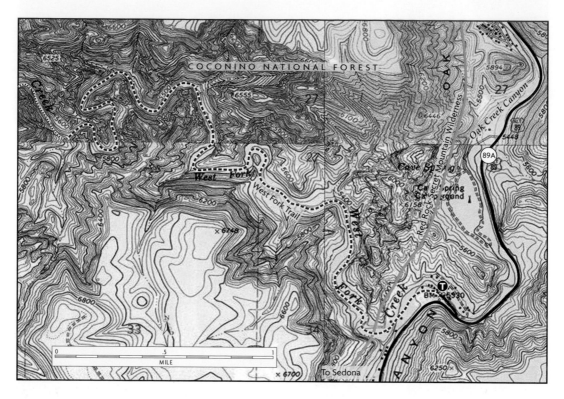

easy. Eventually, any trace of a trail disappears as the route simply follows the creek bottom.

At about the 3-mile mark, a thigh-deep, wall-to-wall pool of water marks this hike's turn-around point. It is possible, however, to continue up the canyon to Forest Road 231—a 14-mile hike in all. The upper portion of the West Fork requires additional wading, some swimming, and lots of boulder hopping, but the hike is well worth the effort.

**Be prepared:** Plan on taking 4 hours to complete the hike described here, a couple of days if you want to go all the way. The stream water should be treated if you plan to drink it. Watch for poison ivy and be mindful of flash flooding, especially in the summer months. Keep in mind that camping is prohibited within the first 6 miles of the canyon to prevent damage to this unique riparian environment.

## 29 *Wilson Mountain*

**Distance:** 11.2 miles roundtrip
**Difficulty:** strenuous
**Hiking time:** 6 hours
**Elevation:** 4600 to 6960 feet
**Management:** Coconino NF

**Wilderness status:** Red Rock–Secret Mountain WA
**Season:** March to November
**USGS maps:** Wilson Mountain, Munds Park
**GPS coordinates:** 34.885791 N, 111.741604 W

***Getting there:*** Purchase a Red Rock Pass in town in participating stores or at a Forest Service visitor center. Drive north from Sedona on Arizona Highway 89A for about 1.5 miles. Immediately after crossing the Midgley Bridge, turn left into a parking area. Don't be alarmed if a lot of cars are parked here. Most belong to people stopping to look at the bridge.

Wilson Mountain, like other high points in the Sedona area, offers a wonderful vantage point from which to enjoy the surrounding red rock terrain. The Wilson Mountain Trail runs mostly within the Red Rock–Secret Mountain Wilderness and was designated as a National Recreation Trail in 1979.

For the first 0.5 mile or so, the trail climbs quickly to gain a ridge just east of Wilson Canyon. This is followed by a stretch of easier grades as the route continues north and approaches the base of the mountain. The terrain along this stretch is dry, open desert. Scattered pinyon pine, juniper, manzanita, agave, yucca, and bear grass are common, but shade is not.

After 1.25 miles, the trail begins switchbacking up a considerably steeper grade as it heads for what appears to be a saddle. This is the First Bench of Wilson Mountain. Along this ascent the trail is steep and rocky in places, and occasionally overgrown with shrub live oak. Although this climb is long, the views of the Midgley Bridge and Sedona far below are spectacular.

Once on top of First Bench, a 0.5-mile stretch of nearly level trail traverses open grassland. This is a good place to take in the ever-changing scenery. The area's century plants bloom in early summer, as do many perennial flowers, and the Mogollon Rim is visible to the east across Oak Creek Canyon. Before leaving the First Bench the

Sedona's redrock scenery is front and center when seen from the Wilson Mountain Trail.

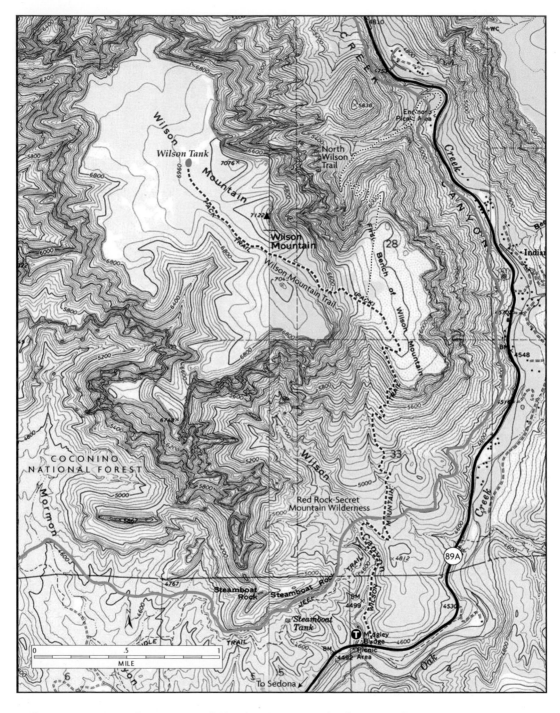

Wilson Mountain Trail connects with the upper end of the North Wilson Trail, a 2-mile alternate route that begins at the Encinoso Picnic Area in Oak Creek Canyon. Keep left at this intersection.

Beyond First Bench the Wilson Mountain Trail begins to make its final ascent to the mountain's summit above. Fortunately, this pitch is neither as steep nor nearly as long as the climb below. As you near the top, you can observe where the trail encounters the mountain's rim of volcanic rock. This cap of dark basalt typifies much of the expansive Mogollon Ridge.

Upon reaching the mostly flat top of Wilson Mountain, the Wilson Mountain Trail continues north for about 1.25 miles to Wilson Tank, which is close to the far end of the mountain. To follow this last stretch of trail, look for stone cairns as the actual tread is faded or nonexistent. Complicating matters on the top of Wilson Mountain is the burn scar left by the Brins Fire, which scorched some 4300 acres in 2006. Be aware of falling trees and expect some deadfall on the trail. Along this last stretch of the hike, the route bypasses the actual 7122-foot summit by a short distance. For the best views you will need to travel a little farther (perhaps 0.25 to 0.5 mile) off the trail to get to the mountaintop's edge. Although Wilson Tank is little more than a glorified water hole, a search for tracks along its banks may reveal signs of some of the wildlife that inhabits the area.

**Be prepared:** During the summer months you may want to set out early to avoid the heat of the day. Lightning may also pose a hazard in July and August. No potable water is found along the way, so bring plenty of your own.

## 30 *Vultee Arch*

**Distance:** 3.4 miles roundtrip
**Difficulty:** easy
**Hiking time:** 3 hours
**Elevation:** 4800 to 5200 feet
**Management:** Coconino NF

**Wilderness status:** Red Rock–Secret Mountain WA
**Season:** year-round
**USGS map:** Wilson Mountain
**GPS coordinates:** 34.937205 N, 111.794320 W

**Getting there:** Drive west from downtown Sedona on Arizona Highway 89A to Dry Creek Road. Turn north and drive 2 miles to the turnoff for Vultee Arch Road (Forest Road 152). Follow this four-wheel-drive road 4.3 miles to its end. The Vultee Arch Trail heads east from the right side of the parking area.

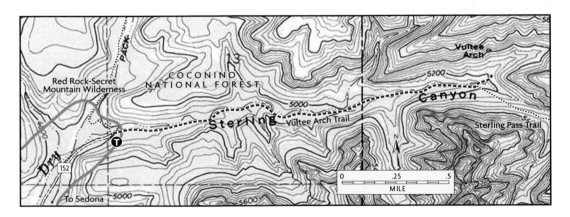

Vultee Arch rises above a forest of low-growing trees.

This short hike allows easy access to a well-known geologic feature of the Sedona area, plus it reveals some of the vegetation that is typical of this red rock country. A favorite among locals, this route sees a lot of activity, especially on weekends.

Entering the Red Rock–Secret Mountain Wilderness almost immediately, the trail follows the gentle bottom of Sterling Canyon. The route is well marked the entire way, and shade is provided by stands of alligator juniper, Gambel oak, and Arizona cypress, or by tall ponderosa pines. White-barked sycamore trees also grow along the normally dry wash bottom.

Within the last 0.25 mile, the Sterling Pass Trail branches off to the right. Keep left, however, and climb a short distance farther to a brass plaque commemorating aviation pioneer Gerard Vultee and his wife, Sylvia. The two died in a plane crash about a mile north of this spot in January 1938. The natural arch that shares their name is located higher on the canyon's north wall and is surrounded by thick brush.

From the plaque you get a good view of the canyon below. It is easy to see how slope aspect plays an important role in this rugged terrain. Because the canyon's north side faces south, it is more arid. Consequently, it supports thickets of manzanita, shrub live oak, and other desert plants. The shadier south side of the canyon supports tall stands of Douglas fir and ponderosa pine.

**Be prepared:** Although this is a short excursion, it is advisable to bring drinking water, especially in the hot summer months.

# 31 *Airport Loop*

**Distance:** 3.3-mile loop
**Difficulty:** easy
**Hiking time:** 2 hours
**Elevation:** 4600 to 4720 feet
**Management:** Coconino NF

**Wilderness status:** none
**Season:** year-round
**USGS map:** Sedona
**GPS coordinates:** 34.855666 N,
111.780153 W

**Getting there:** From Sedona drive about 1 mile west on Arizona Highway 89A to Airport Road. Turn south and drive 0.5 mile to the trailhead on the left side of the road. Parking is limited.

Circumnavigating its namesake, which rises in a very central position in the Sedona area, the Airport Loop Trail provides a nonstop reel of red rock scenery. Yes, there is an airport on the lengthy, flat top of the mesa, but flights are not frequent and the noisy intrusion of spinning propellers is not incessant.

The Airport Loop Trail begins at the left end of the parking area where a large trailhead sign maps out this trail and others in the area. Climb

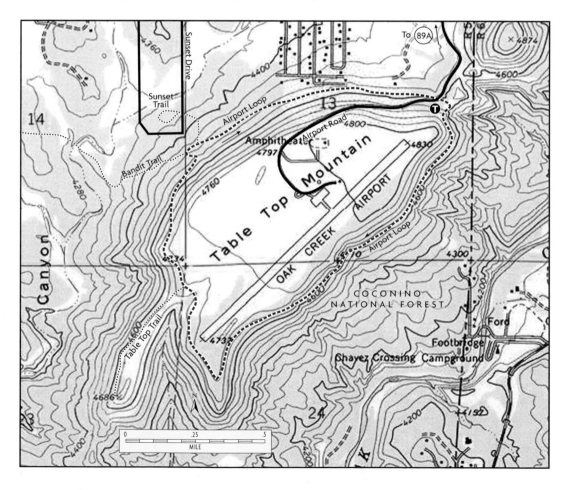

the hill beyond the sign and look for a trail that continues south to begin contouring along the southeast slope of the mesa. Running clockwise around the mesa, the trail maintains a nearly level grade that runs between 150 and 200 feet below the crest of the mesa above. Pinyon pine and juniper grow along the slope of the mesa, but they thin out a bit along the more arid south side where patches of prickly pear cactus take up the slack. The scenery along this section takes in the Munds Mountain area to the east and Courthouse Butte and Cathedral Rock to the south.

After 1.4 miles, the Airport Loop Trail climbs a bit to reach the southwest end of the mesa. Here it turns north to follow along a fence that marks the end of the airport runway. Shortly after passing the fence the trail crosses a shallow drainage before reaching the junction with the 0.4-mile Table Top Trail. Running southwest to a vista point, this side trail reveals some fine scenery to the west. After bearing right at the Table Top Trail junction, the Airport Loop Trail continues north for a little over 0.5 mile to a second trail junction. Branching left, the Bandit Trail accesses a network of trails to the west. Similarly, the Sunset Trail also branches left a short distance beyond the Bandit Trail junction and drops north to access neighborhoods below. At both of these junctions bear right to continue along the Airport Loop Trail.

Running east from the Sunset Trail junction for about 1 mile, the last segment of the Airport Loop Trail continues along a mostly level grade. Here pinyon pines and junipers become more prodigious as these north-facing slopes hold more moisture. Views from this portion of the hike take in Capitol Butte, Coffeepot Rock, and the Soldier Pass area to the north. After 3.3 miles the Airport Loop Trail reaches Airport Road, where you will need to step over the guardrail before crossing the road to return to the trailhead parking area.

**Be prepared:** No water is available along this trail, so bring plenty. Watch for lightning during storms. Use caution when crossing Airport Road.

Redrock scenery as seen from the Airport Loop Trail

## 32 Boynton Canyon

**Distance:** 6 miles roundtrip
**Difficulty:** easy
**Hiking time:** 3 hours
**Elevation:** 4500 to 4850 feet
**Management:** Coconino NF

**Wilderness status:** Red Rock–Secret Mountain WA
**Season:** year-round
**USGS maps:** Wilson Mountain, Loy Butte
**GPS coordinates:** 34.907542 N, 111.848967 W

**Getting there:** Drive west from Sedona on Arizona Highway 89A to Dry Creek Road. Turn north and drive 3 miles to Boynton Pass Road. Turn left at this junction and continue about 2 miles to Boynton Canyon Road. Turn right and drive a short distance to a right turn, which leads to the developed trailhead. A Red Rock Pass is required for trail use. You must purchase the pass in town at participating stores or at a Forest Service visitor center.

Located within minutes of Sedona, Boynton Canyon is a popular hike for locals and visitors alike. Entering a highly scenic canyon boxed in by large red rock buttes and cliffs, this trail accesses some truly outstanding scenery. Wildlife is plentiful, and the flora is fascinating.

The route begins by skirting to the east of a resort that sprawls across the mouth of the canyon. For this first mile the trail traverses dry foothills before dropping back into the canyon bottom. Some minor grade changes can be expected in this first section, but once the canyon bottom is reached, upstream from the resort, the hike is mostly level.

Upon reaching the canyon bottom, the trail is well marked and easy to follow. Although normally dry, this drainage supports a surprisingly thick forest of evergreen trees. Ponderosa pine and Douglas fir make up the larger species of trees, and manzanita, Arizona cypress, and a variety of live oaks constitute the thick understory. Species of wildlife that reside here include mule deer, javelina, and Arizona gray squirrel. Mountain lions no doubt frequent the canyon's rugged upper reaches, and badgers, coyotes, and ringtail cats live throughout.

As the trail nears the canyon's abrupt end, it becomes somewhat overgrown, but it is still easy to follow. Here, where the magnificent canyon walls draw closer, you can really appreciate the amazing scale of Sedona's red rock country.

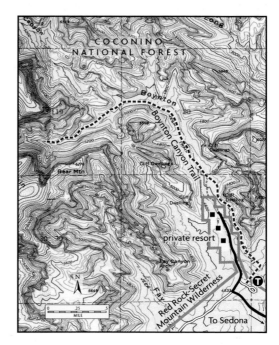

Soaring some 800 feet above are colorful faces of Coconino Sandstone and Kaibab Limestone. Adding a metaphysical complexion to the geology of the area is the reported presence of a "vortex," or a "concentration of electromagnetic energy" within the earth below, near the mouth of Boynton Canyon. The location of four such "vortices" in the Sedona area have made it a mecca for New Age enthusiasts.

Colorful cliffs rise above a thicket of oaks and manzanita along the Boynton Canyon Trail.

**Be prepared:** Because water is nonexistent along this trail, be sure to bring along all that you will need. Don't be surprised to see a lot of cars at the trailhead, especially on weekends. Due to sensitive soils, do not climb around on the sandstone ledges within the canyon itself.

## 33  *Courthouse Butte Loop*

*Distance:* 4.25 mile loop
*Difficulty:* easy
*Hiking time:* 3 hours
*Elevation:* 4200 to 4450 feet
*Management:* Coconino NF

*Wilderness status:* Munds Mountain WA
*Season:* year-round
*USGS map:* Munds Mountain
*GPS coordinates:* 34.791506 N, 111.761626 W

*Getting there:* From downtown Sedona at the intersection of Arizona Highways 89A and 179, drive 6.5 miles south on 179. The signed trailhead is on the east side of the road. If traveling from the south, continue less than a mile north of the village of Oak Creek. A Red Rock Pass is required for trail use. You must purchase the pass at participating stores in town or at a Forest Service visitor center.

Courthouse Butte and adjacent Bell Rock are two of the most popular red rock formations in the Sedona area. Not only do they nestle up to a major roadway where every passing motorist can enjoy their beauty, but an easy trail, the Courthouse Butte Loop, circumnavigates both in a memorable 4.25-mile loop.

Traveling north, the first 0.5 mile of this hike follows the wide and heavily used Bell Rock Pathway. Fencing has been erected along most of this segment to protect fragile desert soils. Once the trail reaches the actual loop, however, the route takes up a single-track trail. At this signed intersection, turn right to follow the loop counterclockwise.

For the next 0.5 mile the Courthouse Butte Loop tracks east along the foot of the butte itself. Gently dipping in and out of shallow drainages, the trail's grade changes are negligible and the scenery is amazing. The two intersections along this stretch mark either end of the Big Park Trail, a short route that loops to the south. Eventually, the Courthouse Butte Loop crosses a more pronounced wash bottom and then begins angling north along the east face of the butte. A little more than 1.5 miles from the trailhead, the route enters the Munds Mountain Wilderness, at which point mountain bikes must turn back.

Along the segment of the trail that crosses through the wilderness (this section passes the northeast side of Courthouse Butte), the route climbs a hundred or so feet before continuing

Courthouse Butte is the scenic centerpiece for its namesake hike.

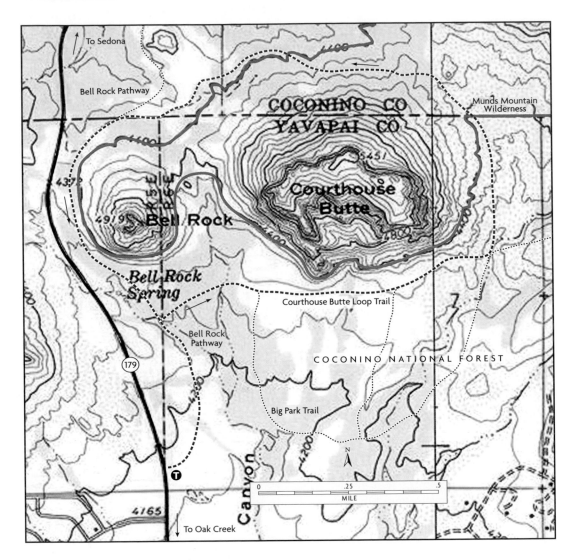

To Sedona

Bell Rock Pathway

COCONINO CO
YAVAPAI CO

Munds Mountain
Wilderness

Courthouse
Butte

Bell Rock

Bell Rock
Spring

Courthouse Butte Loop Trail

Bell Rock
Pathway

COCONINO NATIONAL FOREST

179

Big Park Trail

N

T

4165

0     .25     .5
MILE

Canyon

To Oak Creek

along the north side of the butte. A nice rise of rock along this section makes for a great place to take a break. The trail then leaves the wilderness and continues southwest to circle around Bell Rock. Although considerably smaller than Courthouse Butte, Bell Rock has been of primary interest to New Age enthusiasts for many years. Consequently, heavy visitation to the rock has taken its toll on the surrounding terrain. You may even see a number of people scrambling up the lower slopes of the rock.

Near the northwest corner of Bell Rock, the Courthouse Butte Loop intersects again with the Bell Rock Pathway. Turn left onto this trail and walk south for a little over a mile to return to the trailhead. You will encounter numerous hikers along this stretch of the hike in contrast to the Courthouse Butte Loop portion.

**Be prepared:** Be sure to pack plenty of water, especially in the warmer months. Watch for rattlesnakes and lightning. Also, flash floods could be a possibility during heavy rainstorms.

# 34 *Secret Mountain*

**Distance:** 18.5 miles roundtrip
**Difficulty:** strenuous
**Hiking time:** 2 days
**Elevation:** 4720 to 6600 feet
**Management:** Coconino NF

**Wilderness status:** Red Rock–Secret Mountain WA
**Season:** April to November
**USGS maps:** Loy Butte, Wilson Mountain
**GPS coordinates:** 34.932173 N, 111.924821 W

**Getting there:** Drive 10 miles west of Sedona on Arizona Highway 89A to Red Canyon Road (Forest Road 525). Turn north and continue 3.4 miles on this often washboarded gravel road to a fork. Stay right and continue on Forest Road 525 for another 6.8 miles to the trailhead, following the signs for Loy Butte. The trail takes off to the right just before a cattle guard. The parking area is on the left.

Soaring high above the red rock country west of Sedona, Secret Mountain offers a unique perspective on the surrounding landscape. To the north of the expansive, flat-topped summit is Secret Canyon, and stretching southward is the expansive Verde Valley. This hike begins by following the length of Loy Canyon to a small saddle at its head. From there it is a pleasant walk through pine forests to the mountain's scenic southern edge.

For the first 4 miles, the hike to Secret Mountain follows the bottom of the very scenic Loy Canyon. Maintaining a mostly easy grade, this segment is in itself a worthwhile hike. Rising to the left is Loy Butte. Defining the skyline to the right is Secret Mountain, and straight ahead is the Mogollon Rim. Vegetation along this lower section of the hike includes pinyon pine, juniper, manzanita, shrub live oak, and an occasional ponderosa pine growing along the wash bottom. Wildlife in this arid terrain includes javelinas, coyotes, mule deer, and jackrabbits.

Completing approximately half of its 1700-foot elevation gain in the first 4 miles, the Loy Canyon Trail climbs considerably in its last mile. This steep and narrow stretch of trail ends at the Secret Mountain Trail, which crosses a saddle that connects Secret Mountain with the Mogollon Rim. A left turn at the saddle leads 0.25 mile to a trailhead at the end of Forest Road 538, and

The view into Hartwell Canyon from Secret Mountain

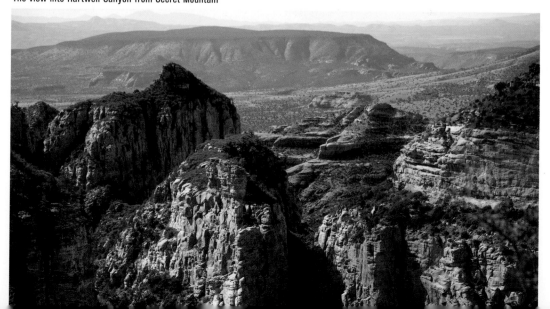

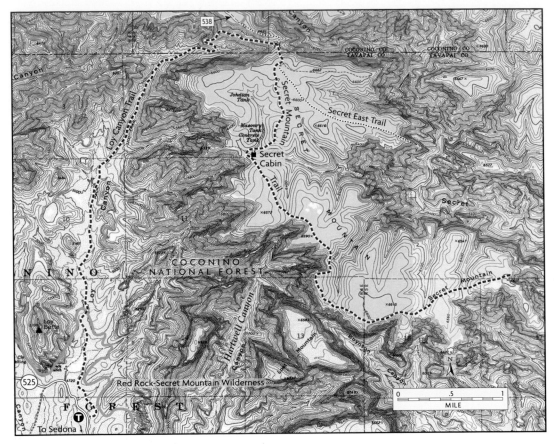

the route to the right accesses Secret Mountain via an easy 200-foot climb. Once on top of the flat summit, the Secret Mountain Trail continues for another 5 miles before reaching the far end of its namesake.

Although the top of Secret Mountain is mostly level, some changes in elevation can be expected when hiking across it. It is mostly shady, thanks to the open forests of ponderosa pine, Gambel oak, and alligator juniper that typify the terrain. Mule deer are plentiful in this high terrain, and elk occasionally migrate to the mountain from the nearby Mogollon Rim. From where it tops out about 0.25 mile south of the saddle, the Secret Mountain Trail first intersects the faded Secret East Trail, which heads off to explore the eastern reaches of the mountaintop. The Secret Mountain Trail then continues south before reaching Secret Cabin, about 1 mile beyond the

saddle. Although the history of this antiquated log structure is sketchy at best, one story claims that horse thieves hid out here, whereas another claims it was home to a group of Mormon polygamists. Be sure not to remove any artifacts from the cabin and surrounding area.

Just beyond the cabin is the first of several viewpoints. Looking down into Loy Canyon, this vista also takes in the Sycamore Pass area, Mingus Mountain, and the Verde Valley. Continuing on, the trail cuts through the forest for less than a mile before again finding the mountain's edge. The views here are of the dramatic Hartwell Canyon drainage. Continue another mile and you can peer into the head of Boynton Canyon. The trail continues a bit farther before ending at the mountain's easternmost point. This neck of land is bounded by Long Canyon to the south and Secret Canyon to the north.

**Be prepared:** Although some small springs are found on Secret Mountain, they are not always reliable, so it is best to bring all the water you will need. Watch for lightning on the rim areas, especially during summer thunderstorms.

## 35 Jacks Canyon

*Distance:* 13.6 miles roundtrip
*Difficulty:* strenuous
*Hiking time:* 7 hours
*Elevation:* 4360 to 6320 feet
*Management:* Coconino NF

*Wilderness status:* Munds Mountain WA
*Season:* March to November
*USGS map:* Munds Mountain
*GPS coordinates:* 34.784730 N, 111.732254 W

*Getting there:* From Sedona, drive about 6 miles south on Arizona Highway 179 to the Oak Creek village center. Turn east on Jacks Canyon Road and drive 0.9 mile to where the road turns right. Continue for about a mile to the signed trailhead.

At 18,150 acres, the Munds Mountain Wilderness encompasses some interesting terrain southeast of Sedona. The primary landmark here is the wilderness area's 6825-foot namesake summit, but a number of scenic canyons also highlight the wilderness. Running the length of one of these is the Jacks Canyon Trail. The drainage got its name from Jack Woods, a railroad engineer from Winslow, Arizona, who grazed sheep here in the latter part of the 19th century.

Except for a 0.3-mile section that climbs around the upper end of a housing development, the first 2.5 miles of the Jacks Canyon Trail follow an old road up a gently ascending canyon bottom. Plant life along this first stretch includes mostly pinyon pine, juniper, and shrub live oak. At the 2-mile mark the road reaches the Jacks Canyon Tank where it ends and the route becomes a single-track trail for the rest of the way. Although it usually contains water, this stock pond is not fit for consumption.

From Jacks Canyon Tank, the trail continues to the dry wash bottom, which it then closely parallels for the next 4 miles. At the many streambed crossings along the way, the trail is marked with cairns on either side to avoid confusion. Otherwise, the route is well established as it passes among beautiful stands of Arizona cypress that are intermixed with an occasional alligator juniper or patch of manzanita.

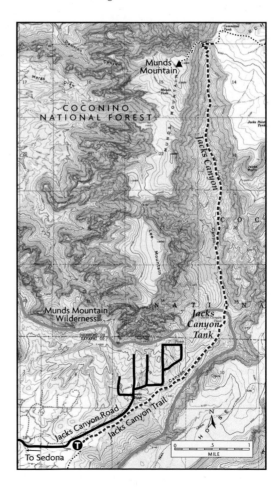

Hikers are treated to a bird's-eye view from the top of the Jacks Canyon Trail.

After climbing along an easy grade for the first several miles, the Jacks Canyon Trail becomes considerably steeper in the last 1.5 miles. Completing nearly half of the route's 2000-foot elevation gain in this final segment, much of the grade is moderate in difficulty, although a few stretches can be considered strenuous. In addition, parts of the trail are badly eroded, and the footing is occasionally loose. Along this upper end, Gambel oaks and ponderosa pines become more common.

Near the trail's end, a saddle is reached that marks the head of Jacks Canyon. Be sure to note the Douglas fir forest growing on the protected north side of the ridge. At the saddle, this hike turns right to access the Mogollon Rim a short distance to the east. A secondary trail turns left, however, and climbs another 500 feet to the top of Munds Mountain. After staying right, continue for another 0.25 mile to reach the rim and its spectacular views. The Schnebly Hill Road lies directly below, and Oak Creek Canyon opens up to the north. Wilson and Secret Mountains rise to the west and, looking back down the Jacks Canyon drainage, you can see part of the Verde Valley far to the south.

**Be prepared:** No potable water is found along the Jacks Canyon Trail, so be sure to bring plenty; the summer months can be hot.

# 36 *Parsons Spring*

**Distance:** 7.4 miles roundtrip
**Difficulty:** easy
**Hiking time:** 4 hours
**Elevation:** 3750 to 3800 feet
**Management:** Coconino NF, Prescott NF

**Wilderness status:** Sycamore Canyon WA
**Season:** year-round
**USGS maps:** Sycamore Basin, Clarkdale
**GPS coordinates:** 34.864135 N,
112.069314 W

**Getting there:** Drive Arizona Highway 89A north from Cottonwood to the turnoff for Tuzigoot National Monument. Turn right toward the monument and take the first left past the bridge. Following the east bank of the Verde River, this good gravel road becomes Forest Road 131 at the Coconino National Forest boundary, 4 miles from the bridge. Continue on this route for another 6.5 miles to the developed trailhead.

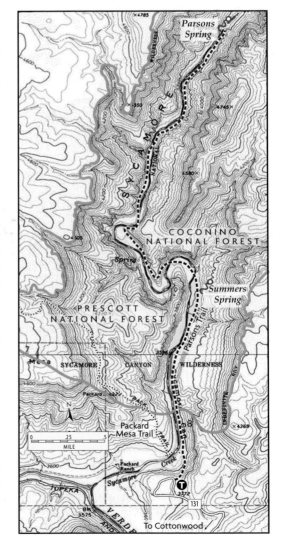

At 55,937 acres, the Sycamore Canyon Wilderness can be a daunting place to explore. That is because many of its finer areas can be reached only after hiking long distances, usually with overnight gear in tow. Heading upstream from the canyon's mouth for nearly 4 miles, however, is the Parsons Trail. Accessing one of the finest riparian areas in the state, this route offers day hikers a golden opportunity to get to know Sycamore Canyon.

Dropping 200 feet in the first 0.1 mile, the Parsons Trail levels off once it reaches the creekbed below. It then remains level as it follows the canyon bottom the rest of the way. Featuring a perennial flow of water, the first 4 miles of the canyon include a wonderful collection of deciduous trees: sycamores, cottonwoods, and Arizona walnuts, to name a few. Wild grape and poison ivy add to this junglelike environment. Fed by several springs, the creek forms pools all along the way, providing dazzling reflections of the verdant canopy above and suitable habitat for great blue herons and river otters.

After 1.1 miles, the Parsons Trail reaches Summers Spring, the first of two signed trailside seeps. Although this steady flow of groundwater comes from under the rocks on the right bank of the stream, it should be treated if you plan to drink it because of the proximity of the trail. Shortly past Summers Spring, the trail makes the first of several crossings over Sycamore Creek. A second crossing follows in less than 0.2 mile. Marked by cairns on either bank, these crossings are easy during normal runoff.

Fall foliage is reflected in the still water of Parsons Spring.

Beyond the second crossing, the route becomes less distinct, as a result of severe flooding. A trail of sorts follows close to the right canyon wall for a little over a mile before crossing to the west bank of the creek. After a short distance, the route crosses back to the right again and continues for roughly another 0.75 mile to Parsons Spring. Although grade changes are nearly nonexistent along the canyon bottom, this route does require some boulder-hopping and route-finding skills.

Identified by an old sign, Parsons Spring is an unimpressive pool of still water that marks the end of the trail and the turnaround point for this hike. It is possible to continue beyond the spring, but the perennial stream ends a short way beyond. In addition, the going can be rough, thanks to thick growth and many large boulders.

**Be prepared:** To protect this fragile riparian environment, camping is prohibited below Parsons Spring. All water along the Parsons Trail should be treated before drinking. Be aware that flash flooding can occur, especially during the summer months. Due to the sensitive nature of this riparian area, it is important to stay on the trail at all times.

## 37 *Wet Beaver Creek*

**Distance:** 6 miles roundtrip
**Difficulty:** easy
**Hiking time:** 3 hours
**Elevation:** 3820 to 4100 feet
**Management:** Coconino NF

**Wilderness status:** Wet Beaver Creek WA
**Season:** year-round
**USGS map:** Casner Butte
**GPS coordinates:** 34.674180 N,
111.713313 W

**Getting there:** To find the trailhead, turn off Interstate 17 at the Sedona exit and drive 2 miles southeast on Forest Road 618. Turn left at the sign for the Bell Trail, and continue 0.25 mile to the parking area. This hike enters the mouth of Wet Beaver Creek Canyon via the Bell Trail.

Slicing deep into the Mogollon Rim, Wet Beaver Creek is a welcome reprieve in this otherwise arid desert terrain. With deep pools of clear water and lush riparian growth, the canyon's oasis-like ambience is a real treat for hikers.

For the first 2 miles, the Bell Trail follows an old road that is closed to most motorized traffic (government maintenance crews do occasionally drive the road) but open to mountain bikes. It crosses arid terrain that is characterized by juniper, prickly pear cactus, and sparse grasses. This section may be quite hot in the summer.

About 1.5 miles from the trailhead, the White Mesa Trail branches off to the north. Within the next 0.25 mile the Apache Maiden Trail branches

north to climb a mesa and, soon after, the Wier Trail appears to your right, paralleling the creek for 0.5 mile. Resist these distractions, and stay on the Bell Trail in both cases to reach the wilderness boundary. At this point the road ends and a single-track trail continues up canyon.

From this point, the Bell Trail climbs for a short distance to gain a narrow bench that runs along the canyon's north wall. From here it is easy to see why the trail was located above the thick tangle of cottonwood, alder, ash, and sycamore that grow in the canyon bottom below. This vantage point also provides a good look at the geology of the canyon. Topping cliffs of the Supai Formation, Kaibab Limestone, Toroweap

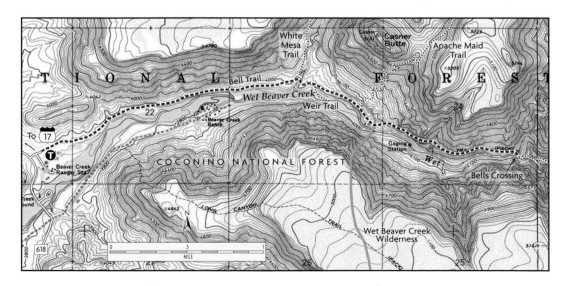

Wetlands along Wet Beaver Creek

Sandstone, and Coconino Sandstone is a layer of dark volcanic rock. Characterizing much of the Mogollon Rim, this basalt was deposited more than a million years ago during volcanic eruptions to the north. The canyon reaches a depth of about 1000 feet in this lower end.

Approximately 3 miles from the trailhead, the Bell Trail drops back down to the canyon bottom where it fords the creek at Bells Crossing. The trail and stream crossing are named after Charles Bell, a local rancher who constructed the route in 1932. From the crossing, the Bell Trail climbs for 1.5 miles to the south rim, where it then continues for another 6.5 miles to Forest Road 214.

Because the canyon bottom is pleasant and shady, this hike description turns around at Bells Crossing, but be sure to venture less than 0.25 mile upstream to a series of deep, crystal-clear pools. Although it is possible to continue upstream from this point, the going is very slow due to thick growth, boulder chokes, and pools that require swimming.

**Be prepared:** Because water is not readily available until you reach Bells Crossing, it is a good idea to bring your own. The creek water should be treated before drinking. Watch for rattlesnakes along the entire hike and poison ivy in the canyon bottom. Keep in mind that it can be quite hot—above 100 degrees Fahrenheit—in the summer. To help prevent damage to riparian areas, do not leave the trail. Bicycles are not allowed within the Wet Beaver Creek Wilderness.

## 38  *West Clear Creek*

*Distance:* 11 miles roundtrip
*Difficulty:* moderate
*Hiking time:* 7 hours
*Elevation:* 3700 to 4100 feet
*Management:* Coconino NF
*Wilderness status:* West Clear Creek WA

*Season:* year-round
*USGS maps:* Walker Mountain, Buckhorn Mountain
*GPS coordinates:* 34.539895 N, 111.704258 W

*Getting there:* From Camp Verde, drive 6 miles southeast on Arizona Highway 260, also known as the General Crook Trail, to the turnoff for Forest Road 618. Turn north and drive 2.2 miles to the signed turnoff for the Bull Pen area. Turn right onto Forest Road 215—rough in places but passable to carefully driven cars when dry, and continue 3.2 miles to its end. The West Clear Creek Trail begins at the Bull Pen Day-Use Area, on the eastern side of the Verde Valley.

Extending east for 30 sinuous miles from the Camp Verde area, West Clear Creek is the longest drainage on the Mogollon Rim. Nearly 2000 feet deep in places, this canyon system is a real delight to explore, for it features not only rugged beauty but also an interesting array of flora and fauna. A good introduction to this spectacular drainage is the West Clear Creek Trail, which extends upstream from the canyon's mouth.

From the trailhead, the route begins by heading east across former pastures of the old Bull Pen Ranch. After reaching the far end of the ranch, the trail then follows the left stream bank rather closely to provide a fine introduction to the lush forest that grows along this perennial

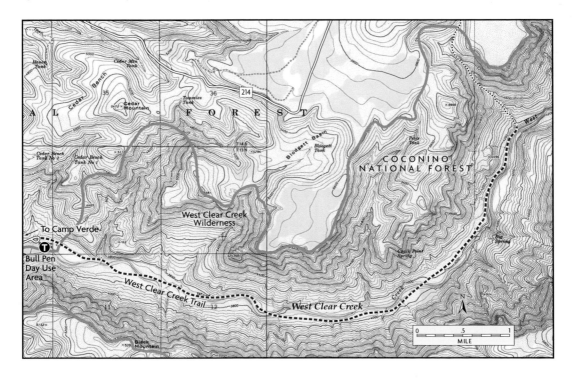

creek. Sycamores grow in the greatest numbers, but cottonwood, Arizona walnut, and ash trees are also prevalent. The first of many deep pools is reached in a short distance. These pools provide habitat for a thriving trout population.

About 1.25 miles from the trailhead, this hike makes the first of four stream crossings. Cairns mark either side of each crossing to make route-finding easier. Under normal runoff conditions, these crossings should not be a problem, and they may even be completed without getting your feet wet if you are good at boulder hopping. During times of snowmelt or after heavy rains, however, they may be dangerous, if not impassable.

A second crossing not far from the first returns the trail to the north bank. From here the route gains a slightly elevated bench where it distances itself from the creek by a few hundred yards. Although still within earshot of the creek, the trail now passes through a plant community that is remarkably different from the leafy growth found along the creekbed. A true desert environment of scattered juniper and mesquite brush typifies this arid topography. Prickly pear cactus are plentiful, as are a number of grasses. Because of the canyon's great diversity, a wide variety of wildlife is found here. Javelinas, ringtail cats, coyotes, mountain lions, deer, and black bears are included in this lengthy list, as

A sandstone wall rises above West Clear Creek at the first crossing.

are bald eagles, red-tailed hawks, and a variety of songbirds.

About 2 miles from the trailhead, the West Clear Creek Trail makes its third stream crossing. It then follows along the south bank for another 2.5 miles before reaching the last ford. From here the trail continues for another mile before turning up a side canyon that extends north from the creek. Although this hike turns around here, the West Clear Creek Trail does continue up the draw to climb nearly 1800 feet in 2 miles. Gaining the Mogollon Rim above, the route ends at a trailhead on Forest Road 214A. It is then possible to return to the Bull Pen trailhead by hiking this road for 1.3 miles to the upper end of the 2.5-mile Blodgett Basin Trail.

Another option is to continue upstream from where the West Clear Creek Trail turns north. Although no established trail exists beyond this point, it is possible to follow the canyon bottom for several miles with a lot of boulder hopping and the wading or swimming of many pools. A portable raft or inner tube is needed to float your pack across these pools, and this trip has to be made during the warmer months. A shuttle would be necessary as well. The rewards of such an adventure, though, are many. As the canyon climbs toward its headwaters, ponderosa pine and Douglas fir grow among the canyon's upper reaches and sheer walls of Coconino Sandstone become much more prevalent as the drainage narrows.

**Be prepared:** Cool, clear water is available all along this hike, but it should be treated first. Watch for flash floods during the rainy months of July and August. To complete the hike from the Bull Pen Day-Use Area to where the West Clear Creek Trail climbs north, plan on a minimum of 3 hours. If you continue upstream, be prepared to spend up to several days longer.

## 39 Woodchute Mountain

*Distance:* 8 miles roundtrip
*Difficulty:* moderate
*Hiking time:* 5 hours
*Elevation:* 7100 to 7700 feet
*Management:* Prescott NF
*Wilderness status:* Woodchute WA

*Season:* April to November
*USGS maps:* Hickey Mountain, Munds Draw
*GPS coordinates:* 34.706796 N, 112.156637 W

*Getting there:* Drive 8 miles south from Jerome on Arizona Highway 89A. Upon topping the pass, turn right at the sign for the Potato Patch Campground and continue 0.3 mile to the signed Woodchute trailhead. This is the official trailhead, but the trail actually begins 0.7 mile farther north along a high-clearance two-wheel-drive road. If you do not want to drive this road or if the gate is closed, park here and walk along the road for 0.7 mile to the signed start of the Woodchute Trail.

Small and often overlooked, the Woodchute Wilderness offers uncrowded hiking along with some spectacular vistas. Reaching the top of Woodchute Mountain, the Woodchute Trail provides the best access to the area.

From its start 0.7 mile north of the developed trailhead, the Woodchute Trail follows an old road for a bit among stands of ponderosa pine. It then climbs gently through more forest before breaking out onto a ridge that runs north toward Woodchute Mountain. For the next mile, this mostly level stretch provides spectacular views of the Verde Valley, Sedona area, Mogollon Rim, and San Francisco Peaks to the right, and the

A plethora of wildflowers grows along the Woodchute Trail.

Woodchute Mountain. Making this ascent in 0.5 mile, the grade is mostly moderate in difficulty.

Upon reaching the relatively level mountaintop, the trail continues for a mile before reaching the north end of Woodchute Mountain. The last 0.3 mile crosses a beautiful meadow. At the north rim of the mountain an awesome view opens up; the San Francisco Peaks, Mogollon Rim, and Sedona's red rock country come into view, as do the upper Verde River, Sycamore Canyon, Bill Williams Mountain, and Kendrick Mountain. This hike turns around here, but beyond this point the Woodchute Trail continues for another 3 miles as it drops to a forest road that runs along the wilderness boundary.

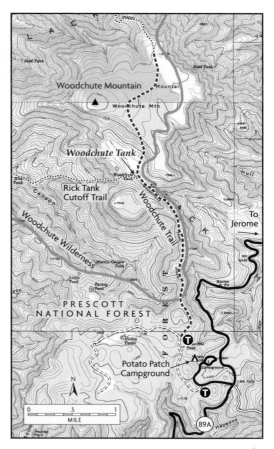

Prescott area to the left. In addition to ponderosa pine, stands of pinyon pine, alligator juniper, and shrub live oak also sidle up to the trail.

After 2.25 miles the route drops moderately before reaching a broad saddle directly south of Woodchute Mountain. A faint trail approaches from the right, but the main trail continues left before reaching Woodchute Tank, a small pond a short distance farther. Surrounded by an open grassy meadow, this area is a good place to spot both deer and elk. Here also is the signed intersection with the Rick Tank Cutoff Trail, which branches west. Beyond the tank the Woodchute Trail begins a 400-foot climb to the south rim of

**Be prepared:** Potable water is not available along the Woodchute Trail, so bring plenty. Watch for lightning during summer showers.

## 40  *Granite Mountain*

*Distance:* 8.2 miles roundtrip
*Difficulty:* moderate
*Hiking time:* 5 hours
*Elevation:* 5600 to 7185 feet
*Management:* Prescott NF

*Wilderness status:* Granite Mountain WA
*Season:* April to November
*USGS maps:* Iron Springs, Jerome Canyon
*GPS coordinates:* 34.615409 N,
112.551064 W

*Getting there:* From downtown Prescott, drive north on North Montezuma Street, which becomes Whipple Street, which then becomes Iron Springs Road. After driving 4.6 miles from the center of town, turn right onto Granite Basin Road (Forest Road 374) and drive 3.6 miles to the Metate trailhead. A trailhead use fee is charged.

Among the more interesting geological features of the Prescott area are the many exposed boulders and buttresses of Precambrian granite. Well rounded by erosion, this pinkish rock is often rendered all the more colorful by lichen. Most visitors to Prescott enjoy the unusual formations of the Granite Dells area just north of town, and hikers will find a whole mountain of this fascinating rock in the Granite Mountain Wilderness to the northwest. The premier hike in this wilderness follows the Granite Mountain Trail up its namesake peak to a vista point near the summit.

From the trailhead it is easy to see that Granite Mountain is popular among rock climbers. Soaring cliffs fortify much of the mountain's south face. These sheer walls are also ideal nesting grounds for peregrine falcons. Although the Forest Service closes off the cliff areas from February 1 to July 31, these restrictions do not apply to trail use.

After crossing a dry washbed, the Granite Mountain Trail intersects with the Clark Spring Trail. It then follows a shallow drainage bottom for about a mile, ascending an easy grade among pinyon pine, alligator juniper, manzanita, a

*Flowers growing in a burn scar along the Granite Mountain Trail*

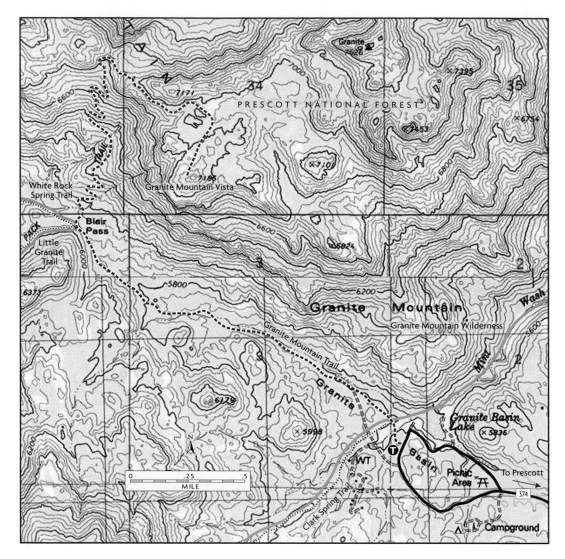

variety of oaks, and scattered ponderosa pine. Shortly after, the route begins to climb along a more moderate grade and then enters the burn scar of the 2013 Doce Fire. The blackened skeletons of what were once mostly shrub-size trees are not particularly scenic, but a riotous display of color can be enjoyed at certain times of the year because a variety of wildflowers have taken root across the otherwise barren hillsides.

After climbing some 400 feet in 1.8 miles, the Granite Mountain Trail reaches Blair Pass, a low saddle that lies between Granite Basin and Long Canyon to the north. From the pass two other trails take off to the left heading in different directions: the Little Granite Trail bears southwest toward Little Granite Mountain, and the White Rock Spring Trail bears northwest crossing into Long Canyon. The Granite Mountain Trail, however, turns right to climb northeast toward Granite Mountain Saddle.

In the next mile or so, from Blair Pass to Granite Mountain Saddle, the route climbs a mostly moderate grade through several switchbacks. Trail conditions include loose rocks in places.

Partway up the mountain, you get an up-close look at the granite of Granite Mountain. Nearly 2 billion years old, these boulders have weathered into beautiful shapes and textures. Upon reaching the Granite Mountain Saddle, the trail turns right and climbs a bit farther. The route then levels off and begins winding toward the mountain's southern edge. A little more than a mile long, this last stretch of the trail dips in and out of shallow washes before reaching Granite Mountain Vista, from which the actual summit (elevation 7626 feet) of Granite Mountain is visible to the east. Situated on a high point above the trailhead area, the vista takes in not only Granite Basin Lake directly below but also the town of Prescott and the Bradshaw Mountains beyond.

**Be prepared:** No drinking water is found along the Granite Mountain Trail. Watch for lightning in the higher, exposed terrain. Campfires are prohibited in the Granite Mountain Wilderness, and campsites must be 200 feet or farther away from trails.

## 41 *Thumb Butte Loop*

*Distance:* 2.1-mile loop
*Difficulty:* moderate
*Hiking time:* 2 hours
*Elevation:* 5700 to 6300 feet
*Management:* Prescott NF

*Wilderness status:* none
*Season:* year-round
*USGS map:* Iron Springs
*GPS coordinates:* 34.551747 N, 112.520854 W

*Getting there:* From downtown Prescott, drive west on Gurley Street, which becomes Thumb Butte Road, for about 3 miles to the Thumb Butte Picnic Area. A trailhead use fee is charged.

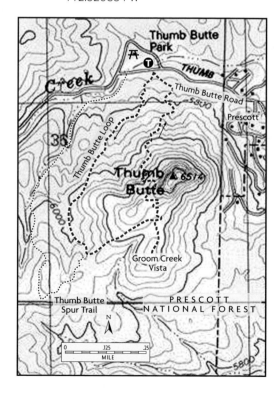

Rising just west of downtown Prescott, the aptly named Thumb Butte is a highly visible landmark beloved by the city's residents. This striking rise of rock is also the centerpiece of a short but very popular hike known as the Thumb Butte Loop Trail.

Gaining some 600 feet in all, the roughly 2-mile-long Thumb Butte Loop is steep in places. To take advantage of the somewhat gentler ascent along the western end of the trail, this description follows the loop counterclockwise. From the trailhead at the picnic area, cross the road to where both ends of the loop join. Keep right here and follow the wide, graveled trail south. Almost immediately the route begins climbing among stands of ponderosa pine. For the next mile, the route tackles most of the route's 600 feet of elevation gain. About 0.3 mile

The prominent Thumb Butte rises just west of Prescott.

in, you will enter an old burn area. Periodic views through the trees of Thumb Butte itself can be enjoyed along this section, but better views are to come so keep walking. All along the trail, interpretive signs explain both the natural and human history of the area.

About halfway through the hike, the Thumb Butte Loop intersects with the Thumb Butte Spur Trail, which runs southwest for 0.7 mile to connect with another trail in the area. Turn left at this intersection and continue climbing a bit farther to where a short side trail leads to the Groom Creek Vista. Complete with benches and numerous interpretive signs, this viewpoint provides a sweeping panorama of Prescott and beyond: the Bradshaw Mountains to the south,

the Spruce Mountain area to the southeast, Mingus Mountain and associated peaks to the northeast, and, to the north, Granite Mountain with the San Francisco Peaks beyond.

Past the Groom Creek Vista turnoff, the Thumb Butte Loop climbs a short distance farther where it crosses the southern ridge of Thumb Butte itself. From here the landmark protrudes skyward just to the north. Beyond this high point of the loop, the trail then begins a definitive drop back to the trailhead. Because of the section's 12- to 18-percent grade change, and because of the heavy use of this trail, this section has been paved with asphalt. Use caution when descending this portion, as loose gravel on the pavement can be slippery.

**Be prepared:** Bring water, as none is available along the hike, and watch for lightning during thunderstorms.

## 42  *Groom Creek Loop*

*Distance:* 8.7-mile loop
*Difficulty:* moderate
*Hiking time:* 5 hours
*Elevation:* 6400 to 7693 feet
*Management:* Prescott NF

*Wilderness status:* none
*Season:* May to November
*USGS map:* Groom Creek
*GPS coordinates:* 34.464541 N,
112.441157 W

*Getting there:* From downtown Prescott, drive a few blocks east on Gurley Street to South Mount Vernon Street. Turn right and follow the road 6.7 miles south to the developed trailhead on the left. Upon leaving Prescott, Mount Vernon Street becomes Forest Road 52, locally known as the Senator Highway.

Circling through the gently rising mountains south of Prescott, the Groom Creek Loop Trail offers both a tranquil hike among beautiful stands of timber and the promise of expansive views from the top of Spruce Mountain.

Following the loop clockwise, the hike begins by turning left at the trailhead. It then parallels Forest Road 52 for about 0.25 mile. After crossing a secondary road, the trail turns east to begin the 1200-foot climb up Spruce Mountain. Following a gentle ridge to the top, this 3-mile ascent is mostly easy, although a few stretches are moderately difficult. Because the route is popular with mountain bikers and equestrians, it is well maintained and easy to follow. In addition, it sticks mostly to shaded forest areas.

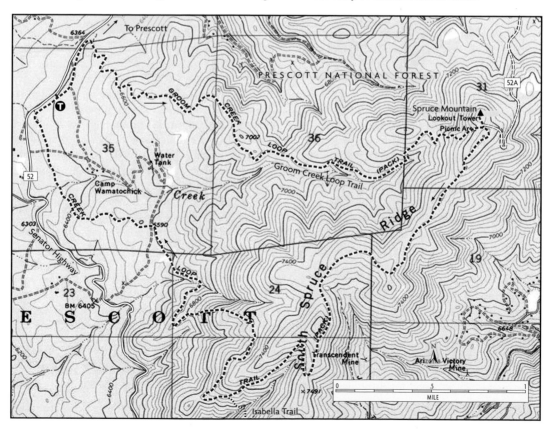

An old cabin along the Groom Creek Loop Trail

For the first couple of miles this timberland features ponderosa pine with some oaks and alligator juniper mixed in. As the trail nears the upper reaches of Spruce Mountain, however, fir trees become more common. In fact, the "spruce" trees of Spruce Mountain are actually white fir—a common misnomer among early settlers throughout the West. Along the climb to Spruce Mountain two intersecting routes are encountered, but the Groom Creek Loop is clearly signed.

On top of 7693-foot Spruce Mountain you will find a dirt road (Forest Road 52A) that also climbs the peak. A few picnic tables are scattered about under the trees, and a small fire lookout sits atop a knoll that is the actual summit. From this high point, the view to the north takes in Prescott, Granite Mountain, Mingus Mountain, the Mogollon Rim, and the San Francisco Peaks. Toward the east is the Verde Valley, and the forested ridges marching southward eventually give way to the more rugged Bradshaw Mountains.

At the summit the Groom Creek Loop continues to the right to follow South Spruce Ridge. Descending easily among a mix of ponderosa pine and fir, the route eventually intersects with the Isabella Trail, which drops for 1 mile to the old mining area of Potato Patch and Forest Road 197. Shortly after this trail junction, the Groom Creek Loop begins dropping a bit more steeply. As the route winds around to south-facing slopes, it enters more arid stands of ponderosa pine and Gambel oak.

After crossing a small ravine, the trail keeps left and, for the most part, levels off for the rest of the way. Within this last 1.5 miles, several old mining roads and trails are crossed. The Groom Creek Loop is marked with small signs (Trail 307) at most of these intersections, but a few may not be signed. At these junctions, look for blaze marks on the trees. For the last 0.25 mile, the Groom Creek Loop again parallels Forest Road 52 as it heads north to the trailhead.

**Be prepared:** Although water is sometimes available at the lookout during the fire season, it is best to bring all that you will need. Lightning may pose a threat on top of Spruce Mountain, especially in the summertime.

## 43  *Pine Mountain*

*Distance:* 10 miles roundtrip
*Difficulty:* moderate
*Hiking time:* 7 hours
*Elevation:* 5100 to 6814 feet
*Management:* Prescott NF

*Wilderness status:* Pine Mountain WA
*Season:* year-round
*USGS map:* Tule Mesa
*GPS coordinates:* 34.326236 N,
111.836873 W

*Getting there:* Drive 5 miles north of Cordes Junction on Interstate 17 to the Dugas exit. Turn east and follow Dugas Road (Forest Road 68) 19 miles to the road's end. The last 8 miles of the drive may require a high-clearance two-wheel-drive vehicle. Parking is available in the Salt Flat dispersed camping area.

As one of Arizona's lesser-known wilderness areas, the Pine Mountain Wilderness offers fine hiking without the crowds. A nice loop hike through the heart of this parcel takes in a section of the Verde Rim as well as Pine Mountain itself. As one might expect, the views are superb along many sections of this hike. Nice stands of the mountain's namesake, the ponderosa pine, are featured all along the way.

From the trailhead, this route follows the Nelson Trail up the usually dry Sycamore Creek drainage. Within 0.5 mile of the start, the trail reaches Nelson Place, an abandoned homestead that includes some dilapidated stone walls. Shortly beyond, the Nelson Trail passes the mouth of Beehouse Canyon, which branches to the south. The Pine Flat Trail turns right here to climb steeply up this side drainage. Continue

Ponderosa pine needles are plentiful along the Nelson Trail.

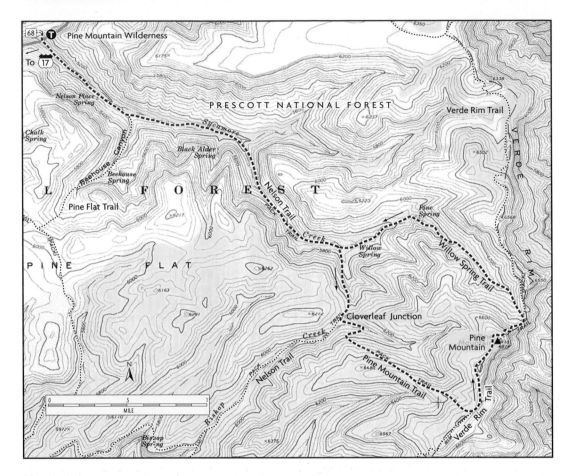

following the main canyon upstream, however, to the vicinity of Willow Spring, 2.7 miles from the trailhead. A forest fire in 2002 has left behind possibly dangerous snags. Just before the spring, the Willow Spring Trail continues straight and the Nelson Trail turns south to climb out of the drainage. Stay right and continue up the Nelson Trail. Whereas the first part of this hike ascends easily along the drainage bottom, this section follows a more moderate grade.

About 0.5 mile from Willow Spring, the Nelson Trail reaches the lower end of the Pine Mountain Trail at what is called the Cloverleaf Junction. Turn left at this intersection and follow the Pine Mountain Trail for 1.2 miles to where it connects with the Verde Rim Trail. Climbing moderate to occasionally steep grades, the Pine Mountain Trail gains about 700 feet in all. Some views of Pine Mountain open up along this trail, and a large burn area that resulted from a 1989 fire is encountered.

Upon reaching the Verde Rim Trail, turn left and follow this route north for 0.9 mile. Near the midpoint of this section of the hike, a short but steep side trail leads to 6814-foot Pine Mountain, the high point of the wilderness. Views from the summit, as well as from most of the Verde Rim, take in the rugged Verde River Canyon and the Mazatzal Mountains farther to the east. The river below is hidden from view, but you can look far to the south to see Horseshoe Lake north of Phoenix. Vegetation along this section of the hike includes a variety of oaks, alligator juniper, and mountain mahogany.

Within half a mile of the Pine Mountain turn-off, the Verde Rim Trail descends some steep switchbacks to reach a saddle at the head of Sycamore Creek. A left turn on the Willow Spring Trail leads 1.6 miles to Willow Spring and the Nelson Trail. The trailhead is another 2.7 miles.

**Be prepared:** Although springs near Nelson Place are perennial, it may be best to bring all the water you will need. Summer days may be too hot for comfortable hiking, and winter rains may make trailhead access difficult. Watch for lightning along the higher portions of this hike.

## 44 *Fossil Springs*

**Distance:** 7.5 miles roundtrip
**Difficulty:** moderate
**Hiking time:** 4 hours
**Elevation:** 5650 to 4250 feet
**Management:** Tonto NF, Coconino NF

**Wilderness status:** Fossil Springs WA
**Season:** year-round
**USGS map:** Hackberry Mountain
**GPS coordinates:** 34.406809 N, 111.568475 W

**Getting there:** In the small town of Strawberry, which is located north of Payson on Arizona Highway 87, turn west on Fossil Springs Road (Forest Road 708) and drive 4.6 miles to the signed turnoff for the Fossil Springs trailhead. Turn right and drive less than 0.25 mile to the developed trailhead. Fossil Springs Road is closed just beyond this turnoff.

Producing over 30 million gallons of water per day, Fossil Springs (actually a collection of several springs) is considered to be one of Arizona's most productive sources of groundwater. The water gushes out at a constant 70 degrees, and the resulting riparian ecosystem is so unique that Congress designated Fossil Creek as a National Wild and Scenic River in 2009. A popular hike to the springs follows the aptly named Fossil Springs Trail.

From the trailhead the Fossil Springs Trail drops some 1200 feet into the Fossil Creek drainage. Because it follows a former four-wheel-drive road, the route is easy to follow the entire way. Nevertheless, along most stretches of the trail, thick growth of Manzanita, live oaks, pinyon pine, and juniper has imbued the route with the feel of a foot trail rather than an old road. Occasional century plants and yuccas add to the variety of plant life. Along the descent grades are mostly moderate, although a few stretches are strenuous and rocky—something to keep in mind when hiking out. In addition, occasional views across the Fossil Creek drainage open up.

Upon reaching the drainage bottom the Fossil Springs Trail intersects the western end of the Mail Trail, which runs for 10 miles to eventually top the Mogollon Rim near Arizona Highway 260. Turn left at this intersection and follow the Fossil Springs Trail less than 0.5-mile farther to reach the first of the several Fossil Springs. Prior to reaching the springs the trail crosses the normally dry Fossil Creek streambed. It also encounters the first of many heavily used camping areas, which is indicative of the hike's popularity. So impacted is the vicinity of the springs that the Forest Service has banned fires of any sort to prevent the stripping of branches and brush for fuel. The creation of new campsites is also prohibited.

Upon reaching the springs you will quickly see why this destination is so popular. Whereas Fossil Creek was bone dry a short distance upstream, it is now a lively, bubbling creek with pools and more. Similarly, the high desert plant life found along the hike in has been replaced by a jungle-like collection of riparian greenery.

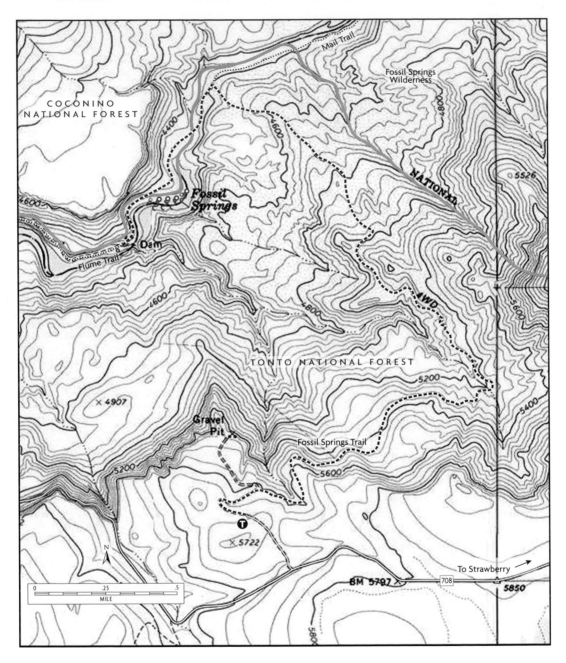

The largest of the trees that grow at streamside are Arizona sycamores, but more than two dozen other species of deciduous trees and shrubs are also found here. So too are a hundred species of birds and such water-loving mammals as beaver and otter. In addition, Fossil Creek is now home to such native species of fish as roundtail chub and the Sonora sucker. To protect this recently established fishery, fishing in the creek is catch-and-release only.

Continuing downstream is a lacework of secondary trails created by hikers intent on finding their own travertine pools to enjoy. The actual trail, however, keeps to the north side of the creek where it climbs a bit to skirt around a narrow bend in the waterway before reaching the old Fossil Creek Dam. Encrusted by deposits of travertine formations, the dam today looks more like a waterfall. It was built as part of an ambitious power-producing project in 1916. From this dam most if not all of the creek water was diverted into a 5-mile-long flume, which in turn fed the Irving Power Plant downstream. Since the project was closed in 2005, the creek flows at full strength, thereby making the native-species-only fishery possible. The 5-mile Flume Trail still follows the flume's route to the old power plant. This hike description turns back at the Fossil Creek Dam for a 7.5-mile roundtrip, but for a much longer hike, follow the 5-mile Flume Trail to the old power plant downstream.

**Be prepared:** Despite the abundance of water at Fossil Springs, bring plenty of water as the hike in and out of the canyon can be hot and dry. Treat water from the creek before drinking. If you are spending the night, be aware that campfires are prohibited and that other rules also apply. Expect to see many other hikers, especially on weekends and on warm days when swimming in the creek is possible.

A large deciduous tree grows at Fossil Springs.

## 45 Horton Creek

**Distance:** 9.4-mile loop
**Difficulty:** strenuous
**Hiking time:** 7 hours
**Elevation:** 5460 to 6700 feet
**Management:** Tonto NF

**Wilderness status:** none
**Season:** May to November
**USGS map:** Promontory Butte
**GPS coordinates:** 34.340121 N, 111.095358 W

**Getting there:** Drive 17 miles east from Payson on Arizona Highway 260. Turn north onto Tonto Creek Road (Forest Road 289) and drive to the Upper Tonto Creek Campground. Although the trailhead is located in the campground, parking is available in the Horton Creek Picnic Site just across the bridge.

Over 50 miles long, the Highline Trail offers a lengthy route for those interested in exploring the Mogollon Rim. Running just below the rim itself, this National Recreation Trail accesses some of Arizona's most scenic backcountry. For a fine day hike along this route, follow a clockwise loop that heads up the Horton Creek Trail to Horton Spring, continues south on the Highline Trail for a few miles, and then returns to the trailhead via the Derrick Trail.

Historically speaking, the Highline Trail was established in the late 19th century as a connecting route between several homesteads below the Mogollon Rim. One homestead was the property of L. J. Horton, who moved to this part of Arizona in 1881 and soon settled in the drainage that bears his name. Building a small cattle business, Horton was running some 200 head on his ranch by 1888. Upon returning from a trip, however, he found that rustlers had stolen the entire herd, forcing him to give up ranching for good.

Today, the 4-mile-long Horton Creek Trail climbs a little over 1000 feet along an easy to

A cascade of water along the upper reaches of Horton Creek

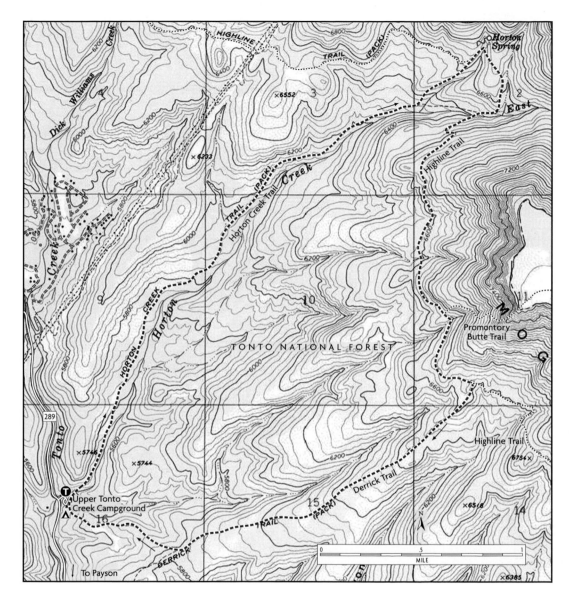

moderate grade. At the start, Horton Creek itself looks to be a dry wash, but this perennial stream actually runs beneath the ground through limestone caverns. Surfacing after the first 0.5 mile, the creek carries enough volume to support a promising population of trout. Forested along most of its route, the Horton Creek Trail passes beneath stands of ponderosa pine and Douglas fir, and among understories of oak, alligator juniper, and maple. Add to this shady ambience a wealth of small pools, cascades, and small waterfalls, and you have a memorable riparian environ.

Upon reaching Horton Spring, be sure to take a moment to enjoy the spring itself. Enclosed by a fence to keep livestock out, Horton Spring gushes from the hillside amid a verdant and pristine community of horsetails, mosses, maples, and giant Douglas firs.

From the spring this route turns right onto the Highline Trail and climbs steeply for a short distance to gain a ridge directly south. The trail then drops into the next drainage before climbing again for about a mile. Steep in places, this stretch has many loose rocks and is less distinct than the Horton Creek Trail.

After 2.2 miles the Highline Trail reaches the downhill end of the Promontory Butte Trail— a challenging 0.75-mile route that climbs to the mesa top. Continue instead on the Highline Trail for less than 0.5 mile from the junction to reach the top end of the Derrick Trail, the return leg of your hike. Dropping 1300 feet in 2.5 miles, this trail descends along a moderate grade through a sunny forest of alligator juniper, manzanita, and small ponderosa pine. Take care; there are loose rocks along this portion of the hike.

**Be prepared:** Water is plentiful along Horton Creek (surface water should be treated before drinking) and at Horton Spring. Beyond the spring there is no water. Although the Horton Creek and Derrick Trails are moderate in difficulty, some parts of the Highline Trail are rugged and should be considered strenuous. Be aware that horse packers and mountain bikers utilize these trails and caution should be used when encountering them.

## 46  Indian Spring Trail

*Distance:* 7.5-mile loop
*Difficulty:* easy
*Hiking time:* 5 hours
*Elevation:* 9100 to 8800 feet
*Management:* Apache–Sitgreaves NF

*Wilderness status:* none
*Season:* May to October
*USGS map:* Big Lake SW
*GPS coordinates:* 33.868869 N, 109.401315 W

*Getting there:* Drive 3.1 miles west on Arizona Highway 260 from Eagar to Arizona Highway 261. Turn south and drive 18.2 miles to Arizona Highway 273. Turn left and continue another 2.5 miles to the end of 273. Continue straight on Forest Road 249 for another 0.7 mile to Forest Road 249E. Turn right and drive 0.5 mile south to the signed trailhead.

The Indian Spring Trail loops through the highlands adjacent to Big Lake, a recreational lake to the northwest. Once beautifully forested, this region was adversely affected by the 538,000-acre Wallow Fire in 2011. Some pockets of unburned timber remain, but much of the Indian Spring Trail was burned over. Nevertheless, the hike is still a pleasure. Scenery abounds, a pair of springs await hikers, and forest succession has already begun.

Following the Indian Spring Trail clockwise, this hike begins by heading south into a mixed forest of ponderosa pine, Douglas fir, Engelmann spruce, and quaking aspen. Along this first section of the hike the burn scar is sporadic at best, leaving a good taste of what this timberland was once like. About 0.5 mile from the start, the trail reaches a 0.5-mile side trail that climbs to where the Big Lake Lookout once stood. Ironically, the tower burned in the fire and splatters of melted aluminum are nearly all that remains. After keeping right at this trail intersection, the Indian Spring Trail continues another 0.5 mile to reach Spillman Spring, where old, hollowed-out logs serve as rustic troughs. Beyond Spillman Spring the burn-over is much more complete, but it is easy to see a variety of undergrowth taking root among the blackened tree trunks. Thanks to some post-fire maintenance, the trail is mostly cleared of deadfall. Nevertheless, use caution

as unstable snags and falling branches can still pose a hazard.

Roughly 3 miles from the trailhead the Indian Spring Trail crosses Forest Road 24 and then reaches its namesake watering hole. Unlike Spillman Spring, Indian Spring is little more than a stock pond and is therefore not a suitable source of drinking water. In the vicinity of Indian Spring the trail follows a grassy meadow in which mule deer and elk might be spotted in the early-morning hours. A reintroduction project conducted by the US Fish and Wildlife Service

has added Mexican gray wolves to the docket of fauna that call these forests home. Because of the large contiguous tracts of wild land that the White Mountains and Blue Mountains present, this area has been identified as suitable for the large carnivores.

About 0.5 mile past Indian Spring the trail takes up the grade of the Old Apache Railroad. Laid in the 1940s to service the area's once-booming logging industry, the tracks were pulled out during the 1970s. After following the railroad grade for 2.5 miles, the Indian Spring

New growth in a burn scar along the Indian Spring Trail

Trail bears right onto a foot trail that eventually enters unburnt timber. In another mile the trail crosses Forest Road 249E and then climbs a bit before reaching a side trail to the Rainbow Campground in the vicinity of Big Lake. After keeping right at this junction, the route crosses Forest Road 249E again just before returning to the trailhead.

**Be prepared:** Although water is available at Spillman Spring, it is best to bring your own as livestock may foul the spring. Watch for falling timber in the burn scars and be aware that mountain bikers occasionally use this trail, especially on weekends.

## 47  *Mount Baldy*

*Distance:* 14 miles roundtrip
*Difficulty:* strenuous
*Hiking time:* 8 hours
*Elevation:* 9200 to 11,350 feet
*Management:* Apache–Sitgreaves NF

*Wilderness status:* Mount Baldy WA
*Season:* June to October
*USGS maps:* Mount Ord, Big Lake
*GPS coordinates:* 33.964927 N, 109.500849 W

*Getting there:* From Eagar, drive about 18 miles west on Arizona Highway 260 to Arizona Highway 273. Turn left and drive 8.4 miles south to the signed West Baldy trailhead.

Reaching an elevation of 11,403 feet, the summit of Mount Baldy features a subalpine environment not typically associated with Arizona. Gnarled krummholz trees grow here, as do various alpine grasses. Although the scenery is nice from this highest of peaks in the White Mountains, if your only intent is to "bag" the summit, you may be disappointed. Because it

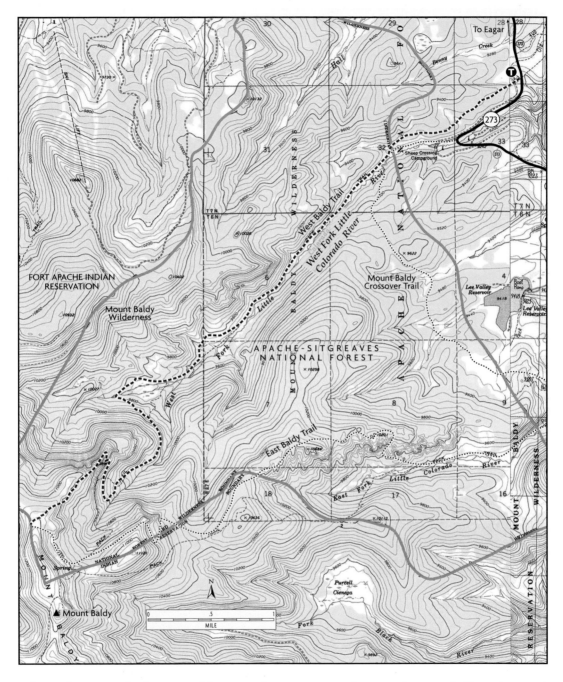

is located just outside the national forest on the Fort Apache Indian Reservation, access to the top is cut short by less than a mile.

Two trails approach Mount Baldy and connect near the highest point within national forest land: the West Baldy and the East Baldy Trails.

Meander in the West Fork of the Little Colorado River.

This hike description follows the West Baldy Trail along the West Fork of the Little Colorado River to its end at the junction with the East Baldy Trail.

From the trailhead, the West Baldy Trail heads southwest along a mostly level grade for about a mile before dropping easily to the valley floor of the West Fork of the Little Colorado River. At this point the route intersects a short side trail that follows the river from a second trailhead at Sheep Crossing. After keeping right at this intersection, follow the West Baldy Trail as it continues upstream along the north side of the river. Over the next 3 miles or so the trail climbs easily through a series of beautiful grassy meadows surrounded by thick forests. The river is diminutive at this point, but it meanders lazily and is quite scenic. Benefiting from the construction of single-log dams that have created small pools, the river is also a popular trout stream.

After the 4-mile mark, the West Baldy Trail crosses a side stream and then begins to climb at a mostly moderate grade through the forested slopes in the upper end of the West Fork drainage. Although the Mount Baldy Wilderness did not suffer the ravages of the massive Wallow Fire in 2011, it did not escape the devastation wrought by a recent beetle infestation. What was once a pristine old-growth forest of Engelmann spruce is today a greatly thinned timberland with plenty of deadfall. Thanks to a lot of trail maintenance, fallen logs have been cleared from the trail, but newly fallen timber will undoubtedly manifest again each spring.

Eventually, after switchbacking a few times, the West Baldy Trail gains a ridge north of Mount Baldy, which it then follows for nearly a mile before reaching the upper end of the East Baldy Trail. As this trail intersection is located at the boundary of the Fort Apache Indian Reservation, it marks the turnaround point of this hike. Although continuing farther to the summit might be tempting, it would involve trespassing on tribal land, and Mount Baldy is sacred to the Apache. In the past the tribe has sometimes issued permits to allow access to the top, but trespassers have had their packs confiscated; it is important to respect the sovereignty of Native American lands. If you want to extend your hike, it would be possible to drop down the 6.5-mile East Baldy Trail and then return to the West Baldy Trail by way of the 3.5-mile Mount Baldy Crossover Trail. Encompassing more than 16 miles, this lengthy loop hike would make for a good overnight trip.

**Be prepared:** Water is plentiful along the first half of the hike but nonexistent up high. Be sure to treat all surface water before drinking. Watch for lightning in open terrain.

## 48 *Escudilla Mountain*

*Distance:* 6 miles roundtrip
*Difficulty:* moderate
*Hiking time:* 4 hours
*Elevation:* 9650 to 10,877 feet
*Management:* Apache–Sitgreaves NF

*Wilderness status:* Escudilla WA
*Season:* June to October
*USGS map:* Escudilla
*GPS coordinates:* 33.919762 N, 109.117148 W

*Getting there:* The trailhead for the Escudilla Trail is located south of the mountain in the vicinity of Terry Flat. From Alpine, drive 5.5 miles north on US Highway 191. Turn right onto Forest Road 8056 and continue on this good gravel road for another 4.5 miles to a junction. Keep left and drive another 0.2 mile to the signed trailhead.

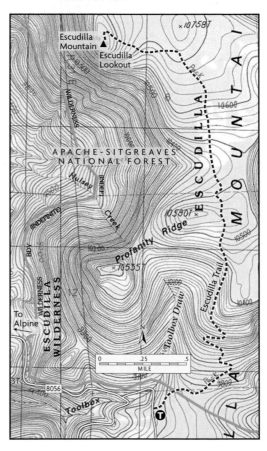

Reaching an elevation of nearly 11,000 feet, Escudilla Mountain maintains a real presence on the skyline of the White Mountains. To early Spanish explorers, Escudilla's broad top resembled a bowl, hence the name. Centuries later, the mountain greatly impressed noted naturalist Aldo Leopold during his tenure with the Forest Service in the White Mountains. In his book *A Sand County Almanac* Leopold wrote, "Life in Arizona was bounded under foot by grama grass, overhead by sky, and on the horizon by Escudilla." He elegantly described the taking of Arizona's last grizzly bear on the mountain. Today Escudilla Mountain is the centerpiece of the 5200-acre Escudilla Wilderness, and the main trail to the top is a National Recreation Trail. Unfortunately, the upper half of the trail was severely affected in 2011 by the 538,000-acre Wallow Fire.

The view of the aspen forest on the slopes of Escudilla Mountain from above

Following an old road that once accessed the fire lookout on top, the hike up Escudilla Mountain is easy to follow the entire way. For the first mile this route climbs gently through prodigious stands of aspen. Among these thickets you may see the charred stumps of giant Douglas firs. This area was scorched by fire in 1951. In the years since, the natural process of succession has spurred new growth of aspen. Indeed, this stretch of the route is quite colorful in mid-autumn. Conifers taking root in the shade of the aspen, however, will eventually crowd out the deciduous trees.

After a mile, the trail begins to steepen a bit as it enters a large meadow that slopes across Toolbox Draw to the left. In itself impressive—especially in the summer when wildflowers are blooming—this break in the forest allows spectacular views to the south and west. Less than 0.5 mile farther, the trail tops Profanity Ridge. From this point on, once pristine stands of Engelmann spruce and fir are now skeleton forests of charred trunks as the burn scar of the Wallow Fire is complete across the upper reaches of the peak.

Continuing north across a meadow, the Escudilla Trail soon reenters the scorched forest and continues for another mile before reaching the Escudilla Lookout. Although the lookout at one time had provided commanding views in all directions, it has since been fenced off and is closed due to severe damage from the Wallow Fire. On a bright note you may see aspen saplings growing in places along the charred forest floor. Similar to what took place along the lower stretch of the Escudilla Trail after the 1951 fire, the process of succession is beginning once again.

**Be prepared:** Because water is not available on this hike, be sure to bring your own. When walking in the burn scar along the upper half of the trail, be aware of the possibility of falling trees, especially when it is windy. Watch for lightning during stormy weather.

## 49 *P-Bar Lake*

| | |
|---|---|
| *Distance:* 2.6 miles roundtrip | *Wilderness status:* Blue Range PA |
| *Difficulty:* easy | *Season:* June to October |
| *Hiking time:* 2 hours | *USGS map:* Hannagan Meadow |
| *Elevation:* 8650 to 8950 feet | *GPS coordinates:* 33.655987 N, |
| *Management:* Apache–Sitgreaves NF | 109.267446 W |

*Getting there:* This hike begins at a signed trailhead 20 miles south of Alpine on US Highway 191. From a gravel parking area on the east side of the highway, the trail crosses a small creekbed before heading into the forest beyond.

In this region of vast spaces and long-distance hikes, the hike to P-Bar Lake is short and sweet. Although the lake itself is quite small, the stands of aspen and spruce that sidle up to it and an accompanying meadow make it ideal for a quick afternoon jaunt.

From the trailhead the 0.6-mile P-Bar Lake Trail climbs an easy to moderate grade to gain the summit of a broad ridge running east of US Highway 191. Shrouded by forest the entire way this route offers a variety of old-growth timber. It also reveals evidence of the massive Wallow Fire that burned through the western half of the Blue Range in 2011. Fortunately, the burn activity in the vicinity of P-Bar Lake was not so complete as to destroy every standing tree. Rather, you will see occasional blackened trunks of still living trees and only a scattering of standing dead timber.

After climbing about 300 feet, the P-Bar Lake Trail levels off before intersecting the Foote Creek Trail. Roughly 16 miles long, the Foote Creek Trail begins at Hannagan Meadow 3.5 miles southwest of this trail intersection and eventually drops to Blue River Road to the east. Although the P-Bar Lake Trail comes to an end

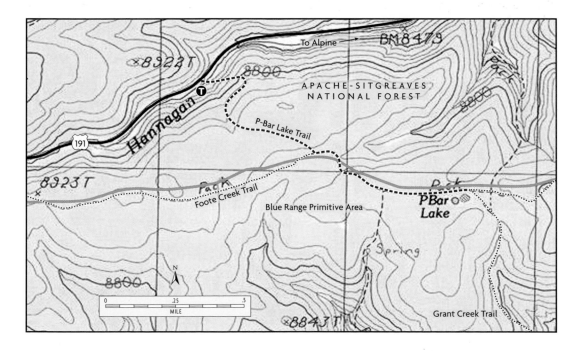

Aspen trees are reflected in P-Bar Lake.

at this point, you still need to walk a bit farther to reach the lake itself. Turn left onto the Foote Creek Trail and continue 0.5 mile or so to the lake.

Although little more than a glorified stock pond, this permanent watering hole is surrounded by an interesting meadow complete with a stand of stately aspen. Fortunately,

evidence of the Wallow Fire is not to be seen in the vicinity of the lake. Look for deer and elk tracks in the lake's muddy edge. Although this hike returns to the trailhead along the same route, further exploration is possible by following the 9.2-mile Grant Creek Trail, which branches south at P-Bar Lake to eventually drop into the Blue River drainage beyond.

**Be prepared:** Water is available at P-Bar Lake but, because it can be muddy and would need to be treated before drinking, it is best to bring your own. Watch for falling timber in forested areas affected by the Wallow Fire.

## 50 Bonanza Bill–Tige Rim Loop

*Distance:* 10-mile loop
*Difficulty:* strenuous
*Hiking time:* 6 hours
*Elevation:* 7250 to 7950 feet
*Management:* Apache–Sitgreaves NF

*Wilderness status:* Blue Range PA, Blue Range WA
*Season:* May to November
*USGS map:* Blue
*GPS coordinates:* 33.617122 N, 109.046940 W

*Getting there:* From the intersection of US Highways 191 and 180 in Alpine, drive east on US Highway 180 3.2 miles to Forest Road 281 (Blue River Road). Turn right and drive 20.2 miles south to Forest Road 232 (Pueblo Park Road). Turn left and drive 4.5 miles to the signed trailhead, which is on the right side of the road, a few yards shy of the New Mexico border. Much of this drive is along gravel roads that are passable to passenger vehicles.

Following a portion of the Bonanza Bill Trail and then the entire length of the Tige Rim Trail, this loop hike explores some of the more remote reaches of the Blue Range. Along the way a number of fine vistas are to be had, especially from Tige Rim. All but a short stretch of the Tige Rim Trail is in New Mexico and, although the Arizona portion of this hike falls within the Blue Range Primitive Area, the jurisdiction changes to the Blue Range Wilderness when the trail crosses into New Mexico.

From the trailhead, the 12.1-mile Bonanza Bill Trail heads south, roughly paralleling the Arizona–New Mexico border for much of the way. From the start the route passes through open forests of ponderosa pines along mostly level

grades. Scattered about the taller pines are stately alligator junipers and a variety of live oaks. The route is easy to find all along the entire portion of the Bonanza Bill Trail followed on this hike.

A little less than a mile from the trailhead, the Bonanza Bill Trail intersects with the northern end of the Tige Rim Trail, which is this hike's return route. Keep right at this intersection and continue another 0.5 mile or so to where the Bonanza Bill Trail drops a couple of hundred feet into the upper end of Steeple Canyon, where water is often found in the form of pools along the drainage bottom. After crossing the streambed, the Bonanza Bill Trail climbs back out of the southern side of the drainage to resume its mostly gentle grade.

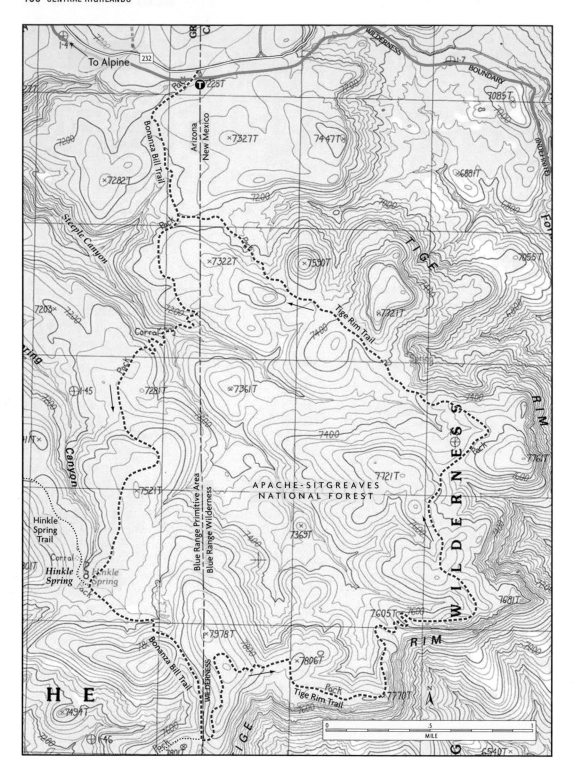

About 3.7 miles from the trailhead, the Bonanza Bill Trail intersects the Hinkle Spring Trail, which leads a short distance to its namesake spring (a dependable water source) before dropping into Cow Canyon and to Blue River Road to the west. Keep left at this signed intersection and continue south along the Bonanza Bill Trail as it climbs up and over a saddle. Gaining nearly 400 feet in this section, the route ascends occasional moderate grades. It also passes by some interesting formations of nearly white volcanic rock. Once over the saddle, the trail begins to closely parallel the state boundary (indicated by a barbed wire fence to the immediate left of the trail) for 0.25 mile or so. A nice view of the Blue River drainage opens up to the west along this portion.

About 4.5 miles from the trailhead, the Bonanza Bill Trail reaches a saddle where it intersects the southern end of the Tige Rim Trail. Although the Bonanza Bill route continues south for several additional miles, this hike turns left to follow the 5.5-mile Tige Rim Trail. At this trail junction, the Tige Rim Trail passes through a gate in the border fence before climbing a couple hundred feet up a small hill to the north. From the top of this ascent, the route turns east to take up its namesake landform. Because the Tige Rim Trail receives little use, this section of the route is very difficult to find and should not be attempted by inexperienced hikers. A topographic map of the area is a must and hikers should watch carefully for very faded stretches of tread, occasional cairns, and old sawn deadfall and stumps. Eventually the trail does become more evident as it begins to skirt the occasionally precipitous edge of Tige Rim. From vista points along the Rim some nice views of the San Francisco River drainage directly east and of the Gila Wilderness beyond can be enjoyed.

Volcanic tuff formations along the Bonanza Bill Trail

Eventually, the Tige Rim Trail turns north and it begins to follow an old road, which is considerably easier to discern. About 3.5 miles from the Bonanza Bill Trail junction, the Tige Rim Trail angles northwest before crossing back into Arizona where it reconnects with the Bonanza Bill Trail. At this point keep right and continue about 0.8 mile to the trailhead.

**Be prepared:** Whereas water can readily be found along the first half of this hike, you should still bring plenty as it is nonexistent beyond Hinkle Spring. Watch for lightning, especially along exposed areas of Tige Rim. Do not attempt to follow the southern end of the Tige Rim Trail if you are not adept at route finding. Given the plentiful signs of black bears along this hike, be sure to follow common sense practices concerning food storage if camping overnight.

## 51  *Bear Wallow*

*Distance:* 15.2 miles roundtrip
*Difficulty:* moderate
*Hiking time:* 2 days
*Elevation:* 8700 to 6700 feet
*Management:* Apache–Sitgreaves NF

*Wilderness status:* Bear Wallow WA
*Season:* May to October
*USGS maps:* Baldy Hill, Hoodoo Knoll
*GPS coordinates:* 33.603237 N, 109.397439 W

*Getting there:* Drive 28 miles south from Alpine on US Highway 191 to Forest Road 25. Turn west and drive 3.1 miles to a signed trailhead on the left.

Named for the many bear wallows that settlers found here in the late 1800s, the Bear Wallow Wilderness encompasses a montane drainage system, complete with a productive trout stream and virgin stands of timber. Unfortunately, Bear Wallow has become known for something else as well. It was here that the massive Wallow Fire began in May 2011. Ignited by an abandoned campfire near the mouth of Schell Creek, this blaze burned 538,000 acres to become the largest wildfire to date in Arizona history. Dozens of homes and buildings were destroyed, and the blaze changed the complexion of a large swath of the Apache–Sitgreaves National Forest for generations to come. Despite this widespread destruction, parts of the 7.6-mile Bear Wallow Trail, which this hike follows, were minimally impacted.

From the trailhead the Bear Wallow Trail drops south at a gentle to moderate grade along a small drainage for 1.5 miles before reaching the North Fork of Bear Wallow Creek. The entire length of this segment of the hike was highly impacted by the Wallow Fire as virtually every tree was torched completely. A lot of new undergrowth beneath the blackened tree trunks signals the start of forest succession.

Upon reaching the North Fork of Bear Wallow Creek, the trail continues downstream along the right side of the creek. Along this stretch

of the route, it is evident that many stands of ponderosa pine, Colorado blue spruce, Douglas fir, and quaking aspen were spared the worst of the fire. Although some blackened trunks of still live trees and an occasional standing dead snag can be found, this riparian forest has mostly retained its pleasant countenance. Alder, ash, willow, Mexican locust, bracken fern, and poison ivy also grow along the canyon bottom. True to the creek's name, you may indeed stumble across places where black bears have rolled in boggy areas to cool off and escape from bothersome insects. In addition to its population of bears, this wilderness is also home to deer, elk, mountain lion, wild turkey, and Mexican gray wolves.

As the trail continues westward, it mostly stays close to the creek, crossing it more than a dozen times. In the quieter pools you may spot small schools of Apache trout, a species officially listed as threatened. The US Forest Service and Arizona Fish and Game have been working to establish a sustainable population of the fish in Bear Wallow Creek. In 1979 a fish barrier was built to prevent the more common rainbow trout from diluting the genetic stock. Flooding four years later opened up the barrier, allowing an influx of rainbow trout. The structure has since been repaired and efforts to establish the Apache trout have continued.

Ponderosa pines that survived the forest fire in Bear Wallow

About 1 mile beyond where the Bear Wallow Trail joins the North Fork, the route reaches the lower end of the Reno Trail, which climbs 1.9 miles north out of the drainage. A second side trail is reached about 3.5 miles from the trailhead, at the junction of the North and South Forks of Bear Wallow Creek. Climbing south to the Mogollon Rim from this point, the 2.8-mile Schell Trail accesses some broad views that are absent along Bear Wallow Creek below. At mile 6.6 is the

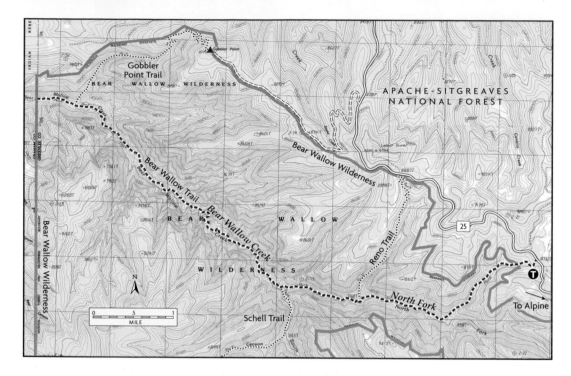

fish barrier mentioned above, and at about mile 7 the 2.7-mile Gobbler Point Trail climbs to the north rim of the drainage.

From the Gobbler Point Trail junction, the Bear Wallow Trail continues for another 0.5 mile to a fence marking the boundary between the Apache–Sitgreaves National Forest and the San Carlos Apache Reservation. The boundary is the turnaround point for this hike, as a permit from the tribe is needed to venture any farther.

**Be prepared:** Water is plentiful along the way, but be sure to treat it before drinking. Watch for falling timber in the burn scars. The hike to the San Carlos Apache Reservation boundary makes for a nice overnight trip, or you can opt for a shorter day hike by turning back where you please.

# 52  *Painted Bluff*

**Distance:** 11 miles roundtrip
**Difficulty:** strenuous
**Hiking time:** 7 hours
**Elevation:** 6200 to 6500 feet
**Management:** Apache–Sitgreaves NF

**Wilderness status:** none
**Season:** year-round
**USGS map:** Coronado Mountain
**GPS coordinates:** 33.170430 N, 109.373127 W

**Getting there:** From Clifton drive 19 miles north on US Highway 191, through Morenci and past the expansive Morenci open pit mine, to a sharp bend in the highway. The trailhead is located up a short, high-clearance road that branches left from the highway.

Exploring a remote reach of the southern end of the Apache–Sitgreaves National Forest, the 11.1-mile Painted Bluff Trail dips in and out of rugged drainages before ending in the vicinity of Eagle Creek, near the San Carlos Apache Reservation to the west. This hike follows this trail about halfway to Wood Canyon before turning around.

From the trailhead, which was once a small open pit mine, the Painted Bluff Trail begins by following an old road that is still open to off-road vehicles despite its poor condition. It is a bit confusing as two other short roads also start here. Climb up and over a small hill just west of the parking area and follow the middle road. Shortly, the Painted Bluff Trail begins to drop moderately as it contours around the head of a broad drainage. After 0.5 mile the trail crosses a normally dry streambed where stands of maple offer splashes of color in late autumn. Away from such drainage bottoms plant life includes a variety of arid land species, such as juniper,

sotol, cholla, and agave—or century—plants. The trail then climbs steadily up the far side of the drainage before entering an old burn scar. About 1.5 miles from its start the Painted Bluff Trail tops out on a ridge before crossing into the drainage beyond. From this high point a second old road branches to the north. Keep left at this junction to continue on the Painted Bluff Trail. From this ridge you will also get an expansive view of the gigantic Morenci open pit copper mine to the south. The collective hum of mining machinery from below is quite audible and remains so for another 1.5 miles.

Beyond this first ridgetop the Painted Bluff Trail drops steeply for a short distance into a small drainage. Here the old road peters out as a single-track trail takes up the route. It then continues to contour around another drainage basin, where it occasionally climbs moderate grades. It also becomes very rocky and difficult to follow in places, especially where it drops into

Century plant along the Painted Bluff Trail

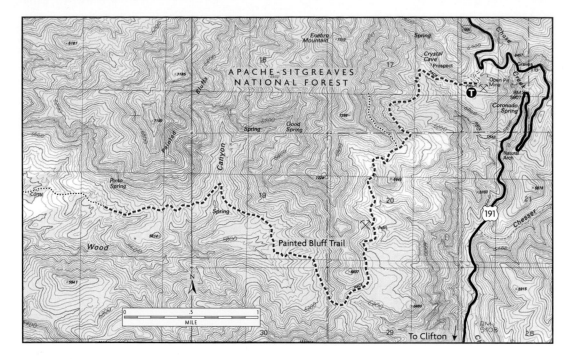

a small drainage that shelters a variety of taller pines and junipers. Along this section the trail climbs through tangled brush that effectively obscures the trail's route. To find the way, hikers should have a topographic map and watch for occasional blazes carved into the tree trunks. Eventually the route climbs out of the drainage and continues another 0.5 mile before reaching a saddle that opens into the expansive Wood Canyon drainage to the west.

Beyond the saddle the Painted Bluff Trail drops about 900 feet in 2 miles to reach the Wood Canyon drainage bottom. You may note that the din of the Morenci mine fades quickly after crossing the saddle. Use caution when descending into Wood Canyon as portions of the trail are rocky and overgrown. Fortunately, the route is periodically marked by large rock cairns.

As you descend into Wood Canyon, you will enjoy nice views of the trail's namesake, the Painted Bluff, which towers above the far side of the canyon. The normally dry Wood Canyon drainage bottom is 5 miles from the trailhead. This hike continues for another 0.5 mile beyond the streambed to the vicinity of Pinto Spring. If you know where to look, you might be able to spot some petroglyphs on a rock wall 500 feet above. Upon turning around, keep in mind that you have a big climb out of Wood Canyon on your return to the trailhead.

**Be prepared:** Although springs are found in the area, do not count on always finding water. Instead, bring all that you will need. Watch for loose, rocky tread in places and possibly overgrown sections of trail.

Opposite, top: Historic petroglyphs on a highpoint in the Superstition Wilderness

Opposite, bottom: Detail of century plants along the Telephone Trail

# Central Deserts

53. Piestewa Peak.................138

54. Hidden Valley.................140

55. Badger Springs Trail..........141

56. Black Canyon Trail............144

57. Cave Creek....................146

58. Pass Mountain Loop...........148

59. Treasure Loop.................151

60. Butcher Jones.................153

61. McDowell Mountain Park.....155

62. The Boulders..................157

63. Browns Saddle................159

64. Mazatzal Peak Loop...........161

65. Upper Cliff Dwelling..........163

66. Hieroglyphic Canyon.........165

67. Peralta Trail..................167

68. Dutchman's Trail..............169

69. Oak Flat......................172

70. Icehouse Canyon..............174

71. Picacho Peak..................177

*Extending north from Mexico into the south-central reaches of the state, Arizona's* portion of the Sonoran Desert is famous for its saguaro cactus stands and its colorful desert wildlife. Within the bounds of Phoenix and the surrounding Sun Valley are a number of urban parks, each remarkable for the extent of its wildlands and its close proximity to a major American urban center. East of the city rise the Superstition Mountains, a range colored as much by its human history as by its natural beauty. North of the Superstitions are the more remote and somewhat loftier summits of the Mazatzal Mountains. Although all of the hikes described in this section are destinations easily reached from Phoenix, they also offer a taste of Arizona's desert wilderness. Keep in mind that many of these hikes take place in extremely arid conditions and should be avoided in the summer months. Take along plenty of water.

## 53  *Piestewa Peak*

*Distance:* 2.4 miles roundtrip
*Difficulty:* strenuous
*Hiking time:* 2 hours
*Elevation:* 1400 to 2608 feet
*Management:* City of Phoenix

*Wilderness status:* none
*Season:* October to May
*USGS map:* North Phoenix
*GPS coordinates:* 33.539510 N,
112.023162 W

*Getting there:* Located in Phoenix Mountains Park, 9 miles northeast of downtown Phoenix, the trailhead is reached by driving north on the Piestewa Parkway to the Glendale exit. Turn right on Lincoln Drive and drive 0.5 mile to Squaw Peak Drive. Turn left and drive 0.7 mile to the signed trailhead. There is no entry fee.

Because Piestewa Peak rises in the midst of Arizona's largest metropolitan area, the trail to the top sees extremely heavy use, especially in the evenings and on weekends. It is, however, a worthwhile hike for anyone visiting Phoenix. The views of the surrounding city are outstanding, especially at sunset. Formerly called Squaw Peak, the prominent mountain was renamed after Lori Piestewa, a Hopi member of the National Guard who was killed in Iraq in 2003.

Although steep and rocky, the Summit Trail is well used and very easy to find. At the start it switchbacks north through the desert foothills of the peak. After 0.5 mile it intersects with the Freedom Trail. Nearly 4 miles long, the Freedom Trail circumnavigates the peak, accessing a variety of vistas along the way. Beyond this junction,

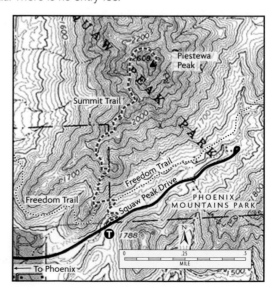

Hikers on top of Piestewa Peak are rewarded with impressive views.

the Summit Trail continues to climb northward along moderate to strenuous grades. The surrounding desert terrain includes impressive saguaro cactus, palo verde trees, barrel cactus, and cholla.

Upon reaching the peak's southwest ridge, the Summit Trail steepens as it continues to climb up the face of the mountain. All along this hike it is possible to take in an ever-changing view of the city below. Although urban development virtually engulfs Phoenix Mountains Park, this panorama is spectacular. Also of interest is the parade of city dwellers who stroll, hike, or jog up the mountain. As you approach the jagged summit, choose your footing well. Armed with a little knowledge about Phoenix and the surrounding Valley of the Sun, you can pick out a variety of landmarks, including South Mountain, the Sierra Estrellas, the White Tank Mountains, the McDowell Mountains, and the Superstitions.

**Be prepared:** Although Piestewa Peak can conceivably be hiked any time of year, the summer months are unbearably hot. Bring plenty of drinking water, and watch for lightning storms.

## 54 Hidden Valley

| | |
|---|---|
| **Distance:** 4.6 miles roundtrip | **Wilderness status:** none |
| **Difficulty:** easy | **Season:** October to May |
| **Hiking time:** 3 hours | **USGS map:** Lone Butte |
| **Elevation:** 2360 to 1950 feet | **GPS coordinates:** 33.342870 N, |
| **Management:** City of Phoenix | 112.044203 W |

**Getting there:** From downtown Phoenix, South Mountain Park is reached by following Central Avenue south to the park entry gate. From the gate continue straight on the main road for 2 miles to a fork in the road. Turn left on Summit Road and drive 3.4 miles. Turn right and continue on to the Buena Vista Lookout at road's end (6.5 miles from the entry gate). There is no entry fee for South Mountain Park. Parking is limited.

Encompassing more than 16,000 acres, Phoenix's South Mountain Park is one of the largest city parks in the United States. It encompasses more than 70 miles of hiking trails. One of the more interesting routes follows the National Trail to Hidden Valley. Situated high above the city, this secluded basin atop South Mountain's east end promises interesting views all around plus a wonderful selection of desert flora.

From the Buena Vista Lookout, the National Trail (a National Recreation Trail that traverses South Mountain Park from end to end) skirts northeast along a ridge before crossing over into a shallow valley. Passing through lower Sonoran desert typical of the Phoenix area, you'll see scattered saguaro, barrel, cholla, and hedgehog cactus, as well as ocotillo and palo verde trees. Spring flowers include brittlebush, globe mallow, and Mexican golden poppy. Scenic vistas from the trail take in much of Phoenix and the Salt River Valley, as well as the Estrella Mountains to the west and the Casa Grande area to the south.

About 1 mile from the trailhead, the route crosses into a second small valley. At the 1.8-mile mark the National Trail reaches the signed turn-off for Hidden Valley. Turn right to drop through Fat Man's Pass—a very narrow passage through some large boulders—and into Hidden Valley itself. Hidden Valley is a shallow and isolated drainage that parallels the main National Trail. Beyond Fat Man's Pass the trail follows along a wash bottom before encountering Window Rock and the Natural Tunnel—two more passageways

A lone saguaro cactus in Hidden Valley

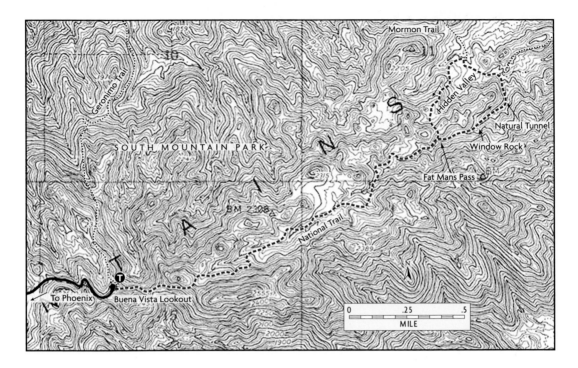

through boulders in the dry streambed. At Window Rock the terrain can be slippery from the wear of countless hikers.

Just beyond the Natural Tunnel, the Hidden Valley Trail reconnects with the National Trail. Whereas a right turn would follow the National Trail 2.7 miles east to Pima Canyon in the park's eastern end, a left turn heads back to the Buena Vista Lookout. Shortly after turning left (west) on the National Trail, an additional trail intersection is encountered. A right turn here leads north to the park boundary on the Mormon Trail. Keep left and continue west on the National Trail. From this point it is 2.2 miles to the trailhead.

**Be prepared:** The National Trail is popular among mountain bikers, equestrians, and hikers. Water is not available along the hike to Hidden Valley, so bring plenty. Rattlesnakes are common in South Mountain Park, and lightning can pose a hazard during thunderstorms. Because this hike falls within the Phoenix Mountains Preserve system, everything (rocks, plants, artifacts, and so on) is protected by law.

## 55 *Badger Springs Trail*

*Distance:* 3 miles roundtrip
*Difficulty:* easy
*Hiking time:* 2 hours
*Elevation:* 3100 to 2900 feet
*Management:* Agua Fria NM, BLM

*Wilderness status:* none
*Season:* October to May
*USGS map:* Joes Hill
*GPS coordinates:* 34.231445 N, 112.100170 W

***Getting there:*** From Phoenix drive north on Interstate 17 about 40 miles to the Badger Springs exit (exit 256). Drive southeast on Badger Springs Road (Road 9287), which is unpaved but passable to all vehicles unless wet, for less than a mile to the trailhead at road's end.

In 2000 President Bill Clinton established the 70,900-acre Agua Fria National Monument. Named for the Agua Fria River, which cuts through the monument lengthwise, this parcel of BLM land embraces both riparian canyon bottom and grassland mesa tops. In addition, numerous cultural sites are scattered across its breadth. Offering quick and easy access into the depths of the Agua Fria River Canyon and the heart of the monument itself is the Badger Springs Trail.

From the trailhead the 1-mile-long Badger Springs Trail quickly finds a shallow wash bottom, which it follows downstream to where it intersects the Agua Fria River. Keeping in the drainage bottom the entire way, the route is very easy to follow. Water occasionally flows in the Badger Spring Wash, and scattered cottonwoods and willows line the way. Slowly, canyon walls grow higher as the wash descends.

Upon reaching the Agua Fria River, the canyon landscape becomes significantly more

Prehistoric petroglyphs can be seen along the Agua Fria River.

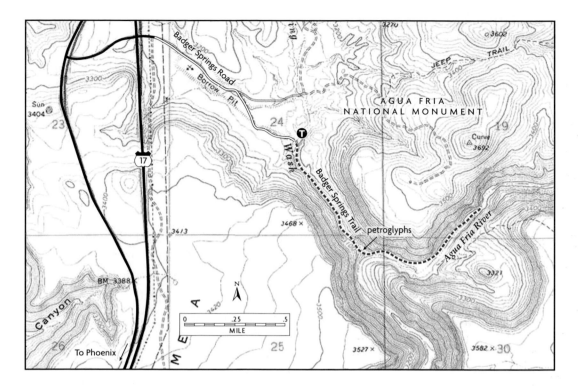

scenic. The mesa tops rise some 600 feet above the river bottom, and scattered stands of cottonwoods and other deciduous trees line the waterway. The river is usually flowing, sometimes so prodigiously that crossing it is not possible. Regardless of its volume, the sound of babbling water as it drops among boulders from pool to pool is quite refreshing in this otherwise desert terrain.

An important feature of the Agua Fria National Monument are its cultural resources. One such example is found at the junction of Badger Spring Wash and the Agua Fria River. Etched into the rock faces just to the left (or east of) the wash's mouth are several petroglyphs. These etched animals and various designs were probably created between 1200 and 1450 A.D. Pueblo-type villages also are found across the mesa tops within the monument.

From the wash/river canyon junction it is possible to follow the Agua Fria River either up- or downstream for as long as you like. This hike description continues upstream for another 0.5 mile to where the canyon narrows and becomes more scenic. From the rock art panel, there is an old trail that follows the north side of the canyon bottom, but it may be difficult to find and soon ends. It is probably best to simply follow the river bottom itself. This will entail some boulder hopping as you pick your way up the river, but exploring the various pools, trickles, and spillways is well worth it.

**Be prepared:** Although water is usually available, it is best to bring all that you will need as any surface water should be treated before drinking. Watch for flash floods during rainy periods. Be aware of venomous snakes, especially when walking among boulders. Because of high temperatures, it is best to avoid this hike during the summer.

## 56 *Black Canyon Trail*

| | |
|---|---|
| *Distance:* 3 miles roundtrip | *Wilderness status:* none |
| *Difficulty:* easy | *Season:* October to May |
| *Hiking time:* 2 hours | *USGS map:* Black Canyon City |
| *Elevation:* 2040 to 1870 feet | *GPS coordinates:* 34.052790 N, |
| *Management:* BLM | 112.151596 W |

*Getting there:* From Phoenix drive north on Interstate 17 to the Black Canyon/Rock Springs exit (exit 242). Cross over the interstate to the frontage road on the west side of the highway. Turn north and drive a short distance to Warner Road. Turn left and drive 0.3 mile to the Black Canyon trailhead. Plenty of parking is available.

The 80-mile-long Black Canyon National Recreation Trail runs north to south from the vicinity of Spring Valley to the Carefree Highway. As a recreation trail it is a relatively new phenomenon as construction of the route began in the 1990s. The corridor itself dates back much earlier as a livestock driveway. Today, the Black Canyon Trail is divided among several access points, and hiking any segment of the trail one way would require a shuttle vehicle. This hike description follows a short section from the popular Black Canyon trailhead to a scenic bend along the Agua Fria River.

From the parking lot, the trail heads west a short distance to a gate, after which it begins contouring across gently sloping hills. Immediately, nice stands of saguaro cactus, as well as cholla cactus, palo verde trees, mesquite, and brittlebush, grace the surrounding desert. Grade changes along this section of the trail are easy, and the trail itself is well delineated, thanks to the route's relatively recent construction.

As the Black Canyon Trail continues southwest, the Agua Fria River comes into view. Along this flow of perennial water a ribbon of greenery follows. Eventually, nearly a mile into the hike, the trail reaches an intersection. Whereas the right fork continues north along the K-Mine section of the Black Canyon Trail, the left fork soon drops south to the Agua Fria River and the destination of this hike. From this intersection to the river, the grade drops about 200 feet before reaching the river itself. As you descend, be sure to note the striking contrast between the

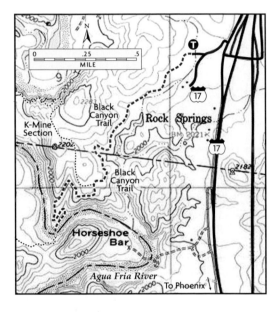

Sonoran Desert plant life in the foreground and the verdant shrubs and trees that find suitable habitat along the waterway below.

Reaching the Agua Fria River at a broad sandy bend, the Black Canyon Trail crosses the river and then climbs up along an old mining road on the other side. Under normal runoff the waterway can be crossed on stepping stones. In the spring or after heavy rains, however, it may require wading or may be uncrossable. As the river disappears around a bend to the east, it is actually beginning its sinuous loop around Horseshoe Bar, the other end of which can be seen from a notch in the hill just south of the river crossing.

Cactus and riparian growth provide contrast along the Black Canyon Trail.

Although this river crossing marks the turn-around point for this hike, it is possible to continue along the Black Canyon Trail and climb easily into the hills to the west before turning south. This optional route crosses the Agua Fria River once again before reaching the Table Mesa trailhead, 12.7 miles from the Black Canyon trailhead. A car shuttle would be required to complete this longer one-way hike between trailheads.

**Be prepared:** Because the water that is available at the Agua Fria River should be treated before drinking, it is best to bring all that you will need. Flash floods are a possibility along the river bottom. Be on the lookout for rattlesnakes throughout the hike. Because the Black Canyon Trail was designed as a multi-user trail, watch for pack horses and mountain bikers.

## 57 Cave Creek

*Distance:* 9.2-mile loop
*Difficulty:* moderate
*Hiking time:* 6 hours
*Elevation:* 3400 to 4080 feet
*Management:* Tonto NF
*Wilderness status:* none

*Season:* October to May
*USGS maps:* Humboldt Mountain, New River Mesa
*GPS coordinates:* 33.972519 N, 111.866551 W

*Getting there:* Drive east from Carefree on Cave Creek Road for 6 miles to the Tonto National Forest boundary. From this point continue another 12 miles on the same route, which is now Forest Road 24. This good gravel road is passable to all vehicles. The trailhead and parking area are just north of the Seven Springs picnic grounds and the CCC campground.

With 35 miles of trails, the Cave Creek trail system offers a variety of hiking terrain a short distance from Phoenix. A nice loop hike here follows perennial Cave Creek for a few miles downstream from the vicinity of the Seven Springs picnic site before returning via the desert foothills to the south.

From the trailhead the route first climbs easily up and over a hillside west of the road. It then crosses a road which leads to a Forest Service administration site. Shortly after, it reaches two trail intersections, the first being a short side trail and the second the north end of the Cottonwood Trail, which is the return leg of this hike. Keep right at both junctions and continue west along Cave Creek Trail as it follows its namesake downstream for 3.4 miles. Because Cave Creek flows year-round it features a variety of riparian vegetation, including Arizona sycamore, alder, and Arizona walnut, to name a few. Although Cave Creek Trail stays mostly above this lush environ, it does cross the stream three times before leaving the drainage. These crossings are easily made under normal runoff.

Nearly 4 miles from its start the Cave Creek Trail intersects the Skunk Tank Trail. Turning left here, this hike takes up the 4.8-mile Skunk Tank Trail, which climbs some 1000 feet in its first 2 miles. As the route ascends, it leaves behind the leafy riparian community to instead encounter saguaro cactus, ocotillo, and a variety of desert grasses. It also passes Skunk Tank itself, which is a usually dry stock pond ringed by verdant growth.

About 2.2 miles from the Cave Creek Trail intersection, the Skunk Tank Trail connects with the Quien Sabe Trail, which heads south. At 4080 feet, this intersection marks the high point

A saguaro cactus along the Cave Creek Trail

of the hike. At this point keep left and continue east along the Skunk Tank Trail. Over the next 2.6 miles the Skunk Tank Trail follows a former mining road which dips in and out of drainages, one of which includes running water that flows from Quien Sabe Spring a short distance south.

The trail also passes skeleton juniper trees decimated by a recent fire.

Nearly 5 miles from its start, the Skunk Tank Trail connects with the Cottonwood Trail. Turn left to follow the Cottonwood Trail 0.4 mile north to its junction with the Cave Creek Trail.

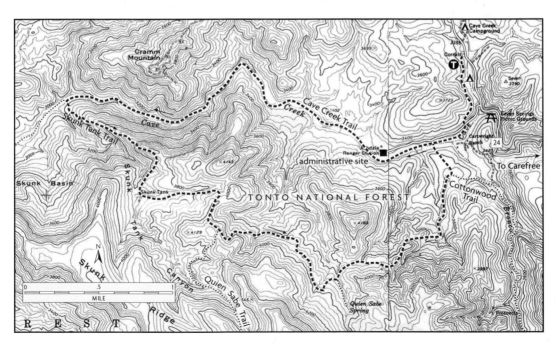

Just before reaching the Cave Creek Trail, the Cottonwood Trail first crosses Cave Creek itself. Like other crossings this one is easy although it may be difficult to find the exact route across the drainage bottom. Simply pick your way directly across and then climb the stream bank on the north side where you should find the Cave Creek Trail. Continue another 0.3 mile north to the trailhead and the end of this hike.

**Be prepared:** Although water is available in Cave Creek, it is best to pack all you will need beforehand. If you are planning a summer hike here, you may want to stick to the Cave Creek Trail, where shade is a bit more prevalent.

## 58 *Pass Mountain Loop*

**Distance:** 7.1-mile loop
**Difficulty:** moderate
**Hiking time:** 4 hours
**Elevation:** 1900 to 2600 feet
**Management:** Tonto NF, Usery Mountain Regional Park

**Wilderness status:** none
**Season:** October to May
**USGS map:** Apache Junction
**GPS coordinates:** 33.465963 N, 111.580924 W

**Getting there:** From US Highway 60 in Apache Junction, turn north on Meridian Road and drive 5.5 miles to the road's end. The Meridian trailhead is one of three trailheads that serve the Pass Mountain Loop Trail. The other two are in Usery Mountain Regional Park, which requires a vehicle fee for entry.

Situated in the Goldfield Mountains, Pass Mountain rises some 1500 feet above the surrounding desert in a rugged and scenic manner. A wonderful way to take in its beauty is to hike the 7.1-mile Pass Mountain Loop, which circumnavigates the entire peak. Along the way both memorable scenery and a variety of Sonoran plant life are in plentiful supply. This hike begins at the southeast corner of the loop and follows it counterclockwise.

From the Meridian trailhead the access trail to the Pass Mountain Loop heads northwest for a short way before reaching a fork in the trail. Keep left and continue a little farther to a ravine where the way in and out of the other side is marked by rock cairns. After crossing the ravine this route intersects the Pass Mountain Loop, which is well defined by the many hikers that follow it. Bear right to follow the trail along the west side of the ravine you just crossed. Dipping in and out of small drainages the gradient along this segment of the hike gains elevation in an easy manner. Eventually, the ascent becomes more pronounced, however, as the route draws closer to a saddle that is 1.5 miles north of the trailhead. From the top of the saddle the views of Pass Mountain's east face are impressive, as are the vistas south into the Apache Junction area and beyond.

Beyond the saddle, the Pass Mountain Loop contours around the northeast slope of its namesake mountain. It then angles west to cross the northern slope of the mountain where a short side trail leads to an overlook that offers fine vistas to the north. The grade changes along this portion of the route are mostly gentle and the trail itself is easy to follow. As the route begins to trend south it crosses a fence, which marks the entry into Usery Mountain Regional Park. From here the Pass Mountain Loop takes up a more southerly track as it traverses bajada lands along the mountain's west side. Although

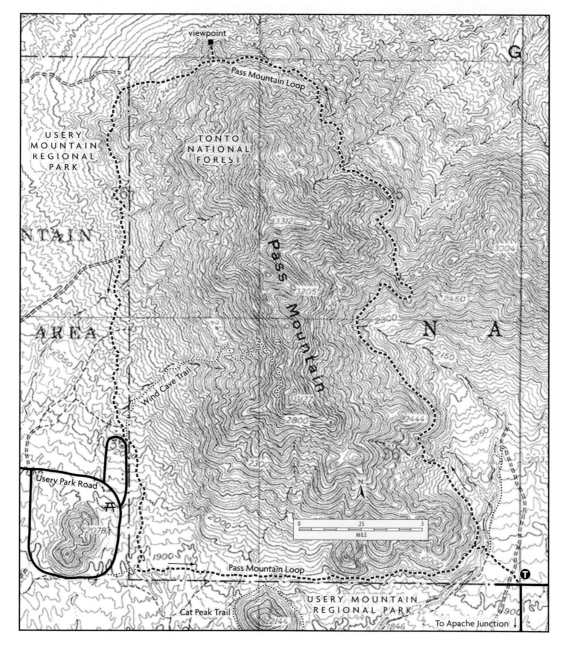

the rich variety of desert plant life is evident all along this hike, it is especially notable along this stretch of the loop. Saguaro cactus, barrel cactus, cholla, palo verde, and ocotillo are just some of the many plant species found along the way.

Within Usery Mountain Regional Park the Pass Mountain Loop reaches the Wind Cave Trail and its accompanying trailhead. Climbing 1.6 miles up the west slope of Pass Mountain, this side trail ends at its namesake, a pronounced

Barrel cactus growing along Pass Mountain Loop

alcove in a cliff face above. The Wind Cave trailhead is used by many hikers to also access the Pass Mountain Loop. Just beyond this trail intersection the Pass Mountain Loop reenters the Tonto National Forest, after which it continues south for another 0.5 mile before turning east. A short access trail runs west from this point to reach a second trailhead in Usery Mountain Regional Park.

For the next 1.5 miles or so the Pass Mountain Loop roughly parallels the national forest boundary back to the hike's start. Along this final segment of the hike the trail intersects the Cat Peak Trail, which turns south to enter Usery Mountain Regional Park, where it circumnavigates its namesake landform. To return to the Meridian trailhead, continue nearly 1 mile east from the Cat Peak Trail intersection and then turn right from the Pass Mountain Loop onto a side trail, cross the ravine, and continue less than 0.25 mile southeast to the parking area.

**Be prepared:** Although potable water can be found at the Wind Cave trailhead, that is quite a ways into this hike so it is best to simply bring all that you will need. Watch for rattlesnakes. This hike is possible throughout the year but it can be quite hot from late spring to early fall.

## 59  *Treasure Loop*

**Distance:** 2.4-mile loop
**Difficulty:** easy
**Hiking time:** 2 hours
**Elevation:** 2080 to 2600 feet
**Management:** Lost Dutchman SP, Tonto NF

**Wilderness status:** none
**Season:** October to May
**USGS map:** Goldfield
**GPS coordinates:** 33.461036 N, 111.477548 W

**Getting there:** From the town of Apache Junction, drive east on Arizona Highway 88 (the Apache Trail) to the entrance of Lost Dutchman State Park, on the right. After entering the park, where an entry fee is charged per vehicle, continue to the Cholla Day-Use Area. The trail begins at the east end of the parking area.

Nestled up to the scenic west end of the Superstition Mountains, Lost Dutchman State Park offers a nice respite from the rush of nearby Phoenix and surrounding suburbs. A handful of trails begin in the park and shortly enter Tonto National Forest. Each of these trails ventures far enough into the lower slopes of the soaring Superstitions to take in spectacular views and a nice stretch of Sonoran Desert. One of these routes is the 2.4-mile-long Treasure Loop.

From the Cholla Day-Use Area, follow the trail a short distance south to an intersection. Turn left and cross through a fence that marks the route's entry into Tonto National Forest. The Treasure Loop Trail then continues southeast to begin a mostly gentle climb into the hills. About 0.5 mile from the start, the loop intersects with the Jacobs Crosscut Trail running north–south. Continue straight at this point.

Because this trail receives a lot of use, its tread is wide and easy to follow. You may also note that it enters an old burn area shortly after leaving the state park. Whereas some nice saguaros populate the park below, the burn area is typified by grasses and scattered brittlebush, which are quite colorful in spring. As you climb, be sure to enjoy the unfolding scenery. To the southwest is the town of Apache Junction, and northwest are the Goldfield Hills. The Four Peaks rise farther to the north, and towering directly above is the impressive Flatiron.

As the trail approaches a sizable rock outcrop known as Green Boulder (because of its coat of lichen), it begins to climb along a moderately steeper grade. Ducking behind Green Boulder, the trail then reaches its high point and an

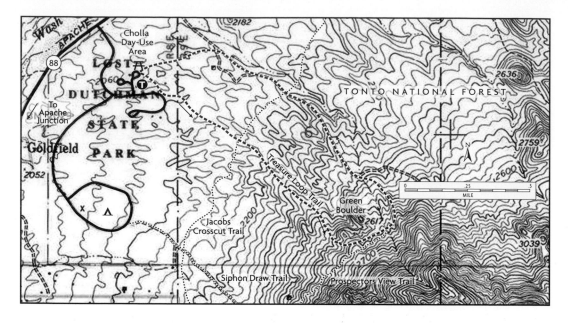

intersection with the Prospector's View Trail. Nice views are indeed to be had from this point, and a bench offers a handy respite. Bear left and continue for another 0.25 mile before turning northwest to return to the park. A great view of the Praying Hands—twin rock spires—can be enjoyed here. Follow Treasure Loop a little over a mile back to the Cholla Day-Use Area.

**Be prepared:** As no water is found in this desert terrain, be sure to fill up your water bottles before setting out. Avoid this hike during the heat of summer, and watch for rattlesnakes.

Looking down on Green Boulder along the Treasure Loop

## 60  *Butcher Jones*

*Distance:* 5 miles roundtrip
*Difficulty:* easy
*Hiking time:* 3 hours
*Elevation:* 1535 to 1700 feet
*Management:* Tonto NF

*Wilderness status:* none
*Season:* October to May
*USGS map:* Stewart Mountain
*GPS coordinates:* 33.575735 N, 111.514492 W

*Getting there:* This hike begins at the Butcher Jones Recreation Site along the north side of Saguaro Lake. From Mesa drive 27 miles north on Arizona Highway 87 to the Bush Highway. Turn right and drive 2 miles to a left turn toward Butcher Jones. Drive another 2 miles to this developed recreation area. It is also possible to access the Bush Highway from the Apache Junction area by driving north on Ellsworth Road (which becomes Usery Pass Road). Turn right onto the Bush Highway and drive 6.7 miles to the turnoff for Butcher Jones Recreation Area. There is a fee per vehicle for day use of the facility. Called the Tonto Pass, this permit may be purchased from participating stores and Forest Service offices and visitors centers, but not at the trailhead itself.

Saguaro Lake as seen from the Butcher Jones Trail

The Butcher Jones Trail was designed in part to allow land access to some shoreline spots for anglers. For hikers this trail provides some great vistas of Saguaro Lake and the surrounding desert topography, plus it reveals a nice collection of desert plant life.

From the trailhead, the Butcher Jones Trail follows a paved nature trail south along the water's edge for a short distance, passing a boat dock along the way. At Peregrine Point the trail passes through a gate and becomes an actual backcountry route. It then turns east to contour around Peregrine Cove, after which it climbs easily to the south before turning east again. The trail passes through riparian growth at the head of the cove, where it encounters some impressive specimens of saguaro, barrel, and cholla cactus once it leaves the water's edge.

At nearly 2 miles from the trailhead the Butcher Jones Trail intersects a side trail that accesses the lakeshore at Campers Cove. From this portion of the hike you will get a nice view of the rugged cliff faces that crowd along the south side of Saguaro Lake. Keep left at this intersection and continue east for a little more than half a mile to reach this hike's end at a rocky vista point overlooking Burro Cove. In addition to enjoying views of the bright blue water below, you will also enjoy an unobstructed vista of the Four Peaks, which rise impressively to the east. From this point, backtrack 2.5 miles to your starting point.

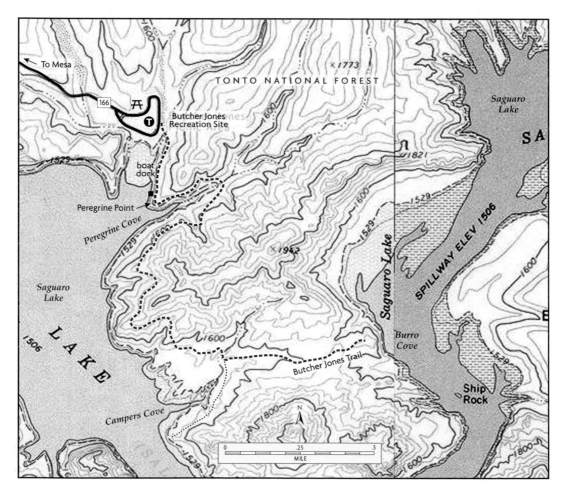

**Be prepared:** Although the lakeshore is accessible in a few places, lake water should be treated before drinking, so it is best to bring all the water that you will need. Watch for venomous snakes, and be prepared for very hot temperatures from late spring to early fall. In addition, be sure to purchase a Tonto Pass for the day before driving to the trailhead.

## 61  McDowell Mountain Park

**Distance:** 5.2-mile loop
**Difficulty:** easy
**Hiking time:** 3 hours
**Elevation:** 1985 to 2200 feet
**Management:** McDowell Mountain
Regional Park

**Wilderness status:** none
**Season:** October to May
**USGS map:** Fort McDowell
**GPS coordinates:** 33.694245 N,
111.731085 W

**Getting there:** From Mesa, drive northeast on Arizona Highway 87 to the turnoff for Fountain Hills. Turn north onto Shea Boulevard, drive to the first traffic light and turn right onto Saguaro Boulevard. Occasional signs point the way to the park along the drive, which continues past Fountain Park. Saguaro Boulevard ends at an intersection with Fountain Hills Boulevard. Turn right and continue 4 miles to the park entrance. After entering the park and paying a per vehicle day-use fee, drive to the campground and park at the Wagner trailhead at the campground entrance.

Spanning more than 21,000 acres of scenic desert terrain northeast of Phoenix, McDowell Mountain Regional Park offers hikers 68 miles of trails within a short distance of downtown Phoenix. The hike described here follows a loop that incorporates portions of the Wagner, Granite, and Bluff Trails.

From the Wagner trailhead, begin by hiking north and then west on the Wagner Trail, which loops around the large campground. After

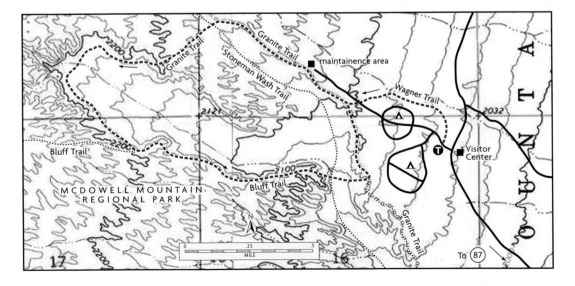

Burned-over cholla cactus along the Wagner Trail

1.1 miles the Wagner Trail intersects with the Granite Trail. As with all trail intersections in the park, this one is well signed. Turn right onto the Granite Trail and continue northwest across gently sloping bajada lands (eroded alluvial gravel and sand deposits). This desert terrain still shows signs of the 22,000-acre Rio Fire that swept through the area in July 1995. Today you will see a few saguaro cactus that managed to survive the flames, along with thriving creosote bush. Numerous charred stands of cholla cactus highlight the destruction that the park endured, and you will see mesquite trees that the park staff has since planted.

About 1 mile from the Wagner–Granite Trails intersection, the Granite Trail drops into shallow Stoneman Wash, which was named after the first military commander of the Arizona Territory. The route then loops around the head of a small basin where some nice granite boulders and cliff faces are encountered. After climbing out of the shallow basin, the Granite Trail reaches the Bluff Trail. True to its name, the Bluff Trail follows along the crest of bluffs that define the south side of Stoneman Wash.

From this intersection, hike east on the Bluff Trail, which drops to cross Stoneman Wash before intersecting the Granite Trail. Bear left on the Granite Trail and continue for 0.3 mile to an intersection with the Wagner Trail. Turn right and continue 1.1 mile to the trailhead. As you make your way back, be sure to take in the expansive views: directly west are the rugged McDowell Mountains, to the east rise the Four Peaks and the Mazatzal Range, and to the southwest you can see Weavers Needle, which lies in the heart of the Superstition Mountains.

**Be prepared:** Because all trails in McDowell Mountain Regional Park are well maintained and signed, routefinding should not be a problem. Be sure to pack plenty of water, however. Watch for rattlesnakes during the warmer months and lightning during stormy periods. Flash flooding may also occur along Stoneman Wash.

## 62  *The Boulders*

*Distance:* 8 miles roundtrip
*Difficulty:* moderate
*Hiking time:* 5 hours
*Elevation:* 2250 to 4000 feet
*Management:* Tonto NF

*Wilderness status:* none
*Season:* October to May
*USGS map:* Boulder Mountain
*GPS coordinates:* 33.764427 N,
111.493411 W

*Getting there:* From Mesa drive north about 40 miles on Arizona Highway 87 to just beyond milepost 210 (about 8 miles south of the small enclave of Sunflower) and the signed Ballantine trailhead on the east side of the highway.

This hike climbs away from the traffic noise along the Pine Creek Loop before taking up the Ballantine Trail itself. The eventual destination is The Boulders, a sprawling garden of sculpted rocks and formations that are quite picturesque.

At the trailhead you are immediately faced with a choice of two routes to follow. Actually, these two trails are the two western ends of the Pine Creek Loop, and both continue for 1.5 miles east to where they meet and connect with the much longer Ballantine Trail. This hike description follows the right-hand or southern route in and returns by way of the northern leg of the loop.

After a short jaunt across the gentle lower slopes, the Pine Creek Loop soon begins climbing steadily along mostly moderate grades. The higher it climbs, the rockier the footing becomes, and the farther you go, the less noticeable the

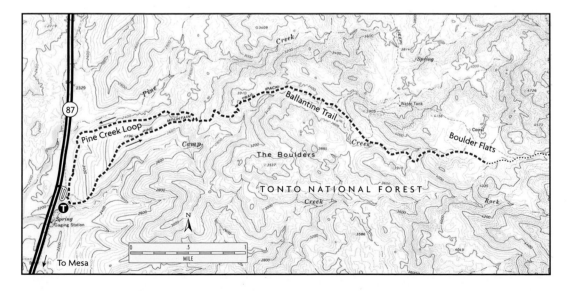

traffic noise is, and eventually the din fades away completely. All along the Pine Creek Loop, and then along much of the Ballantine Trail, you will enjoy a nice variety of Sonoran Desert plant life. Tall saguaros are most prominent, especially along south-facing slopes. Various cholla and prickly pear cactus are also present, as are palo verde trees with their green bark.

After climbing about 500 feet in elevation and then following a ridgeline a bit, the southern segment of the Pine Creek Loop reaches its easternmost point at a small saddle 1.5 miles from the trailhead. From here this hike takes up the Ballantine Trail, which extends east for 10 miles to eventually reach Forest Service Road 143 near the crest of the Mazatzal Mountains (beyond this hike's terminus). Climbing steadily higher, the Ballantine Trail soon begins following along the north side of the normally dry Camp Creek drainage. It also enters what are known as The Boulders, an expansive collection of mostly rounded granite formations of varying sizes.

After continuing to wind its way among a multitude of rock formations, the Ballantine Trail eventually reaches Boulder Flats, the destination of this hike. Here the drainage bottom opens up considerably and becomes much more level. An old, well-weathered trail sign lying on the ground indicates that it is 4 miles back to the trailhead and 8 miles to Four Peaks Road (Forest Road 143).

Situated at about 4000 feet in elevation, Boulder Flats is 1750 feet higher than the trailhead, and this gain in elevation is reflected in the surrounding plant life. Although a handful of saguaro cactus still grow at this elevation, the predominant plant types are shrubs and grasses. To return to the trailhead, follow the Ballantine Trail back and down to the eastern edge of the Pine Creek Loop. Keep right at this junction and follow the north segment of the loop back to the trailhead. This route contours along the south slope of the Pine Creek drainage before paralleling the highway south to the parking area.

**Be prepared:** Bring plenty of water as no reliable sources are found along the way. Also, watch for rattlesnakes during the warmer months.

Granite boulders and formations in The Boulders grace the hike along the Ballantine Trail.

## 63 *Browns Saddle*

**Distance:** 4 miles roundtrip
**Difficulty:** moderate
**Hiking time:** 3 hours
**Elevation:** 5700 to 6760 feet
**Management:** Tonto NF

**Wilderness status:** Four Peaks WA
**Season:** April to November
**USGS map:** Four Peaks
**GPS coordinates:** 33.705485 N,
111.337899 W

**Getting there:** This hike begins at the Lone Pine Saddle trailhead. To reach Lone Pine Saddle, drive north from Mesa on Arizona Highway 87 for 21 miles to Four Peaks Road (Forest Road 143). Turn right and continue east for 20 miles to the Mazatzal Divide. Turn right again onto Forest Road 648 and continue 1.4 miles to the road's end. A high-clearance two-wheel-drive vehicle is recommended from the turnoff on Highway 87 to the trailhead.

Rising abruptly to 7657 feet from desert elevations of less than 2000 feet, the Four Peaks comprise a well-known landmark throughout central Arizona. Forming the southern end of the Mazatzal Mountains, reaching these rugged summits requires some scrambling skills. A short and scenic hike that accesses the heart of the massif follows the Browns Trail to Browns Saddle.

From Lone Pine Saddle, the Browns Trail sets off to roughly follow a ridgeline south toward Browns Peak. An additional trail that also begins at this trailhead is the 10-mile Four Peaks Trail, which contours around the eastern slope of the Four Peaks. Following easy to moderate grades from the start, the Browns Trail leads through scattered taller pines and thicket upon thicket of manzanita, Gambel oak, Arizona white oak, and alligator juniper. This ecosystem is one that is in transition thanks to the Lone Fire, which burned 61,000 acres in 1996. Today the most telling remnants of the burn scar are widely scattered dead and blackened snags.

Shortly, the trail begins to cross from one side of the ridgetop to the other. In so doing it offers some nice views on either side of the divide. To the west, vistas take in the Valley of the Sun, Phoenix, the Superstitions, and a myriad of lesser ranges. To the east lies the sparsely populated Tonto Basin with its band of blue water that is Roosevelt Lake. It is also rewarding

to occasionally look to the north where the Mazatzal Mountains march away in spectacular fashion.

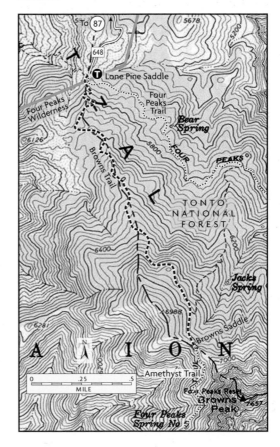

The rugged northwest face of Browns Peak

After covering 2 miles and climbing about 1000 feet, the Browns Trail reaches its destination, Browns Saddle, which sits directly beneath 7657-foot Browns Peak. The peak itself rises above the saddle as an impressive wall of Precambrian shale and quartzite. Many hikers opt to scramble up to the summit by way of a route that follows a couloir to the right of the summit. Because the climb does involve loose rock, some exposure, and a bit of technical scrambling, it should not be attempted by novice hikers.

From the saddle, the views that were periodically enjoyed along Browns Trail really come into focus, especially those to the west. In addition, a second, less utilized trail, the Amethyst Trail, continues south from the saddle for a little more than 1 mile to reach its namesake mine. Situated on private land that is surrounded by designated wilderness, the Amethyst Mine is fenced off and closed to the public.

**Be prepared:** No water is available along the Browns Trail, so bring all that you will need. Watch for lightning in exposed higher terrain. Do not attempt the scramble to the summit if you are not experienced in off-trail travel. Take necessary precautions when storing food for the night if you are camping—this is bear country.

# 64  *Mazatzal Peak Loop*

*Distance:* 15-mile loop
*Difficulty:* strenuous
*Hiking time:* 2 days
*Elevation:* 4200 to 6550 feet
*Management:* Tonto NF

*Wilderness status:* Mazatzal WA
*Season:* March to November
*USGS map:* Mazatzal Peak
*GPS coordinates:* 34.092882 N,
111.422116 W

*Getting there:* From Payson, drive 14.5 miles south on Arizona Highway 87 to the signed turnoff for the Barnhardt trailhead, along the eastern front of the range. Turn right onto Forest Road 419 and drive west for nearly 5 miles to its end. Although rocky, the road is passable to most vehicles.

At more than 252,000 acres, the Mazatzal is one of the largest wilderness areas in the state. Encompassing the Mazatzal Mountains, it ranges in elevation from 2100 feet along the Verde River in the west to the 7903-foot summit of Mazatzal Peak in the east. One of the premier hikes in this expansive parcel of pristine terrain follows the Barnhardt, Mazatzal Divide, and Y Bar Basin Trails around Mazatzal Peak.

Three trails take off from the Barnhardt trailhead. This hike begins by following the Barnhardt Trail, which starts at the west end of the parking area. Heading west up a mostly easy but rocky grade, the Barnhardt Trail reaches the wilderness boundary within the first 0.5 mile. It then continues west along the southern side of Barnhardt Canyon. Vegetation along this first portion of the hike includes Arizona white and Emory oaks, two species of juniper, century plants, sotol, and nolina. Unfortunately, evidence of a wildfire also comes into play here. In 2004 the 119,500-acre Willow Fire devastated most slopes of Mazatzal Peak. Although its impact is minimal at this point of the hike, it really becomes evident farther along.

Near the 1.5-mile mark the Barnhardt Trail begins climbing along the south wall of the canyon through a series of switchbacks at a mostly moderate grade. This ascent continues as the route skirts around a side drainage of the canyon. Along the way velvet ash, Arizona walnut, sycamore, and ponderosa pine are found. And, during the rainy seasons when streams are flowing, waterfalls further grace these rocky drainages.

Pause to admire the bedrock with veins of quartzite along the Y Bar Basin Trail.

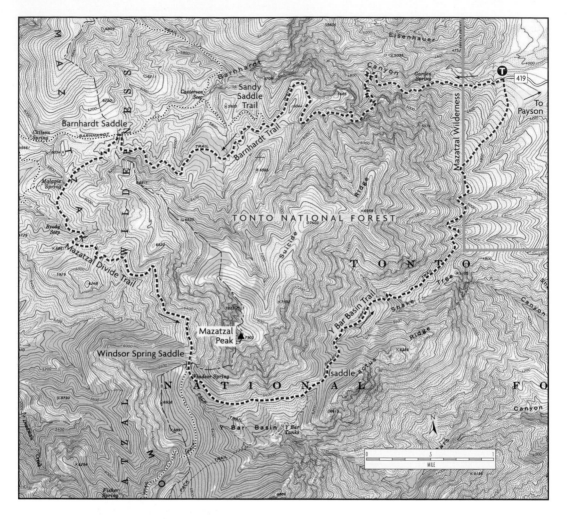

Roughly 3 miles from the start, the Barnhardt Trail tops out above the rim of the canyon to contour west along more gently sloping terrain. Along this section the trail intersects the very faded Sandy Saddle Trail, which continues northwest for 3 miles before connecting with the Mazatzal Divide Trail. Whereas the effects of the Willow Fire are spotty within Barnhardt Canyon, it becomes painfully clear that the fire reduced every patch of tall timber on the north slope of Mazatzal Peak into sporadic clusters of blackened tree trunks. Regrowth since has resulted in thickets of live oaks and manzanita, and the trail itself is often encroached upon by thick brush. Such is the scene for the next several miles of the hike.

A little over 6 miles from the trailhead, the Barnhardt Trail ends at its intersection with the Mazatzal Divide Trail at Barnhardt Saddle. Nearly 30 miles long, this major north–south route stretches across the entire east side of the wilderness. It is also part of the trans-state Arizona Trail.

From Barnhardt Saddle continue south on the Mazatzal Divide Trail across the west-facing slopes of Mazatzal Peak. The trail is often overgrown in this section, but it is not too difficult to follow. At first the scenery is uneventful, but eventually the first of many nice views of Mazatzal Peak's impressive west face open up, as do vistas to the west. These take in the Verde River Valley and Horseshoe Reservoir far below. Farther on, the hike runs directly below the impressive west face of Mazatzal Peak. Consisting mostly of shale and rhyolite, these spectacular cliffs have withstood the effects of erosion quite well.

As the Mazatzal Divide Trail passes Mazatzal Peak, it climbs slightly before reaching Windsor Spring Saddle. At 6550 feet, this is the high point of the hike. It is also 9.5 miles from the start of the hike. Although Windsor Spring is intermittent at best, some suitable spots nearby make this a possible place to camp.

From Windsor Spring Saddle the Mazatzal Divide Trail continues south along the crest of the range. This hike, however, bears left onto the Y Bar Basin Trail (also known as the Shake Tree Trail). At first the Y Bar Basin Trail is very faint, but eventually cairns mark the route and an actual tread becomes discernable. Originally this trail dropped some 500 feet in elevation into the Y Bar Basin, but it has since been rerouted to contour east toward a saddle between Mazatzal Peak and Cactus Ridge, thereby eliminating a climb of a few hundred feet. From this last saddle, the Y Bar Basin Trail continues northeast for about 3.5 miles before ending at the Barnhardt trailhead and the hike's end. Dropping from an elevation of 6300 feet to 4200 feet, this last leg of the hike is difficult in places, not because of its steepness but because of the prevalence of loose rocks, which make for uncertain footing. On the plus side, the route has finally left behind the burn scar of the Willow Fire. Scattered stands of tall ponderosa pines shade the trail and old-growth oak, juniper, and pinyon pine hint at what the Mazatzal Range was like before the fire.

**Be prepared:** Because water sources in the Mazatzal are not always reliable, it is best to bring along all that you will need. A sign at the trailhead warns of unstable trail conditions due to the Willow Fire. Watch for lightning in higher terrain. Long pants are highly recommended due to thick, thorny brush along many stretches of the route.

## 65  *Upper Cliff Dwelling*

**Distance:** 3 miles roundtrip
**Difficulty:** moderate
**Hiking time:** 4 hours
**Elevation:** 2787 to 3390 feet
**Management:** Tonto NM

**Wilderness status:** none
**Season:** November to May
**USGS map:** Windy Hill
**GPS coordinates:** 33.644327 N, 111.112713 W

**Getting there:** From Globe drive northwest on Arizona Highway 188 for about 30 miles to the entrance of Tonto National Monument. This hike begins at the Visitor Center, which is about 1 mile in at the end of the monument road. The hike to the Upper Cliff Dwelling is led by rangers and by reservation only. One tour per day, limited to fifteen participants, is conducted on weekends and some weekdays from November to April. Phone ahead for a reservation (see Appendix A, under "National Parks and Monuments").

Perched high above the Tonto Basin in two protective alcoves, the Lower and Upper Cliff Dwellings in Tonto National Monument offer some of the best preserved glimpses of prehistoric life in Arizona. Constructed by the Salado people, these cliff dwellings have survived quite

The Upper Cliff Dwelling bathed in morning light

well, but they are only the tip of the archaeological iceberg in the Tonto Basin. The Lower Cliff Dwelling is accessible to all visitors via a paved 0.5-mile trail, whereas the longer route to the Upper Cliff Dwelling accesses a nice slice of the monument's backcountry.

Beginning at 10:00 A.M. and lasting between three and four hours, the guided hike to the Upper Cliff Dwelling follows a 1.5-mile trail that ascends some 600 feet. The pace, which is set by the ranger, is typically easy as informative commentary is offered along the way.

From the south end of the parking lot, the hike begins by following Cave Canyon upstream for about 0.75 mile. The first portion of this drainage bottom features a steady trickle of water thanks to a reliable spring partway up. Because of this perennial presence of water, a bit of rock hopping may be required along the way. There is also a shady riparian community of sycamore, Arizona black walnut, and hackberry to be enjoyed. Once the trail climbs beyond the spring, it continues to follow a dry canyon bottom a bit

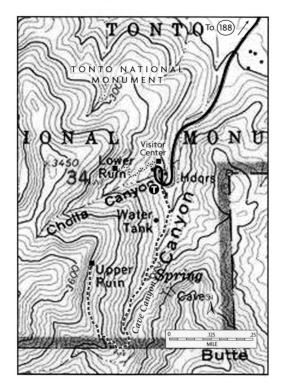

farther until it reaches the southern boundary of the monument, which is indicated by a barbed-wire fence.

As the trail leaves the drainage bottom it passes a nice stand of sotol plants. It then turns north to begin climbing through some switchbacks. Although the route climbs another 450 feet, the grades are mostly easy to moderate. From this point to the top, plant life is strictly Sonoran: stately saguaro cactus, teddy bear cholla, prickly pear cactus, palo verde, and brittlebush are common. In the spring, mid-March into April to be exact, the wildflower display can be quite colorful. In addition, views from this last stretch of the trail take in Roosevelt Lake, which is framed by sloping canyon walls.

Upon reaching the Upper Cliff Dwelling, the ranger will unlock the gate and open the dwelling for visitors. With some thirty ground floor rooms, this dwelling is quite large when compared to neighboring cliff dwellings. Some structures are two stories high. Many metates, or grinding stones, have been found here. The dwelling even had a cistern for storing water. The cave measures 70 feet wide by 60 feet deep. Construction began around 1300 A.D., and occupancy continued until the Salado left the Tonto Basin between 1400 and 1450 A.D. Why the Salado lived in this lofty perch is not known, nor is the exact reason why they left the region. Possible causes include environmental degradation, unfriendly neighbors, and persistent drought.

**Be prepared:** Be sure to bring plenty of water on this hike. As with most backcountry areas within National Park Service units, dogs are not permitted along this trail. If you cannot make a reservation for the hike to the Upper Cliff Dwelling, or if you do not have the time, it is still worth visiting Tonto National Monument because the Lower Cliff Dwelling is quite spectacular as well. It is accessed by a paved trail that climbs 350 feet in 0.5 mile. Although a bit smaller than the Upper Cliff Dwelling, this dwelling is well preserved and the views from it are similarly memorable. When visiting any archaeological site, please help protect fragile dwellings by not touching them, leaning on them, or climbing on the walls. In short, leave everything as you found it.

## 66  *Hieroglyphic Canyon*

**Distance:** 2.8 miles roundtrip
**Difficulty:** easy
**Hiking time:** 2 hours
**Elevation:** 2100 to 2800 feet
**Management:** Tonto NF

**Wilderness status:** Superstition WA
**Season:** October to May
**USGS map:** Goldfield
**GPS coordinates:** 33.389644 N, 111.424681 W

**Getting there:** From Apache Junction drive 7 miles southeast on US Highway 60 to Kings Ranch Road. Turn left and drive 2.8 miles. Turn right onto Baseline Avenue, drive 0.2 mile, and turn left onto Mohican Road. Drive 0.3 mile, and turn left onto Valley View Drive. Drive 0.5 mile on Valley View Drive (which shortly becomes Whitetail Road) to Cloudview Avenue. Turn right onto Cloudview, and drive 0.5 mile to the trailhead.

For a short and easy jaunt through nice desert terrain to some interesting rock art panels, the hike into Hieroglyphic Canyon is hard to beat. Contrary to what early settlers may have believed, these carvings on the rock walls are not hieroglyphics but rather petroglyphs.

From the trailhead, the Hieroglyphic Trail climbs easily up a low ridge to the east. There it intersects the western end of the 5.7-mile Lost Goldmine Trail, which traverses the foothills of the Superstition Mountains before reaching Peralta Road. Keep left at this intersection

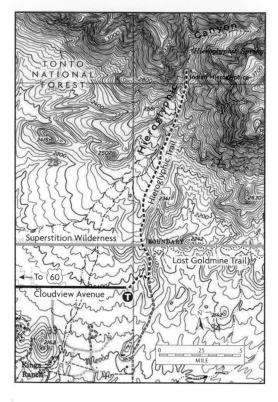

and continue north along the gently ascending bajada terrain. Shortly, the Hieroglyphic Trail passes through a gate, which indicates the boundary of the Superstition Wilderness. Beyond the gate the trail continues on toward the mouth of Hieroglyphic Canyon, which is visible ahead. Along the way you will pass some rather stately saguaro cactus, plenty of cholla cactus, and brittlebush, which blossoms brightly in the spring.

Shortly after entering the canyon itself, the trail reaches a narrow section where the drainage bottom passes between cliffs and boulders. It is here that the so-called hieroglyphics are found etched into a number of rock faces; hieroglyphics are Egyptian in origin and represent an actual alphabet, whereas these petroglyphs tell their stories through strictly visual means. Depicted are a variety of animals, such as desert bighorn sheep. This rock art is attributed to the Hohokam people who inhabited the lower Sonoran Desert from around 1 A.D. to 1450 A.D. From the trailhead this hike ascends about 700 feet in 1.4 miles. Return the way you came.

**Be prepared:** Although pools of water are often found in the streambed in Hieroglyphic Canyon, it is best to bring all the water you will need. Watch for snakes. Summer months are typically quite hot.

A plethora of animals graces this rock art panel in Hieroglyphic Canyon.

## 67 *Peralta Trail*

*Distance:* 4.8 miles roundtrip
*Difficulty:* moderate
*Hiking time:* 3 hours
*Elevation:* 2400 to 3766 feet
*Management:* Tonto NF

*Wilderness status:* Superstition WA
*Season:* October to May
*USGS map:* Weavers Needle
*GPS coordinates:* 33.397377 N, 111.348026 W

*Getting there:* Drive 8.5 miles southeast of Apache Junction on US Highway 60/89, and turn east at the signed turnoff for the Peralta trailhead. Follow this good gravel road (Peralta Road) for 8 miles to its end. Although a large parking area is provided at the trailhead, it may be necessary to use auxiliary parking nearby.

Few, if any, mountain ranges in the American West have stirred the imagination like the Superstitions. Rising east of Apache Junction in a great jumble of volcanic rock, these mountains have earned what geologists say is an erroneous reputation as an area rich in gold. At the center of this mistaken identity is the legend of the Lost Dutchman's Mine. The Peralta Trail evokes that legend in no uncertain terms. Although it is one of the more heavily used trails in the state, the Peralta Trail offers an introduction to the 159,700-acre Superstition Wilderness that hikers will not want to miss.

Two different trails are accessed from the Peralta trailhead. The Dutchman's Trail runs east toward Miners Needle, and the Peralta Trail heads northwest along its namesake canyon to climb 1300 feet in 2.25 miles. The route

Weavers Needle rises impressively above the Superstition Mountains.

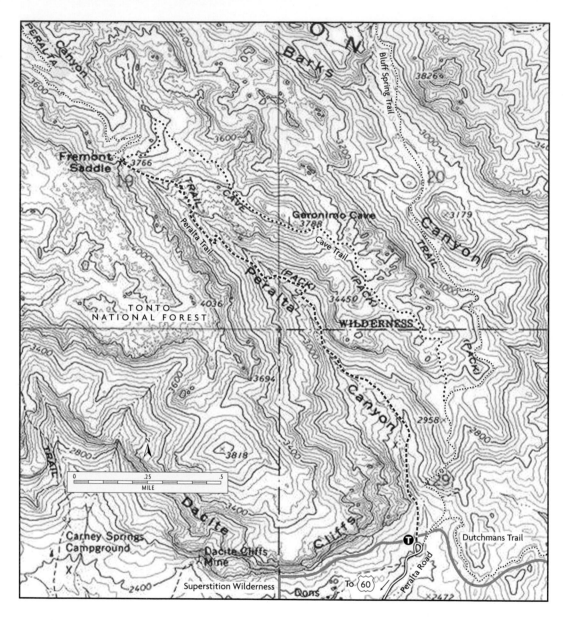

immediately enters the Superstition Wilderness, after which it continues up Peralta Canyon. Easy to follow, the Peralta Trail is well delineated by the countless number of hikers who have made the ascent to the Fremont Saddle. In some places the tread has been eroded down to bedrock. Several stretches are rocky, and a few steep pitches are encountered. The surrounding desert scenery is memorable, especially as the trail draws closer to the top.

Upon reaching the Fremont Saddle, the view to the north is one of the most spectacular in the state, for towering 1000 feet above a wilderness of rock is Weavers Needle. As the most identifiable landmark within the Superstitions, this volcanic plug is indicative of the fiery origins of these mountains. Today, most of the range consists of well-weathered tuff, a rock that geologists contend does not produce much in the way of precious metals. Nevertheless, the legends persist. Don Miguel Peralta reportedly discovered a prodigious lode of gold in 1845. A few decades later, Jacob Waltz, a German immigrant whom locals called the "Dutchman," supposedly rediscovered Peralta's mine. Although Waltz never revealed the exact whereabouts of the mine, stories claim that it lies within the shadow of Weavers Needle. Since Waltz's death in 1891, the Lost Dutchman's Mine has eluded hundreds of would-be prospectors.

From the Fremont Saddle, the Peralta Trail drops north into Boulder Canyon for several miles before connecting with the Dutchman's Trail. Because the saddle commands some great views, however, it makes for a great destination for day hikers. If you are prepared for a very rugged route (seemingly too rugged to be called a trail), you could return to the trailhead via the Cave Trail. Branching east from the Fremont Saddle, the Cave Trail skirts along the ridgetop that bounds Peralta Canyon to the east. Not maintained, this route is difficult to find as well as dangerous in spots due to drop-offs and steep descents on smooth bedrock. Although this route is strictly for sure-footed adventurers (don't attempt it alone), it does provide a scenic and seldom-used alternative to the main trail.

**Be prepared:** Be sure to bring plenty of drinking water. Avoid this hike in summer because of very hot temperatures. Watch for rattlesnakes throughout the hike, and be forewarned that this trail receives exceptionally high use, especially on weekends. The Forest Service discourages campfires in the entire western portion of the Superstitions due to a shortage of fuel.

## 68  *Dutchman's Trail*

*Distance:* 18.2 miles one-way
*Difficulty:* strenuous
*Hiking time:* 3 days
*Elevation:* 2280 to 3250 feet
*Management:* Tonto NF

*Wilderness status:* Superstition WA
*Season:* October to May
*USGS maps:* Goldfield, Weavers Needle
*GPS coordinates:* 33.480250 N, 111.443046 W

*Getting there:* This hike description begins at the First Water trailhead and travels east and south to the Peralta trailhead. To reach the First Water trailhead, drive 5 miles north from Apache Junction on Arizona Highway 88 (the Apache Trail). Turn right just past the Lost Dutchman State Park entrance and follow Forest Road 78 for 2.6 miles. Camping is prohibited along this graded road. A shuttle vehicle can be left at the Peralta trailhead as described in Hike 67.

For an extended hike into the heart of the Superstition Wilderness, the lengthy Dutchman's Trail is not to be missed. Like the Peralta Trail, this well-established route offers some incredible views of the stunning Weavers Needle. Because the Dutchman's Trail winds for 18-plus miles across the western third of the Superstition Range, it also offers a peek at a number of other impressive landmarks, some nice canyon walls, and some surprisingly verdant riparian communities. Add to this a number of connecting trails, and you have a wealth of hike possibilities.

To begin the hike, follow the Dutchman's Trail for 0.25 mile to the first junction. Turn right and continue southeast on the Dutchman's Trail for

A hiker explores some rock sculptures along the Dutchman's Trail.

another 3 miles. A favorite among horse packers, the Dutchman's Trail can receive heavy use. Within this first segment the trail climbs an easy 350 feet to Parker Pass. Nice views are possible in all directions from this high point.

From Parker Pass the trail drops into Boulder Basin, where it connects with the south end of the Black Mesa Trail. Within its 3 miles, the Black Mesa Trail climbs about 400 feet before traversing an interesting basin on top of Black Mesa. Continue on the Dutchman's Trail to intersect with the Boulder Canyon Trail, which travels 7.3 miles along its namesake canyon from Canyon Lake and along Arizona Highway 88. Shortly after, the Dutchman's Trail intersects with the Bull Pass Trail, which climbs up and over Bull Pass to connect back up with the Dutchman's Trail in La Barge Canyon. On the map this route may look like a shortcut, but the 1.6-mile route climbs some 500 feet, making it a bit of a grunt.

Climbing more steadily up East Boulder Canyon, the Dutchman's Trail circles south around the impressive Black Top Mesa. Along this stretch it connects this time with the northern end of the Peralta Trail. If you want to cut your Superstition traverse short, follow this 6.3-mile trail to the Peralta trailhead. Within a mile of the Peralta Trail intersection, the Dutchman's Trail meets up with the northern end of the more rugged Terrapin Trail. Like the Peralta Trail, the Terrapin Trail cuts south past the base of Weavers Needle. It then connects with the Bluff Spring Trail, which takes you to the Peralta trailhead.

After intersecting the east end of the Bull Pass Trail, the Dutchman's Trail takes up a steady ascent along the La Barge Creek drainage. Although the creek is not always flowing, some more reliable springs along the route offer possible places to fill canteens. You may also find some nice camping spots among the trees.

This section of the Dutchman's Trail intersects with the west ends of two other trails. The first is the 7.2-mile Peters Trail, which climbs up and over Peters Mesa to Tortilla Well at the end

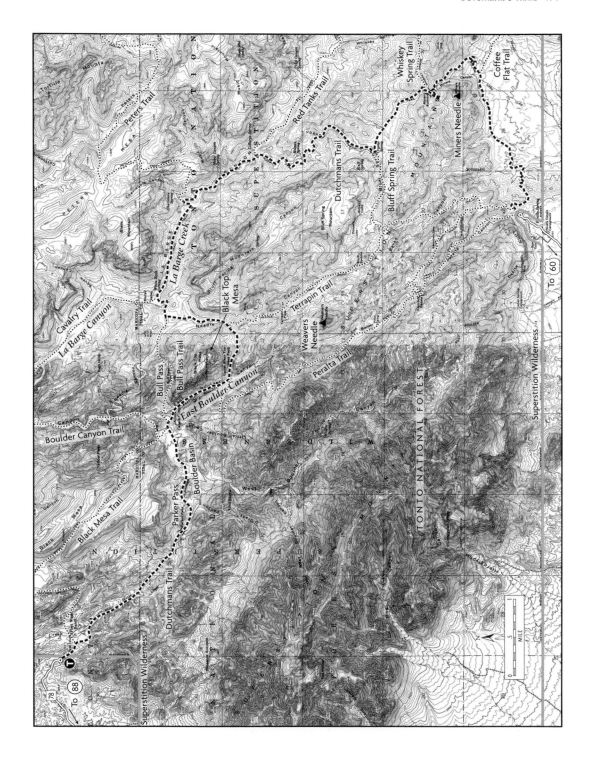

of a 3-mile four-wheel-drive road. The second is the Red Tanks Trail, which will take you into the central portion of the Superstition Wilderness. These two routes would be of interest to experienced hikers intent on traversing the range west to east. After the intersection with the Red Tanks Trail, the Dutchman's Trail begins climbing away from the canyon bottom. Within 2 miles it passes Bluff Spring and then connects with a trail by the same name. The Dutchman's Trail turns left to angle southeast, and the Bluff Spring Trail offers some different route possibilities. After 3.4 miles, the Bluff Spring Trail nearly reaches the Peralta Trailhead (actually, it intersects with the Dutchman's Trail less than 0.25 mile from the trailhead). It also hooks up with the Terrapin Trail, which makes its way over Bluff Saddle and Terrapin Pass before dropping to the Dutchman's Trail below Black Top Mesa. By following the Bluff Spring and Terrapin Trails, it is possible to return to the First Water trailhead and avoid the necessity of a shuttle. Although the going is

slow along this rugged route (use caution), the scenery is outstanding.

From the intersection with the Bluff Spring Trail, the Dutchman's Trail takes in one more important landmark before terminating at the Peralta trailhead: Miners Needle. A bit smaller than the better-known Weavers Needle, Miners Needle is nevertheless impressive. Just north of this landmark the Dutchman's Trail intersects with the west end of the Whiskey Spring Trail and reaches its high point at 3250-foot Miners Summit.

South of Miners Needle the Dutchman's Trail connects with the Coffee Flat Trail, after which it runs an additional 2 miles to reach its end at the Peralta trailhead. With a prearranged shuttle, you can be content with the 18.2 miles of walking that the Dutchman's Trail has provided. If no shuttle is available, however, you can return to the start of the hike via the Bluff Spring and Terrapin Trails (about 11 miles) or by way of the Peralta Trail (about 10 miles).

**Be prepared:** Because of the remote nature of this hike, it is best to hike with another person. Pack plenty of water, as it is not always available. Check with the Forest Service about the status of springs in the Superstition Mountains. The Forest Service discourages campfires in the entire western portion of the Superstitions due to a shortage of fuel. Watch for rattlesnakes, and avoid this area during the hotter times of year.

## 69  Oak Flat

*Distance:* 4.2 miles roundtrip
*Difficulty:* easy
*Hiking time:* 3 hours
*Elevation:* 3450 to 3677 feet
*Management:* Tonto NF

*Wilderness status:* Superstition WA
*Season:* year-round
*USGS map:* Haunted Canyon
*GPS coordinates:* 33.437638 N, 111.067721 W

*Getting there:* From the intersection of US Highway 60 and Arizona Highway 188 in Miami, drive 7.4 miles west on US Highway 60 to Pinto Valley Road. Turn right and drive 2.8 miles north to Forest Road 287. Turn left onto Forest Road 287 and drive 4 miles through the sprawling Pinto Mine to the National Forest border. Some of the many intersections along this portion of the drive are signed as public access; others are not. Basically, you will know which way to go because the mine entry roads are gated and Forest Road 287 is not. Upon entering the National Forest continue across a narrow bridge, then turn left on Forest Road 287A. Follow this high-clearance two-wheel-drive road 5.8 miles to its end.

Entering the southeast corner of the Superstition Wilderness, the hike to Oak Flat explores a nice riparian community along West Pinto Creek. Because this is an easy hike into the Arizona outback, it is a good choice for kids.

From the signed trailhead the West Pinto Trail heads west up canyon. Almost immediately the route enters the Superstition Wilderness where it intersects the Bull Basin Trail, which branches southwest. Keep right and continue following the main canyon upstream. For the first 0.25 mile or so, the West Pinto Trail skirts along the perimeter of some former pastureland. It then climbs a bit to contour along the south side of the canyon. Growing across the drier surrounding hillsides is a collection of pinyon pine, juniper, live oaks, and manzanita. The canyon bottom features many fine Arizona sycamores as well as several other deciduous species and in places is home to poison ivy growing at trailside.

Upon dropping back to the canyon bottom, the trail follows the streambed in places and crosses the creek. Although no actual trail tread exists in this portion of the route, the way is sufficiently marked with cairns. Some stone stepping may be required when water is flowing. After crossing to the north side, the trail climbs again to squeeze through a narrow portion of the canyon.

A sycamore tree along West Pinto Creek

About 1.5 miles in, the West Pinto Trail crosses back to the south side of the stream and then climbs a couple of hundred feet to contour along the canyon wall for a short distance. After passing through an old fence, it drops back to the canyon bottom, which has opened up considerably. Eventually, the West Pinto Trail intersects the Cuff Button Trail, which heads north. The West Pinto Trail soon intersects the Campaign Trail, which continues northwest. This intersection is situated in the middle of Oak Flat and marks the turnaround point for this hike. Although live oaks do grow in this open junction of drainages, plenty of junipers and sycamores are here as well. An item of interest that lies on

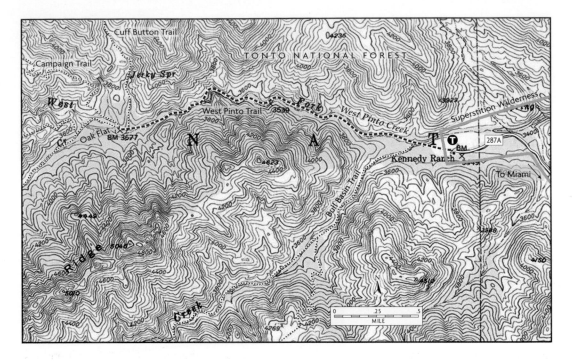

the north side of the creek is an old corral fashioned from wire and juniper logs. From Oak Flat the West Pinto Trail continues west for nearly 8 miles before terminating at the Rogers Trough trailhead in the central portion of the Superstition Wilderness.

**Be prepared:** Although water is typically available along this hike, it should be treated before drinking. Flash floods are a possibility along this streambed. Watch for poison ivy and rattlesnakes along the way.

## 70 *Icehouse Canyon*

| | |
|---|---|
| **Distance:** 9.5 miles roundtrip | **Wilderness status:** none |
| **Difficulty:** strenuous | **Season:** March to November |
| **Hiking time:** 6 hours | **USGS map:** Pinal Peak |
| **Elevation:** 4557 to 7580 feet | **GPS coordinates:** 33.326341 N, |
| **Management:** Tonto NF | 110.805314 W |

**Getting there:** In downtown Globe on US Highway 60, turn south onto Hill Street. Drive a short distance and turn right on Walliman Road. Turn left a short way farther to cross the railroad tracks and continue southwest on Jesse Hayes Road, which soon becomes Pioneer Drive. Turn right onto Icehouse Canyon Road, which becomes Forest Road 112, and drive 4.8 miles to the Icehouse CCC recreation area. The trailhead is on the west side of the road as it enters the campground.

Rising impressively above the town of Globe, Pinal Peak presents a surprising and thoroughly refreshing montane environ in the southwest corner of the Tonto National Forest. Four different trails that ascend the mountain's north slope offer a variety of hiking experiences as they trend southwest toward a forest road that is draped across the mountain's summit. This hike explores the cool and forested upper reaches of Icehouse Canyon.

The Icehouse Trail lies within its namesake drainage for the entire way, but the lower portion of the trail actually follows a ranch road, which is occasionally driven by vehicles. Consequently, this hike description follows the Telephone Trail for the first half of the hike before connecting with the Icehouse Trail near its midway point. From the trailhead begin by following the Telephone Trail a short way west to where it intersects the lower end of the Icehouse Trail. Keep left to continue up the Telephone Trail as it begins a mostly moderate ascent along an established foot trail. Growth along these lower slopes includes a tangle of manzanita and live oaks. Occasional yuccas and century plants add variety here and there. In addition, as the route climbs, some nice views of the Globe area to the north come into play.

A little more than 0.5 mile in, the Telephone Trail intersects a buried power cable right-of-way, which services radio towers on top of the mountain. In 2014 this right-of-way was reworked, but new growth should eventually mask the bulldozed swath. Upon reaching the right-of-way follow it uphill a hundred yards or so to a gate on the right. Pass through this gate to take up the foot trail again. About 0.5 mile or so farther, the Telephone Trail encounters the right-of-way a second time where, as before, this hike follows it uphill a short distance to another gate on the right. After passing through the second gate the Telephone Trail then contours southwest toward Icehouse Canyon. As the trail progresses, scattered taller pines begin to add verticality to the vegetation.

About 2 miles from the trailhead, the Telephone Trail intersects the Icehouse Trail within the canyon's drainage bottom. At this point a right turn heads down the lower half of the Icehouse Trail, and a left turn continues up the canyon along the same trail. Turn left and follow the route for a short distance to where the Telephone and Icehouse Trails separate again. Branching left the Telephone Trail climbs up and out of the drainage bottom to follow a ridgeline to the east. The Icehouse Trail, however,

An old trail sign in Icehouse Canyon

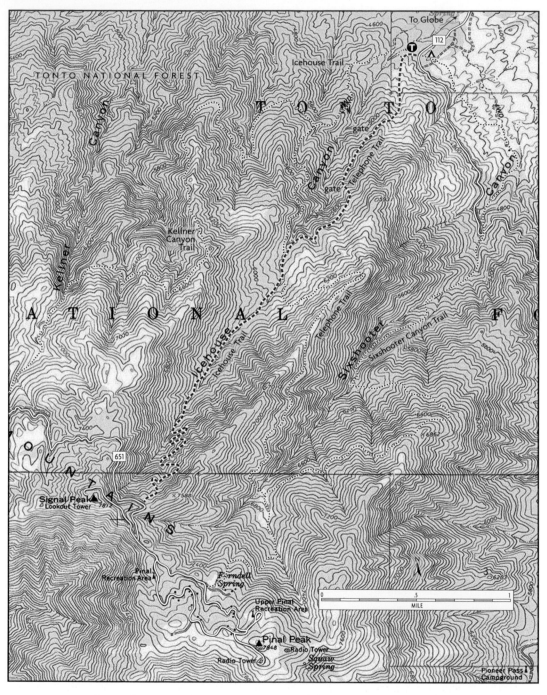

continues straight up the canyon bottom. Keep right at this intersection to continue along the Icehouse Trail.

Climbing steadily up Icehouse Canyon, the route crisscrosses the creekbed, which occasionally features flowing water. Thanks to the many tall pines, firs, and deciduous trees that grow within this drainage, the trailside environ all of the way to the top is shady and cool. This is a big plus since the route climbs quite a bit in these last miles. Thanks to the coolness of this canyon, an entrepreneur in the late 1800s was able to cut ice from frozen ponds and sell it to saloons in town.

Eventually the trail leaves the canyon bottom to switchback up the mountainside east of the drainage. Shade-bearing trees continue, and you will encounter a nice stand of quaking aspen near the top. Although most grades along the upper half of the Icehouse Trail are moderate in difficulty, the last 0.5 mile to the top is strenuous in several places. After 4.75 miles this hike reaches a signed trailhead along Forest Road 651, a short distance northwest of the Pinal Mountain summit. From here you can return to your vehicle via the same route. For a change in scenery, you could follow the Icehouse Trail the entire way down.

**Be prepared:** Because any water found within Icehouse Canyon should be treated before drinking, it is best to simply bring all that you will need. These Pinal Mountain trails are open to mountain bicycles, so remain aware, especially since riders most often enjoy their rides in the downhill direction.

## 71  *Picacho Peak*

*Distance:* 4 miles roundtrip
*Difficulty:* strenuous
*Hiking time:* 4 hours
*Elevation:* 2000 to 3374 feet
*Management:* Picacho Peak SP

*Wilderness status:* none
*Season:* October to May
*USGS map:* Newman Park
*GPS coordinates:* 32.642732 N, 111.402528 W

*Getting there:* This hike is located in Picacho Peak State Park, which lies along Interstate 10 (at exit 219) between Phoenix and Tucson. Follow the signs into the park from the highway, then turn left onto Barrett Loop Road, 0.2 mile beyond the park entrance. A fee is collected upon entering the park.

No doubt serving as an important landmark for as long as humans have inhabited this part of the Southwest, Picacho Peak features one of the more challenging short hikes in Arizona. First built by the CCC in 1933 and then improved by Boy Scouts in 1972, the Hunter Trail reaches the top of this fortified summit in only 2 miles. Although not recommended for children under ten or inexperienced hikers of any sort, this route offers rewards that few other hikes in the state can.

From the trailhead, the Hunter Trail climbs quickly through a desert community of saguaro, cholla, palo verde, and ocotillo. From this angle Picacho Peak seems like an unapproachable stone fortress, and yet, after climbing through a series of switchbacks, the trail reaches the base of some high cliffs. A bit farther—approximately 1 mile from the start and over 900 feet in elevation gain—the route reaches a saddle west of the summit.

Blessed with wonderful views, this saddle marks the halfway point of the hike up. From here the trail drops considerably (nearly 400 vertical feet) down the back side of the mountain. Cable handrails provide much-needed assistance along this stretch. Not until reaching the 2500-foot level does the trail again turn uphill to head for the summit. At this point a junction with the Sunset Vista Trail is reached. Keep left to continue up the Hunter Trail, which then climbs very steeply (900 feet in about 0.5 mile) to arrive

A saguaro cactus near the summit of Picacho Peak

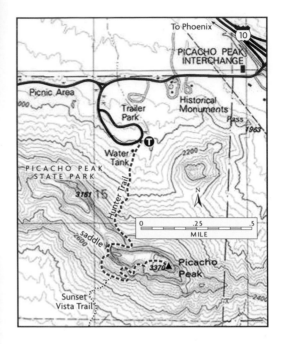

Because the summit is mostly barren and cliffs drop straight down toward the desert floor below, the views are superb. Interstate 10 cuts an arrow-straight path close to the base of the peak. It was in this area that Arizona's most significant Civil War battle took place in April 1862. The Central Arizona Project Canal can be seen running along the base of the Picacho Mountains to the north. The Santa Catalina and Rincon Mountains rise in the vicinity of Tucson to the southeast. Telescope-studded Kitt Peak looms to the south, and countless desert mountain ranges march farther south into Mexico.

at the top. Again, cable handholds provide assistance along steeper stretches. Leather gloves would be very helpful.

**Be prepared:** Bring plenty of drinking water, sturdy hiking boots, and leather gloves. Avoid this hike during summer, when daytime temperatures can reach well above 100 degrees Fahrenheit. Be prepared for loose footing and precipitous drop-offs.

Opposite, top: Broad grasslands typify the start of the hike to Powers Garden.

Opposite, bottom: Saguaro cactus at dusk along the hike to Brown Mountain

# Southeastern Basin and Range

72. Wasson Peak...............180

73. Brown Mountain.............182

74. Bridal Wreath Falls...........185

75. Seven Falls..................187

76. Sabino Canyon..............189

77. Finger Rock Canyon.........191

78. Romero Canyon.............193

79. Green Mountain.............196

80. Aspen Loop.................198

81. Bog Springs................200

82. Mount Wrightson...........203

83. Cochise Trail...............206

84. Heart of Rocks.............207

85. Echo Canyon...............210

86. Chiricahua Peak............212

87. South Fork Cave Creek.......215

88. Rucker Canyon.............216

89. Pole Bridge Canyon.........218

90. Fort Bowie.................220

91. Arcadia National
    Recreation Trail.............222

92. Powers Garden.............224

*As with other parts of Arizona, the Basin and Range region of the southeastern* portion of the state is a truly unique land. The area appeals to hikers of many persuasions because the geography here is typified by a number of sharply rising mountain ranges that oversee broad desert basins. So definitive are these mountain chains that they are often referred to as "sky islands." The largest of these ranges, the Santa Catalinas, which create a dramatic backdrop for the city of Tucson, provides backcountry jaunts among everything from cactus gardens to aspen glades. Other mountain ranges, including the Santa Ritas and Chiricahuas, offer equally dramatic profiles in elevation and ecological diversity. Add to this the array of seemingly exotic species of wildlife and the unique history of the region, and you have an abundance of alluring hikes.

## 72  *Wasson Peak*

*Distance:* 8 miles roundtrip
*Difficulty:* strenuous
*Hiking time:* 6 hours
*Elevation:* 2850 to 4687 feet
*Management:* Saguaro NP

*Wilderness status:* Saguaro WA
*Season:* October to May
*USGS map:* Avra
*GPS coordinates:* 32.246930 N, 111.167128 W

*Getting there:* To reach the western unit of Saguaro National Park, drive west from Tucson on West Speedway Boulevard, which eventually turns into Gates Pass Road (closed to oversize vehicles, such as RVs). After crossing over Gates Pass, turn right on Kinney Road and continue for another 2 miles to the Arizona–Sonora Desert Museum. The King Canyon trailhead is located a short distance north of the museum entrance on the east side of the road.

Divided into east and west units, Saguaro National Park encompasses tracts of desert mountain terrain on either side of Tucson. Saguaro National Park West takes in part of the Tucson Mountains, whose highest summit is Wasson Peak (elevation 4687 feet). Providing the shortest access to the top is the King Canyon Trail.

For the first 0.9 mile, the trail follows an old mining road along the south side of King Canyon to the backcountry Mam-a-Gah Picnic Area and the intersection with the Esperanza Trail, which is the return portion of this hike. Keep right at the trail junction and continue following the King Canyon Trail. This section of the route starts out by following a dry wash bottom for a few hundred yards but then turns right to begin climbing into the foothills. The grade is moderately steep along this section. Continue for another 1.4 miles to the top of a ridge to the east. Upon reaching the ridge, the King Canyon Trail intersects with the Sweetwater Trail, which approaches from the east. After staying left at this junction, the King Canyon Trail climbs north for 0.9 mile through a series of steep switchbacks. At the next trail junction, a right turn leads 0.3 mile to the summit of Wasson Peak, and the left-hand fork provides the return route.

The view from the top of Wasson Peak is spectacular. Tucson spreads out to the east, as

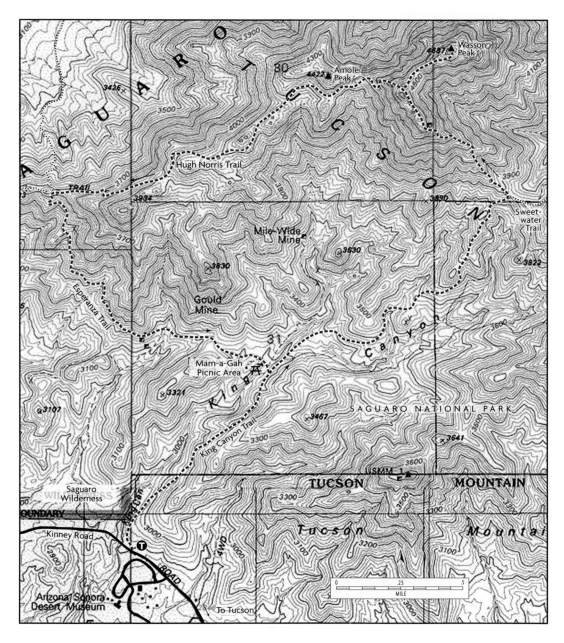

do the Santa Catalina and Rincon Mountains. Mount Wrightson is visible toward Mexico, and Kitt Peak, with its collection of telescopes, rises to the west. Both military and commercial aircraft use nearby air space while making their approach to the airport in Tucson. Although the noise can be disturbing, from the Wasson Peak summit it seems as if you are almost at eye level with the pilots.

To return to the trailhead, turn right a short distance from the summit and follow the Hugh Norris Trail west for 1.9 miles to where

Saguaro cactus with fruit on the slopes of Wasson Peak

it intersects with the Esperanza Trail. Springtime along this stretch of the route reveals a plethora of wildflowers, including lupine and Mexican golden poppies. Other species of flora found along the entire hike include palo verde, barrel cactus, cholla, and, of course, saguaro. Keep left on the Esperanza Trail and continue southeast for 1.4 miles to return to the Mam-a-Gah Picnic Area. From there it is 0.9 mile to the trailhead.

**Be prepared:** Avoid this hike in summer, when temperatures can be quite hot. Bring plenty of water, for none is found along the way. Be wary of lightning along exposed ridges and mountaintops. Watch for rattlesnakes.

# 73 *Brown Mountain*

*Distance:* 4.4-mile loop
*Difficulty:* moderate
*Hiking time:* 3 hours
*Elevation:* 2650 to 3098 feet
*Management:* Tucson Mountain Park

*Wilderness status:* none
*Season:* October to May
*USGS map:* Brown Mountain
*GPS coordinates:* 32.223720 N, 111.144600 W

*Getting there:* To reach Tucson Mountain Park, drive west from Tucson on West Speedway Boulevard, which eventually turns into Gates Pass Road (closed to oversize vehicles, such as RVs). After crossing over Gates Pass, turn right on Kinney Road and continue a short distance before turning left onto McCain Loop Road. The trailhead is 0.3 mile down McCain Loop on the right side of the road, nearly opposite the entrance to the Gilbert Ray Campground.

Administered by Pima County, Tucson Mountain Park serves as a 20,000-acre extension of Saguaro National Park West, or perhaps it is the other way around since the county park was established in 1928, five years prior to Saguaro National Park's designation as a national monument. Among the many miles of hiking trails that lace the county park, a particularly nice loop route climbs up and over its namesake, Brown Mountain. In addition to providing plenty of fine

desert scenery, this trail also accesses some nice desert plant life.

From the trailhead, the Brown Mountain Trail traverses relatively level terrain north for about 0.3 mile before reaching a wash that circumnavigates the southwest end of Brown Mountain. Along this stretch some very nice examples of hanging fruit cholla are encountered. Upon crossing the wash, the trail begins climbing the mountain itself. Ascending a few hundred feet in

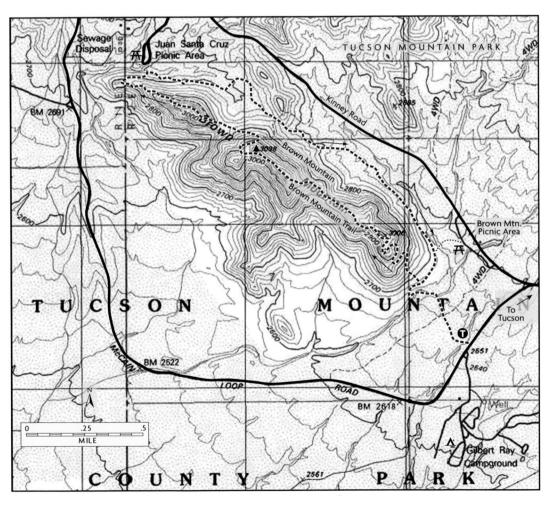

Hanging fruit cholla cactus grows on the hike to Brown Mountain.

about 0.25 mile, this segment of the route presents some moderate grades and rocky tread in places. Upon reaching the first of three summits, the Brown Mountain Trail continues northwest to follow the spine of this elongated peak for 1.5 miles or so. All along this portion of the trail, the views are nice in every direction: Gates Pass to the southeast, the Arizona–Sonora Desert Museum and Saguaro National Park to the north, and Kitt Peak with its collection of telescopes to the west.

A little more than halfway along the Brown Mountain summit, the route reaches the actual 3098-foot high point of the mountain, after which it drops through a switchback as it begins a gradual descent down the northwest end of the mountain. After dropping through a few more short switchbacks, the trail reaches the toe of the mountain, a little over 2 miles from the trailhead. At this point a short side trail branches north to access the Juan Santa Cruz Picnic Area. Keeping right at this intersection, the Brown Mountain Trail begins following the east slope of the mountain where it continues southeast for 1.7 miles before closing the route's loop near the large wash crossed earlier in the hike. This section of the trail dips gently in and out of shallow drainages along the toe of the mountain. It also encounters some nice stands of saguaro cactus and a short spur trail, which runs east to the Brown Mountain Picnic Area, which is also accessed by Kinney Road. Upon crossing the wash, it is a short jaunt back to the trailhead.

**Be prepared:** Bring plenty of water as none is available along the way and it can be quite hot, especially during the warmer months. Watch for rattlesnakes.

## 74 *Bridal Wreath Falls*

**Distance:** 5.4 miles roundtrip
**Difficulty:** moderate
**Hiking time:** 3 hours
**Elevation:** 2749 to 3800 feet
**Management:** Saguaro NP

**Wilderness status:** Saguaro WA
**Season:** October to May
**USGS map:** Tanque Verde Peak
**GPS coordinates:** 32.235185 N,
110.686970 W

**Getting there:** This hike begins at the Douglas Spring trailhead, which is at the east end of Speedway Boulevard, nearly 17.5 miles from the Speedway exit on Interstate 10 in Tucson. The trailhead includes a medium-size parking area, which often fills up because of the trailhead's popularity among locals. Additional parking is often available along the roadway.

Even when only a small amount of water is flowing, Bridal Wreath Falls makes for a nice destination in the foothills of the Rincon Mountains. If the flow is dried up, this hike nevertheless accesses some scenic and pristine Sonoran Desert lands within the east unit of Saguaro National Park.

For most of this hike the route follows the Douglas Spring Trail, which heads east from the trailhead. From the start the ecological countenance of this hike is one of beautiful lower Sonoran plant life. First and foremost are the plentiful giant saguaros. Prickly pear cactus, a variety of cholla cactus, palo verde, ocotillo, and brittlebush round out the list.

For the first 0.7 mile or so the trail treks easily across rolling bajada lands where it intersects the Garwood and Converse Trails. At each of these intersections, keep left. Shortly after, the Douglas Spring Trail begins climbing along moderate to occasionally steep grades as it ascends the foothills of the Rincon Mountains to the east. Although steep in a few places, the trail is well maintained and easy to follow. About 1.5 miles in, the Douglas Spring Trail intersects the Carrillo Trail, which, like the two previous side routes, heads south where a tangle of trails spreads out across the park's northwest corner. Keep left at this intersection and continue east.

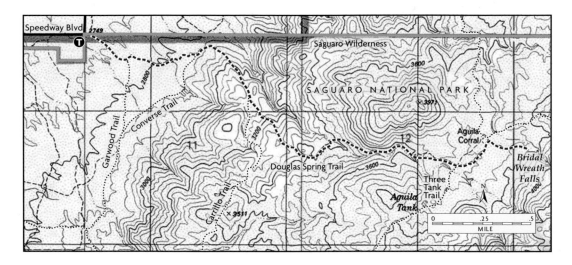

A study in contrast: sotol plant and saguaro cactus near Bridal Wreath Falls

At the 2.3-mile mark the Douglas Spring Trail connects with the Three Tank Trail, which branches off to the southwest. Keep left here and continue a short distance to a side trail that branches right to continue 0.2 mile to a grotto and the destination of this hike, Bridal Wreath Falls. Typically, water flows through this drainage in spring or after periods of rain, and when it does, it tumbles off a 25-foot-high pour-off to splash on the rocks below. The grotto is often shady and offers a cool respite to hikers. Interestingly, riparian growth is scant in this protected area. Upon returning to the Douglas Spring trailhead, be sure to enjoy the broad vistas of the Tucson area and the Santa Catalina Mountains to the northwest.

**Be prepared:** Although water may be available at times, it is best to bring all you will need as any that you might come across should be treated first. Summer temperatures are typically quite high at this elevation.

## 75 Seven Falls

*Distance:* 5.4 miles roundtrip
*Difficulty:* moderate
*Hiking time:* 4 hours
*Elevation:* 2800 to 3400 feet
*Management:* Coronado NF

*Wilderness status:* Pusch Ridge WA
*Season:* October to May
*USGS map:* Sabino Canyon
*GPS coordinates:* 32.309912 N, 110.822841 W

*Getting there:* The hike to Seven Falls begins at the Bear Canyon Overlook Picnic Area, which is a 10-minute ride on a shuttle bus from the Sabino Canyon Recreation Area Visitor Center. A parking fee is charged per vehicle, and a fee per adult is charged for the shuttle bus ride. To reach the visitor center from downtown Tucson, drive east on Speedway Boulevard to Wilmont Road. Turn north and follow Wilmont, which eventually becomes Tanque Verde Road, to Sabino Canyon Road. Turn left and follow Sabino Canyon Road for about 8 miles to the signed right turn for the Sabino Canyon Recreation Area. If you forego the shuttle bus and begin your hike at the visitor center, add an extra 1.5 miles each way to the mileage total.

Surrounded by soaring canyon walls, Seven Falls is one of the more alluring places in the Santa Catalina Mountains. Dropping through a staircase of pools, the cool water of Bear Creek tempts hikers to linger a bit. Because it is short, this hike is quite popular. Regardless of the crowds, Seven Falls is a destination well worth a visit.

From the Bear Canyon Overlook Picnic Area, this hike follows the Bear Canyon Trail, which drops easily into its namesake canyon, and then continues along the mostly level canyon bottom for about 1.5 miles. Growing here are stands of giant saguaro cactus, along with other lower Sonoran flora such as palo verde, cholla, prickly pear cactus, mesquite, and brittlebush. In addition, cottonwood and sycamore trees intermittently shade the creek bottom. Shortly into the hike, the first of several stream crossings

is encountered. Although Bear Creek is easy to cross at most times of the year, heavy rains and melting snow occasionally swell the flow considerably. Flash floods are also a possibility. For current conditions, check with the staff at the Sabino Canyon Visitor Center before heading out.

Eventually the trail climbs out of the canyon bottom along the east wall. After making one long switchback, it traverses along a contour a few hundred feet above the canyon bottom. This climb is initially moderate in difficulty, but it soon levels off. At 2.2 miles the trail arrives at a signed junction where a left turn leads 0.2 mile to Seven Falls. The Bear Canyon Trail continues to the right and eventually climbs over into Sabino Basin.

Although the falls at Seven Falls are often reduced to a trickle (and are sometimes dried up completely), the pools are usually filled with

Reliable pools of water make Seven Falls a popular hike.

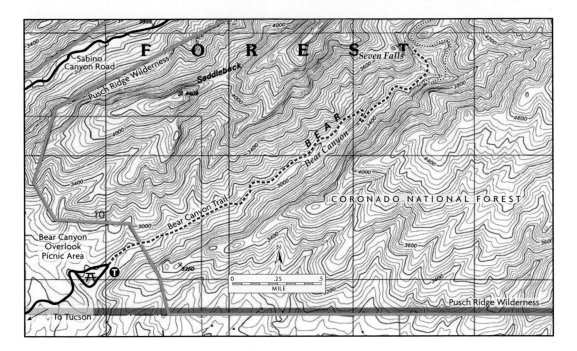

clear, cool water. Care should be taken when entering them because of the slippery bottoms and
hidden obstructions. Similarly, caution should be
used when climbing to each successive pool.

**Be prepared:** Because all water in Bear Creek must be treated before drinking, it is best to pack in all
that you will need. Temperatures can reach well above the century mark in summer. Flash floods are a
possibility, especially in the summer monsoon season. Keep in mind that the Coronado National Forest
does not encourage swimming in the creek. In addition, dogs are not permitted along this hike.

## 76  *Sabino Canyon*

*Distance:* 8.2 miles roundtrip
*Difficulty:* moderate
*Hiking time:* 5 hours
*Elevation:* 3330 to 3900 feet
*Management:* Coronado NF

*Wilderness status:* Pusch Ridge WA
*Season:* October to May
*USGS map:* Sabino Canyon
*GPS coordinates:* 32.309912 N,
110.822841 W

*Getting there:* This hike begins at the end of Upper Sabino Canyon Road in the Sabino
Canyon Recreation Area. To reach the recreation area from downtown Tucson, drive
east on Speedway to Wilmont Road. Turn north and follow Wilmont, which eventually
becomes Tanque Verde Road, to a left turn onto Sabino Canyon Road. Follow Sabino
Canyon Road for about 8 miles to the signed right turn for the Sabino Canyon
Recreation Area. From the visitor center you will need to take a shuttle bus to the
trailhead. A parking fee per vehicle and a per adult fee for the shuttle bus are charged.

A flowering saguaro cactus in Sabino Canyon

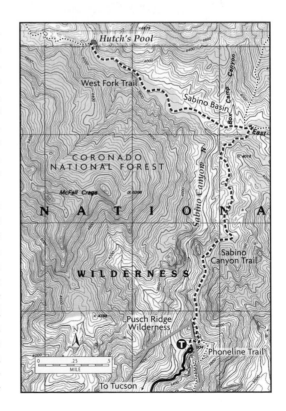

Of all the drainages along the Santa Catalina's front range, Sabino Canyon is by far the most popular. Accessed by a narrow paved road that extends 3.8 miles into the canyon, it attracts countless folks who come to stroll, jog, bicycle, or ride a shuttle bus through this scenic desert canyon. From road's end, the Sabino Canyon Trail ventures beyond the crowds and noise to reveal a rugged and beautiful wilderness. An ideal destination for day hikers along this route is Hutch's Pool.

Within the first 0.5 mile the Sabino Canyon Trail climbs through some short switchbacks before connecting with the upper end of the Phoneline Trail. Turning left at this junction, the Sabino Canyon Trail continues upstream along the canyon's east side. Although dipping occasionally, the next 2 miles follow a mostly easy grade. About 2.5 miles from the trailhead the route drops easily into Sabino Basin. An open area where several canyons converge, Sabino Basin is quite beautiful. Just after the first stream crossing, a trail junction is reached. Branching to the right, the East Fork Trail eventually drops into Bear Canyon and a left turn takes up the West Fork Trail leading to Hutch's Pool. Although flowing intermittently, this stream can be difficult to cross during periods of high runoff.

Beyond the crossing, the hike follows the open bottom of Sabino Basin. Typified by grasslands interspersed with sotol, agave, manzanita, and stands of oak, Sabino Basin lies at the boundary between two ecological life zones. You may note a few saguaros growing among rocky areas of the basin. These stragglers mark the upper limit of the lower Sonoran life zone. The grassland community that now prevails is indicative of the upper Sonoran zone.

About 1 mile from the East Fork/West Fork trail junction, the route makes a second stream crossing (this one may also be difficult to cross during periods of high water), after which it follows the left bank of the creek for another 0.3 mile to Hutch's Pool. Along the way a nice glade of tall Arizona cypress is encountered. Situated in an elongated, rock-rimmed basin, Hutch's Pool is quite scenic and does receive a lot of use. The Coronado National Forest suggests that overnight visitors not camp in the vicinity of the pool.

**Be prepared:** Although this hike can be completed year-round, summers often bring hot temperatures to all of Sabino Canyon. High water (typical during the monsoon season in the summer and after periods of snowmelt in the winter) may make stream crossings impossible. Be sure to treat any surface water before drinking. Because this hike is within a desert bighorn sheep management area, dogs are not allowed.

## 77 Finger Rock Canyon

| | |
|---|---|
| **Distance:** 10 miles roundtrip | **Wilderness status:** Pusch Ridge WA |
| **Difficulty:** strenuous | **Season:** year-round |
| **Hiking time:** 7 hours | **USGS maps:** Tucson North, Oro Valley |
| **Elevation:** 3070 to 7255 feet | **GPS coordinates:** 32.336237 N, |
| **Management:** Coronado NF | 110.910070 W |

**Getting there:** The Finger Rock trailhead lies at the end of Alvernon Way, about a mile north of Tucson's Skyline Drive. From Speedway Boulevard, drive north on Swan Road. Turn left onto Skyline Drive, and continue west for about a mile to Alvernon Way. Turn right and continue to the Richard McKee Finger Rock trailhead. A large parking area is located on the left side of the road, and the trail's start is a short distance up the road on the right.

The Finger Rock Trail offers the quickest access to Mount Kimball—the top of the Santa Catalinas' impressive front range. This steep and rugged route reveals some interesting geological formations and provides some particularly spectacular vistas of Tucson and beyond.

For the first mile the trail climbs easily among the foothills before reaching the bottom of Finger Rock Canyon. Dominated by saguaro cactus, the surrounding desert plant community also includes sotol, ocotillo, patches of prickly pear cactus, and yucca. Wildflowers include penstemon, groundsel, and brittlebush. Various riparian plant species also grow along the streambed.

At the 1.1-mile mark, the trail reaches Finger Rock Spring. Beyond this point it begins a long and difficult ascent along the rugged southeast face of the canyon. Steep and rocky for the next 2 miles, this section includes a few switchbacks plus areas of loose rock. There are also some precipitous drop-offs along the way. Despite its ruggedness, however, the route does afford

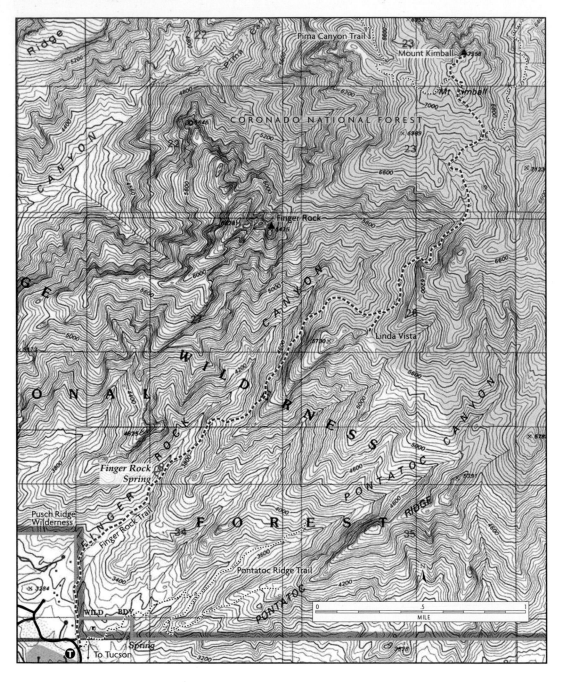

views that become more spectacular the higher up it climbs. For the first few miles, Finger Rock is visible along the high skyline to the north. As the canyon deepens, the city of Tucson is nicely framed by sheer rock walls. You may also get a chance to observe some desert bighorn sheep as the canyon beyond Finger Rock Spring has been designated as a bighorn management area.

Finger Rock rises above its namesake canyon.

After 3 miles and 2500 feet of climbing, a short side trail leads to Linda Vista, a notch in the ridgeline that opens up to even broader views of the city. Beyond Linda Vista, the Finger Rock Trail passes among stands of oak and juniper as it traverses around the head of the canyon. At the 4.5-mile mark a saddle is reached. Here, keep left at the junction of the Finger Rock and Pima Canyon Trails to continue another 0.5 mile to the top of Mount Kimball. Beyond the summit, the Pima Canyon Trail continues northwest, eventually dropping into its namesake drainage.

**Be prepared:** Some exposure and slick bedrock are encountered. Dangerous electrical storms can crop up suddenly, so watch for lightning in exposed higher terrain. Do not expect to find water during drier months, and watch for rattlesnakes. Although this is considered a year-round hike, summers usher in temperatures over 100 degrees Fahrenheit, and winters may see the upper end of the trail snow-covered for short periods of time. Because this is a desert bighorn sheep management area, dogs are not permitted on this hike.

## 78 Romero Canyon

**Distance:** 14.4 miles roundtrip
**Difficulty:** strenuous
**Hiking time:** 10 hours
**Elevations:** 2800 to 6100 feet
**Management:** Catalina SP, Coronado NF

**Wilderness status:** Pusch Ridge WA
**Season:** year-round
**USGS maps:** Mount Lemmon, Oro Valley
**GPS coordinates:** 32.425218 N, 110.908527 W

**Getting there:** Drive 5 miles north of the Tucson city limits on US Highway 89 to Catalina State Park. Enter the park (an entry fee is charged per vehicle) and drive to the day-use area. The trail begins near the information board at road's end.

Like other routes in the Santa Catalina Mountains, the Romero Canyon Trail begins at the base of the range but eventually climbs to its upper reaches. The canyon itself is quite rugged and beautiful, and a surprising variety of flora is encountered.

For the first 1.1 miles the Romero Canyon Trail follows an old roadbed across relatively level terrain. Beyond a point that overlooks the Montrose Canyon drainage, the route passes through the boundary fence of the Coronado National Forest and then takes up a narrow foot trail. Climbing steeply, the route occasionally switchbacks as it gains the rugged north face of Montrose Canyon. Traversing a lot of rocky terrain, the trail is rough in places but easy to follow. Along the way saguaro cactus, ocotillo, and palo verde trees abound. Spring often brings a plethora of wildflowers along this stretch of trail, including brittlebush and paperflower. It is also possible to spot coyotes, desert bighorn sheep, javelinas, and perhaps even an elusive mountain lion along this hike.

Approximately 2.5 miles from the trailhead, the route passes through a small notch before dropping into Romero Canyon proper. As the trail approaches this high point, a nice vista of Pusch Ridge opens up to the south. Forming the dramatic southwest façade of the Santa Catalina Range, Pusch Ridge consists mostly of Catalina Gneiss, a hard Precambrian rock banded with veins of white quartz.

Nearly 3 miles from the trailhead, the trail reaches the bottom of Romero Canyon. Just downstream from this point are several pools that occasionally have water in them. Here you can also get an up-close look at the riparian plant life that grows along drainages like Romero Canyon. Veritable jungles compared to the sparse lower Sonoran Desert ecosystem, these verdant communities include sycamore, cottonwood, velvet ash, cattails, and other water-loving flora.

Continuing up Romero Canyon, the trail soon enters a narrow section of canyon where it ascends a series of switchbacks along the drainage's north wall. Gaining 800 feet in less than a mile, this stretch is steep, but it is followed by a gentler traverse high above the canyon bottom. About 5 miles from the trailhead, the route drops down to the canyon bottom, where a short spur

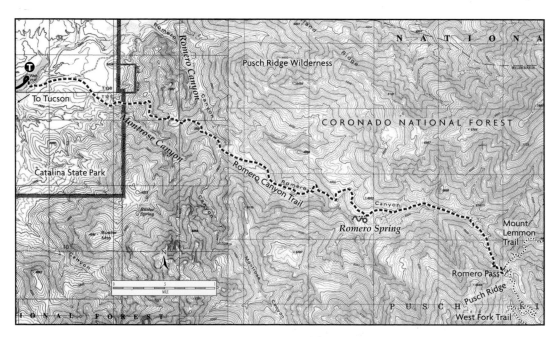

A water hole, complete with cattails, along the Romero Canyon Trail

trail runs downstream to Romero Spring. The spring is unreliable in the drier months, so don't count on always finding water here.

Beyond Romero Spring, it is another 2 miles and 1300 vertical feet to the top of 6100-foot Romero Pass. At first following the main branch of Romero Canyon, the trail takes up a steep side tributary for the last mile. At the pass itself, the Romero Canyon Trail connects with the Mount Lemmon and West Fork Trails. The Mount Lemmon Trail continues north to the summit of the range. At this elevation, pinyon pine, alligator juniper, Arizona white oak, and even ponderosa pine replace the desert flora that grows below.

**Be prepared:** Be sure to bring plenty of drinking water because streams along the route are not always flowing and the water is not potable without treatment. Be wary of rattlesnakes, and watch for lightning in higher terrain. Dogs are prohibited along this trail.

## 79  Green Mountain

*Distance:* 7.8 miles roundtrip
*Difficulty:* moderate
*Hiking time:* 5 hours
*Elevation:* 7300 to 6000 feet
*Management:* Coronado NF

*Wilderness status:* none
*Season:* April to November
*USGS map:* Bellota Ranch
*GPS coordinates:* 32.397773 N, 110.689318 W

*Getting there:* Take the turnoff on Tanque Verde Road in Tucson for the Catalina Highway and drive about 22 miles north to the signed Green Mountain trailhead, which is about 0.25 mile before the San Pedro Vista. A fee is charged for trailhead use along the Catalina Highway.

A large boulder like this might stop you in your tracks along the upper end of the Green Mountain Trail.

Accessing some spectacular views from the Santa Catalina Range's east side, the Green Mountain Trail makes for a nice day hike.

The Green Mountain Trail begins by climbing easily among ponderosa pines to a ridgetop 0.3-mile east of the trailhead. Once on the ridge,

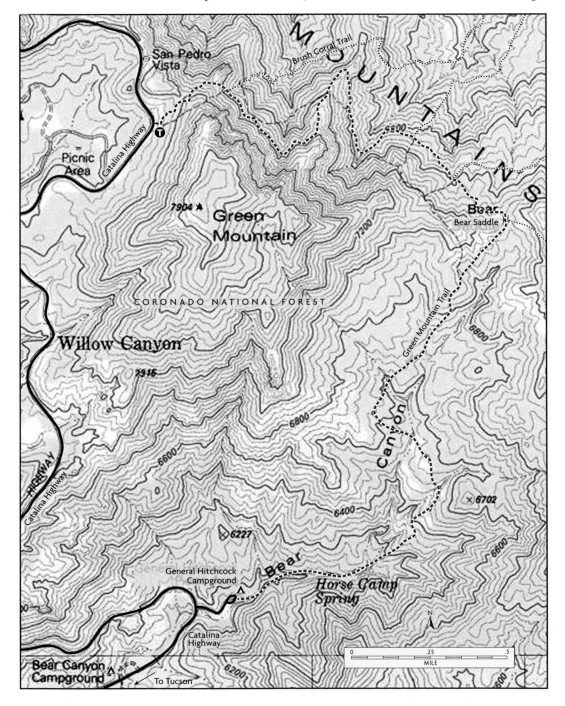

the Green Mountain Trail intersects the upper end of the Brush Corral Trail, which drops down the east slope of the Santa Catalina Range. Turning right at this junction, the Green Mountain Trail then contours around the east slope of its namesake mountain where drier terrain is home to lower-profile forests.

After 1.5 miles the Green Mountain Trail intersects the Brush Corral Shortcut Trail, which is a spur route to the Brush Corral Trail. Keep right here and continue nearly 0.5 mile to another side trail, which leads to Maverick Spring. Located 0.4 mile away, the spring is usually flowing.

Keep right again to continue along the Green Mountain Trail.

A little over 2 miles from its start, the Green Mountain Trail reaches 6950-foot Bear Saddle. From this point, a secondary route leads 1.2 miles to Guthrie Mountain, a summit with fine views of the San Pedro Valley to the east. From the saddle, the Green Mountain Trail continues south an additional 1.8 miles before ending at the General Hitchcock Campground. Descending a mostly easy grade, this final segment of the trail passes mostly among ponderosa pine forests and along a dry streambed.

**Be prepared:** With a shuttle this hike could end at the campground, making it 3.9 miles long. Without a shuttle, however, it is necessary to hike back up the Green Mountain Trail, a climb of 1300 feet. Bring plenty of water, and watch for lightning during thunderstorms.

# 80  Aspen Loop

**Distance:** 3.7-mile loop
**Difficulty:** easy
**Hiking time:** 3 hours
**Elevation:** 7500 to 8100 feet
**Management:** Coronado NF

**Wilderness status:** Pusch Ridge WA
**Season:** May to November
**USGS map:** Mount Lemmon
**GPS coordinates:** 32.428184 N, 110.755789 W

**Getting there:** From its intersection with Tanque Verde Road in northeastern Tucson, drive 30.5 miles north on the Catalina Highway to the Marshall Gulch Picnic Area, less than a mile south of the enclave of Summerhaven. A fee is charged for trailhead parking.

This pleasurable walk through a variety of mountain terrain is quite popular among local hikers. Unfortunately, the 85,000-acre Aspen Fire swept across much of this portion of the Santa Catalina Mountains in 2003. Despite being broadly affected by the blaze, the Aspen Loop hike is still a worthwhile endeavor.

This hike description follows the loop counterclockwise and thus begins by following the Marshall Gulch Trail, which takes off just to the right of the outhouse. Climbing along mostly easy grades, the Marshall Gulch Trail heads west from the picnic area along an often shady

drainage bottom. Blessed with an intermittent stream, this relatively lush area features towering firs, leafy bigtooth maples, and Arizona alders. Along the first portion of the Marshall Gulch Trail, evidence of the Aspen Fire is scant as most trees survived and the undergrowth is still thick. Near the upper end of Marshall Gulch, however, the burn becomes much more evident as entire mountainsides feature mostly standing dead timber.

After 1.2 miles the Marshall Gulch Trail tops out on Marshall Saddle, where it connects with other routes. The Wilderness of Rocks Trail continues west from the saddle, and the Aspen

A thicket of pine saplings growing along the Aspen Trail in the wake of a large forest fire

Trail runs north and south. The Aspen Loop hike takes up the latter route by turning left onto the Aspen Trail.

From Marshall Saddle, the Aspen Trail continues south and then east along a ridgeline that was once thickly forested by pine, fir, and oak. Sporadic tall stands of timber are still intact, and bushy thickets of pine saplings are coming up in burn areas. Such is the process of succession after wildland fires. Also along this stretch of

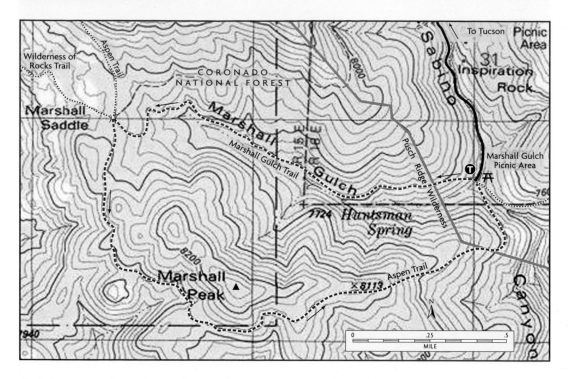

the hike, vistas take in the southern and western flanks of the Santa Catalinas and the Tucson area beyond. Nearly 1 mile from the saddle, a faint trail branches off to the right. Keep left on the main trail, however, and continue to where the trail begins switchbacking downhill.

As the trail bottoms out in this last segment of the hike, sporadic stands of aspen, many of which are saplings, sidle up to the trail. In the final 0.5 mile the trail contours along the upper reaches of Sabino Canyon. The Aspen Loop then ends back at the Marshall Gulch Picnic Area.

**Be prepared:** Although water is usually available along the Marshall Gulch Trail, it should be treated before drinking, so it is best to bring your own. Watch for poison ivy, especially in and around the picnic area. Because of the Aspen Fire, be aware of possible falling timber and eroded stretches of trail.

# 81 *Bog Springs*

| | |
|---|---|
| *Distance:* 5-mile loop | *Wilderness status:* Mount Wrightson WA |
| *Difficulty:* moderate | *Season:* year-round |
| *Hiking time:* 4 hours | *USGS map:* Mount Wrightson |
| *Elevation:* 5100 to 6600 feet | *GPS coordinates:* 31.726727 N, |
| *Management:* Coronado NF | 110.874953 W |

*Getting there:* The Bog Springs Trail begins in the Bog Springs Campground. Take Interstate 19 south from Tucson to the Continental exit just south of the retirement community of Green Valley. There is also a sign for Madera Canyon here. Drive southeast on a paved road for 13 miles to Madera Canyon. Turn onto the road to the Bog Springs Campground and drive another 0.5 mile. The trail begins at site 13, but parking spaces are at the upper end of the campground loop. A day-use fee is charged in Madera Canyon.

Nestled among the high summits of the Santa Rita Mountains south of Tucson, Madera Canyon is one of the premier bird-watching areas in the country. In all, more than 200 species of birds have been spotted here, many of which are considered rare north of the Mexico border. A primary reason for the canyon's attraction to birds is that it offers cool refuge from the desert heat in the summertime. Providing a wonderful introduction to the natural beauty of Madera Canyon is the hike to Bog Springs and Kent Spring. Unfortunately, the 23,000-acre Florida Fire devastated the upper reaches of this hike in July 2005.

The Bog Springs Trail begins by climbing moderately along an old road (closed now) for 0.7 mile to a signed junction. The route then turns left to follow a foot trail for 0.8 mile to Bog Springs. This section climbs at a steeper pace as it approaches the spring. Along the first part of the hike a low-profile forest of alligator juniper, Mexican pinyon pine, Arizona white oak, silver-leaf oak, and Emory oak predominates. Scattered yucca and sotol also grow here. In the vicinity of

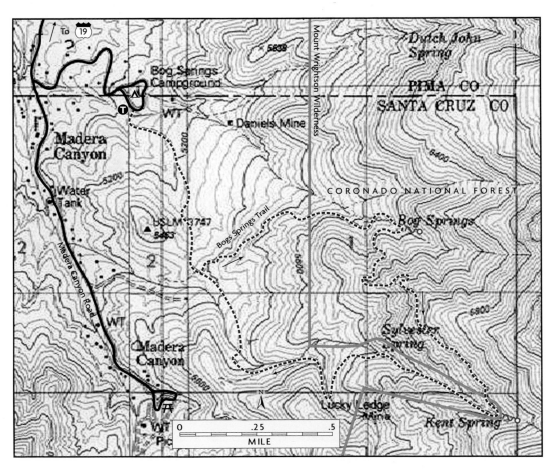

A noisy waterfall along the Bog Springs Trail

Bog Springs, a wonderful riparian community of stately sycamores and Arizona walnut trees is encountered.

It is in riparian areas such as that found at Bog Springs, and Kent Spring farther on, that you might spot some of the birds for which Madera Canyon is known. Topping the list for most birders is the elegant trogon. A relative of the quetzal, this colorful bird migrates here from Mexico in late spring and does not leave until summer's end. Of course, many other species of birds have enthusiasts scouting the treetops with binoculars from April to September. A variety of mammals, including white-tailed deer, black bears, javelinas, and coatimundis, also frequent the area.

From Bog Springs the trail continues south toward Kent Spring, 1.2 miles away. Climbing another 800 feet, this leg of the route is steep in places but does open up to some nice views of Madera Canyon and beyond. It also reveals a change in plant communities as taller Chihuahua pines become more common.

From Kent Spring the route drops quite rapidly for 1.6 miles before reaching the trail junction encountered earlier. Following an old access road that is used to maintain the springs, this part of the hike parallels a beautiful stream that tumbles through picturesque waterfalls and cascades. It is 0.7 mile from this junction back to the trailhead.

**Be prepared:** Although water is usually available at both Bog Springs and Kent Spring, check first with the Forest Service before setting out. Also, watch for falling snags in the burn areas.

## 82  *Mount Wrightson*

*Distance:* 11.7 miles roundtrip
*Difficulty:* strenuous
*Hiking time:* 8 hours
*Elevation:* 5400 to 9453 feet
*Management:* Coronado NF

*Wilderness status:* Mount Wrightson WA
*Season:* April to November
*USGS map:* Mount Wrightson
*GPS coordinates:* 31.713023 N, 110.873675 W

*Getting there:* From Tucson, drive south on Interstate 19 to the Continental exit, where a sign points the way to Madera Canyon. Drive southeast on the paved route for 13 miles to the Roundup Picnic Area. Turn left here to find the developed trailhead. A day-use fee is charged in Madera Canyon.

Towering above the surrounding desert floor, Mount Wrightson (elevation 9453 feet) and the Santa Rita Mountains offer a superb example of what are often called "sky islands." By providing a considerably cooler and wetter climate, these desert ranges feature ecosystems that are strikingly different from those of the desert below. In addition to finding shady oak and pine forests, hikers may also discover a surprising selection of fauna. Madera Canyon, in which this hike begins, is world-renowned for the great number of birds that frequent its wooded environs, including the elegant trogon and Lucifer hummingbird. In 2013 a jaguar was sighted in the Santa Rita Mountains. Unfortunately, several portions of this hike were burned over by the 23,000-acre Florida Fire in July 2005.

This hike combines segments of two different trails that climb Mount Wrightson. The Super Trail (8.1 miles from trailhead to summit) takes its time making the 4000-foot ascent, and the shorter Old Baldy Trail (5.4 miles) makes a more direct assault. Both begin at the Roundup trailhead at the end of Madera Canyon Road (Forest Road 70).

Taking advantage of its mostly gentle ascent, this hike follows the Super Trail for the first 3.7

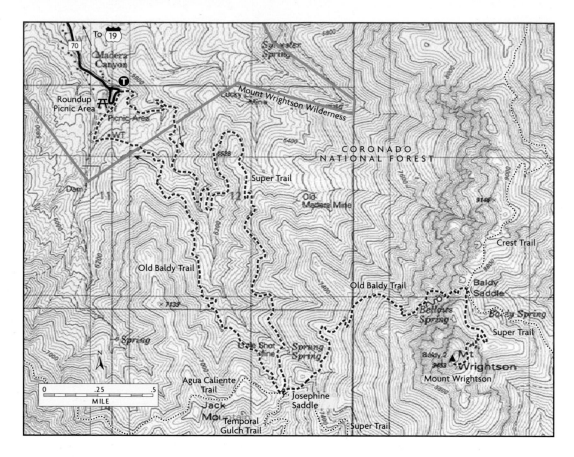

miles. Climbing just over 1600 feet, this leg of the hike makes a few long switchbacks as it contours along the upper reaches of Madera Canyon. Just short of Josephine Saddle the Super Trail reaches Sprung Spring, a developed watering hole that is usually flowing.

At 7080-foot Josephine Saddle, the Super Trail meets the Old Baldy Trail, which this hike description follows during the descent. A number of other trails take off from here as well. The Agua Caliente Trail continues west toward Agua Caliente Saddle and Rattlesnake Canyon, and the Josephine Canyon and Temporal Gulch Trails drop into drainages to the south. Josephine Saddle was the scene of a rather tragic episode. In November 1958 three Boy Scouts perished here when they were caught by a sudden snowstorm. A memorial at the intersection of the Super and Old Baldy Trails serves to remind hikers of the mishap.

From Josephine Saddle, the Super and Old Baldy Trails continue as one heading northeast for 0.2 mile to a second junction. This hike description bears left on the Old Baldy Trail for 1.8 miles to reach Baldy Saddle, whereas the Super Trail loops around the south side of the summit to reach Baldy Saddle in 3.3 miles at easy to moderate grades. Both routes climb 1800 feet, but the Old Baldy Trail cuts across the steeper north face of the peak.

Upon parting with the Super Trail, the Old Baldy Trail wastes little time in gaining elevation. Moderate to strenuous grades can be expected, not to mention several switchbacks. Soon, impressive cliffs that ring the summit come into view. The trail then passes Bellows

Pine trees along the hike up Mount Wrightson

Spring and soon after tops Baldy Saddle. The Crest Trail runs north from Baldy Saddle, and the upper end of the Super Trail is found a short distance to the south. Baldy Saddle is open and scenic, and it features some nice camp spots.

From Baldy Saddle it is a 0.9-mile, 600-foot climb to Mount Wrightson's summit. Keep right at the Super Trail junction and continue south to climb through a few short switchbacks. Whereas evidence of the Florida Fire can be found along several stretches of the hike up to this point, it becomes especially obvious along this final sprint to the summit.

The open summit was, for the first half of the 20th century, home to a fire lookout. Active until the 1950s, the structure was eventually removed, and all that remains now is a concrete foundation and an interpretive sign. From the top you can enjoy a spectacular 360-degree view. To the north lie Tucson, Mount Lemmon, and the Rincon Mountains. Along the western skyline rise Baboquivari and Kitt Peaks, and nearby Mount Hopkins features the Smithsonian Astrophysical Observatory. To the east the Whetstone, Dragoon, and Chiricahua mountain ranges rise from the valley floor. Miller Peak and the Huachuca Mountains are visible to the southeast. The Patagonia Mountains march south toward Mexico, and stacking up on the horizon south of the border are seemingly countless other ranges, each impressive in its own respect.

Although the upper segment of the Super Trail would offer a different perspective, this hike description takes the quickest way back down to the Roundup trailhead by following the Old Baldy Trail for its entire 5.4-mile length.

**Be prepared:** Water is usually available at Sprung and Bellows Springs. Watch for lightning, especially on the summit, and sudden changes in weather throughout the year. Watch for deadfall in the burn areas and do not leave the trail for any reason. Watch for poison ivy, especially along the Baldy Trail below Josephine Saddle.

# 83 *Cochise Trail*

*Distance:* 6 miles roundtrip
*Difficulty:* moderate
*Hiking time:* 4 hours
*Elevation:* 4900 to 6000 feet
*Management:* Coronado NF

*Wilderness status:* none
*Season:* year-round
*USGS map:* Pearce
*GPS coordinates:* 31.922153 N, 109.967724 W

*Getting there:* Located on the east side of the Dragoon Mountains, Cochise Stronghold is reached by driving 12 miles south from Interstate 10 on US Highway 191 to Ironwood Road. Turn west at the sign for the Stronghold and drive 8 miles to the Cochise Stronghold Campground. There is a charge for trailhead parking. The Cochise Trail actually begins at the end of a short nature trail that is easy to follow.

Named for the famed Apache chief, Cochise Stronghold is an alluring and mysterious place. Ringed by salmon-tinted granite domes and faces, this wilderness of rock provided safe haven for Cochise during the years that he and his warriors fought the US Army. Never surrendering, Cochise agreed to peace only in exchange for land in 1872. Cochise died on June 8, 1874, and he was buried somewhere among the rocks of the Stronghold by friends, although to this day no one is sure where. Heading south from a Forest Service campground to Stronghold Divide, the Cochise Trail offers a wonderful look at this legendary locale.

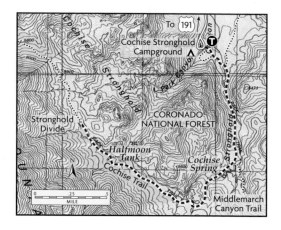

From the trailhead, this hike immediately crosses a footbridge and then encounters a fork in the trail. These two routes are actually either end of a loop nature trail. To reach the Cochise Trail, which sets off from the back end of this loop, stay left. For the first mile the Cochise Trail climbs up a gentle grade along the canyon bottom. Thick woodlands of Mexican pinyon pine, Arizona white oak, alligator juniper, and manzanita persist. A few sycamores also grow in the creek bottom. The Cochise Trail also intersects the 2.3-mile Middlemarch Canyon Trail, which heads southeast to its namesake drainage. Keep right at this trail junction.

Nearly a mile in, the Cochise Trail cuts through some rocky terrain where it scrambles a bit among large boulders. These colorful granite formations are often clad with lichens, which add wisps of green to the pink rock. With literally thousands of nooks, crannies, and crevices here, it is easy to understand how Cochise's body has lain undisturbed for more than a century.

After 1 mile the trail passes Cochise Spring and then climbs moderately through a few switchbacks for 0.75 mile to Halfmoon Tank. Complete with cattails, this small stock pond is an important source of water for wildlife in the area. Beyond the tank, the trail generally levels off before reaching Stronghold Divide, 3 miles from the trailhead. Because this saddle lies behind the rocky façade that towers over the campground, it offers a very different view of the picturesque Stronghold. Beyond the divide, the trail continues down Stronghold Canyon west for another 1.75 miles to the end of a four-wheel-drive road. The divide, however, makes a logical turnaround point for the hike.

The rugged Cochise Stronghold at sunset

**Be prepared:** Bring drinking water on this hike. Cochise Spring is not always flowing, and water from Halfmoon Tank must be treated. Watch for lightning during thunderstorms. Expect hot temperatures in the summer.

## 84  *Heart of Rocks*

*Distance:* 7.1 miles roundtrip
*Difficulty:* moderate
*Hiking time:* 5 hours
*Elevation:* 5400 to 6860 feet
*Management:* Chiricahua NM

*Wilderness status:* Chiricahua WA
*Season:* year-round
*USGS maps:* Cochise Head, Rustler Park
*GPS coordinates:* 32.005657 N, 109.356119 W

*Getting there:* Drive 32 miles southeast from Willcox on Arizona Highway 186. Turn east onto Arizona Highway 181 and continue another 4 miles to the monument entrance where Highway 181 becomes Bonita Canyon Drive. This hike begins at the Chiricahua National Monument visitor center.

Revealing some of the most interesting geological formations that Chiricahua National Monument has to offer is the Heart of Rocks area. Punch and Judy, Pinnacle Balanced Rock, and Duck on a Rock are but three of several aptly named formations found within this large garden

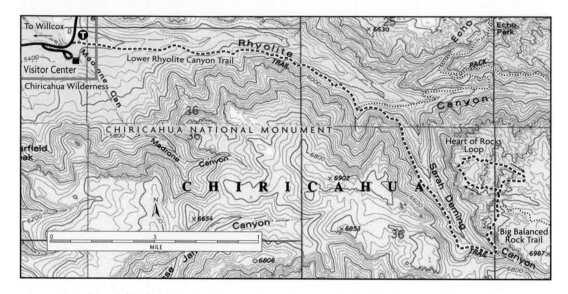

of naturally sculpted statuary. In reaching the Heart of Rocks, this hike also reveals some interesting plant communities within Rhyolite and Sarah Deming Canyons.

Beginning at the east end of the parking lot next to the visitor center, the first 0.25 mile of the route follows the level bottom of Rhyolite Canyon. Although the stream is intermittent in this canyon, there is enough groundwater to support a generous overstory of Apache and Chihuahua pines, Arizona cypress, alligator juniper, and several oaks—Emory, silverleaf, and Arizona white, to name a few. You may also note some scorched tree trunks in this canyon bottom. In 2011 the 223,000-acre Horseshoe II Fire briefly swept into this section of the monument. Fortunately, however, most of the timber survived the burn. A similar scenario is found farther on, along the Sarah Deming Trail portion of this hike.

The route continues up the Lower Rhyolite Canyon Trail and begins climbing gradually in the process. Rhyolite is the volcanic rock of which the monument's formations are made. Geologists believe that it originated as ash from a fiery volcanic explosion 27 million years ago. Eroding at different rates, countless hoodoos of many shapes and sizes resulted. The first of these come into view as the Lower Rhyolite Canyon

Trail climbs out of the canyon bottom along the south side of the drainage. Well maintained, this trail is a breeze to follow, despite its occasionally moderate grade.

After following the Lower Rhyolite Canyon Trail for 1.5 miles, the route then turns right up Sarah Deming Canyon along the Sarah Deming Canyon Trail. Continuing on for a little over a mile, this leg of the hike climbs an easy to moderate grade. Along the way some rather stately Apache pine forests and a few large Arizona cypress add to the scenery, as do more rock formations. Shortly after crossing the drainage bottom, the trail begins to climb a series of short switchbacks as it gains the north face of the canyon. Upon passing some impressive stone spires, the trail reaches a saddle of sorts and a trail junction, 3.1 miles from the trailhead. The right-hand route, the Big Balanced Rock Trail, continues east toward Totem Canyon and Inspiration Point. And a short distance to the left is a sign marking the start of the 0.9-mile Heart of Rocks Loop.

Although you can follow this loop trail in either direction, this description turns left to trace it clockwise. After climbing a short distance, the trail reaches Pinnacle Balanced Rock, a massive totem precariously balanced on the left side of the trail. Beyond this impressive

Pinnacle Balanced Rock is one of many unusual formations along the Heart of Rocks Loop.

formation are others, including Camel's Head, Thor's Hammer, Punch and Judy, Duck on a Rock, and the Kissing Rocks. The Heart of Rocks Loop also provides spectacular views of the rugged north end of the Chiricahua Mountains. Of particular prominence is Cochise Head, a large face of rock that rises northeast of the monument.

Take note of the vegetation in the Heart of Rocks area. In comparison to the canyon bottom below, this drier basin supports diminutive Apache pines, Mexican pinyon pines, stunted oaks, small Arizona cypress, and manzanita bushes. Upon finishing the Heart of Rocks Loop, return to the trailhead by retracing the Sarah Deming Canyon and Lower Rhyolite Canyon Trails.

**Be prepared:** Water is not available along this hike, so bring plenty. Summers may see temperatures in the 90s, and winter snowfall may make the trail difficult to follow. Watch for lightning in exposed terrain.

## 85 Echo Canyon

| | |
|---|---|
| **Distance:** 3.5-mile loop | **Wilderness status:** Chiricahua WA |
| **Difficulty:** moderate | **Season:** year-round |
| **Hiking time:** 3 hours | **USGS map:** Cochise Head |
| **Elevation:** 6780 to 6330 feet | **GPS coordinates:** 32.011961 N, |
| **Management:** Chiricahua NM | 109.315762 W |

**Getting there:** Drive 32 miles southeast from Willcox on Arizona Highway 186. Turn east onto Arizona Highway 181 and continue for another 4 miles to the monument entrance where Highway 181 becomes Bonita Canyon Drive. This hike begins at the Echo Canyon Trail Parking Area, 5.5 miles past the Chiricahua National Monument visitor center.

Winding among a stunning collection of strange rock formations, the loop hike through Echo Canyon offers a short yet memorable introduction to the wonders of Chiricahua National Monument. Add to this lesson in geology some fine vistas and a fascinating variety of plant life, and you have a great hike. Constructed by the Civilian Conservation Corps in 1936 and 1937, the Echo Canyon Trail has that sturdy, comfortable feel that most CCC projects seem to possess.

Shortly after starting out, this hike reaches the first of four trail junctions along the way. Turn right onto the Echo Canyon Trail, which begins winding among lichen-covered rocks and pinnacles. After 0.5 mile the grade drops slightly and the trail enters an area known as the Grotto. Crowded in by towering columns of rock, this stretch of the hike reveals several secretive passageways and up-close rock formations. Although these passageways may be inviting places to explore, it is imperative to be extra cautious because of dangerous drop-offs.

About 1 mile from the trailhead, the route descends some short switchbacks into Echo Canyon where the trail enters Echo Park. Whereas Mexican pinyon pine, oaks, manzanita, and other low-profile trees grow among the rock formations above, the availability of groundwater in this drainage bottom originally allowed for towering Apache pine, Douglas fir, and Arizona cypress. Unfortunately, the 223,000-acre Horseshoe II Fire devastated the Echo Park area in 2011.

At 1.6 miles, the route reaches a second junction. The trail to the right leads down Rhyolite Canyon to the Chiricahua National Monument visitor center. Turning left here, however, this hike loops back to the Echo Canyon trailhead by

Rock walls crowd over portions of the Echo Canyon Trail.

way of the Hailstone Trail. Climbing easily along the semi-arid south-facing wall of Rhyolite Canyon for 0.8 mile, this section of the hike passes mostly among pinyon pine and juniper forests.

At a third trail junction near the upper end of Rhyolite Canyon, keep left to follow a shallow drainage along the easy grade of the Ed Riggs Trail. After 0.7 mile there is yet another junction; keep left again and continue another 0.2 mile to the trailhead. A right turn at this last intersection leads 0.2 mile to Massai Point and the end of Bonita Canyon Drive. From this viewpoint it is possible to look out over much of the monument.

**Be prepared:** Be sure to bring plenty of drinking water as none is found along the Echo Canyon hike. Ice and snow may be encountered in winter. Watch for lightning, especially in higher areas.

## 86  *Chiricahua Peak*

*Distance:* 10 miles roundtrip
*Difficulty:* moderate
*Hiking time:* 7 hours
*Elevation:* 8400 to 9796 feet
*Management:* Coronado NF
*Wilderness status:* Chiricahua WA

*Season:* May to October
*USGS maps:* Rustler Peak, Chiricahua Peak
*GPS coordinates:* 31.906690 N, 109.277235 W

*Getting there:* From Willcox, drive 32 miles southeast on Arizona Highway 186 to Arizona Highway 181. Turn east on Highway 181 and drive 3 miles, following the signs for Chiricahua National Monument. Just before entering the monument, keep right on the graveled Pinery Canyon Road (Forest Road 42) and continue nearly 12 miles to Onion Saddle and the turnoff for Rustler Park. From this junction drive 2.8 miles south on Forest Road 42D to the trailhead, which is at the entrance of the Rustler Park Campground.

Topping out at nearly 10,000 feet, the Chiricahuas are the second-highest mountain range in southeastern Arizona. Despite their lofty status, reaching the summit is a relatively simple task, thanks to the Crest Trail. In just 5 miles of mostly easy grades, this hike will put you on top of 9796-foot Chiricahua Peak. Unfortunately, much of the Crest Trail was greatly affected by two major forest fires. First in 1994 the 27,500-acre Rattlesnake Fire swept across portions of the mountain range. Then in 2011 the 223,000-acre Horseshoe II Fire added insult to injury. Although this devastation has resulted in charred stands of dead timber and a lot of deadfall across the trail, it has also opened up some nice vistas of the surrounding basin-and-range topography.

From the trailhead this hike begins by skirting around the north end of the Rustler Park Campground. At first the trail crosses a mostly open area that was cleared of standing fire debris. It soon enters stands of burnt timber as it begins to circle south from Rustler Park. Sadly, both the campground and the surrounding mountain slopes were completely inundated by the flames in 2011. This has resulted in a lot of undergrowth that now encroaches on the trail. Near the top of the ridge just west of the campground, the trail reaches the Crest Trail itself. Whereas a right turn accesses Barfoot Lookout to the north, this hike bears left onto the southbound Crest Trail.

After continuing for 1.5 miles the route reaches Bootlegger Saddle, where a short side trail accesses the four-wheel-drive Long Park Road. The Crest Trail continues south for another mile before reaching an intersection of routes. One spur trail leads 0.7 mile north to the end of Long Park Road. Another trail heads east from this point for 1.9 miles to the scenic Centella Point. Still another route climbs to the top of nearby Flys Peak (elevation 9666 feet).

Continuing south, the Crest Trail covers another 0.6 mile before connecting with the upper end of the Saulsbury Trail, a popular route that begins at Turkey Creek to the west. In another 0.3 mile the Crest Trail crosses a small opening known as Round Park. A 0.2-mile spur trail turns left shortly beyond Round Park to find Booger Spring, which, like most springs in the area, is usually flowing.

From Round Park, the Crest Trail continues for 0.7 mile to Cima Park, where the Greenhouse Trail drops off to the east and the Mormon Ridge Trail descends west. Following that is the turnoff for Anita Park and Anita Spring. A short distance farther, the Crest Trail reaches Junction Saddle and a final intersection of routes. At this point it is not difficult to find the trail that makes the moderate 0.5-mile climb to the top of 9796-foot Chiricahua Peak.

In spite of the devastation that the Rattlesnake and Horseshoe II Fires caused, it is still possible to find stands of Chihuahua and Apache pines, ponderosa pine, and Douglas fir in places. Although damaged by the fires, stands of Engelmann spruce can still be found near Chiricahua Peak. This

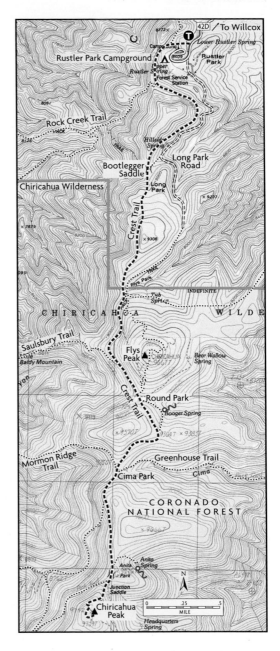

marks the southernmost extent of the species in North America. Among the burn areas, you can now see grasses and a variety of other plants being reestablished. Where stands of aspen once stood, thickets of aspen saplings now grow.

An early morning look east from the Crest Trail

**Be prepared:** Two different springs within a mile of the Crest Trail—Booger and Anita—usually provide adequate drinking water, although arid years have seen them dry up. As with water collected in streams, water from these springs should be treated before drinking. Lightning may be hazardous during summer thunderstorms. Because the trail is often sided by standing dead timber, hikers should be wary of falling trees, especially during strong winds. Expect to negotiate a lot of deadfall all along the route.

## 87 *South Fork Cave Creek*

**Distance:** 3.2 miles roundtrip
**Difficulty:** easy
**Hiking time:** 2 hours
**Elevation:** 5300 to 5600 feet
**Management:** Coronado NF

**Wilderness status:** Chiricahua WA
**Season:** year-round
**USGS map:** Portal Peak
**GPS coordinates:** 31.868848 N,
109.188404 W

**Getting there:** To reach the South Fork Cave Creek, drive north from Douglas on Arizona Highway 80 to Rodeo, New Mexico. Continue another 2 miles to the road to Portal, turn left, and drive 7 miles to the small enclave of Portal, Arizona. Continue another 3 miles or so west on Forest Road 42 to the left-hand turn for the South Fork Picnic Area. In another mile you will reach the road's end and the trailhead. There is a per vehicle fee for trailhead parking.

A beautiful area, Cave Creek Canyon on the eastern slope of the Chiricahua Mountains, is home to a varied selection of flora and fauna. One of the best places to enjoy the area's ecology is along the South Fork Cave Creek. Accessed by a nice, easy trail, this drainage bottom makes for a wonderful outing.

Tracing the nearly level canyon bottom the entire way, the South Fork Trail is easy to follow, freeing you up to concentrate on enjoying the natural wonders of the canyon. This riparian environment offers an interesting mix of deciduous trees (sycamore, live oak, ash, Arizona walnut, and bigtooth maple) and evergreens (alligator juniper, Arizona cypress, sizable Douglas fir, and ponderosa pine). Add to this an occasional yucca, patches of poison ivy, and other understory species, and you have an ecosystem conducive to an array of wildlife, including black bears, white-tailed deer, javelinas, and coatimundis. Certainly, however, the South Fork's most fabled residents are of the feathered variety. This canyon ranks right up there with Madera Canyon in terms of biological diversity. Here, too, it is possible to spot several different species of hummingbirds, painted redstarts, sulfur-bellied flycatchers, and elegant trogons, among other showy species. You can almost count on running across at least a handful of birders on this hike.

Although the South Fork Cave Creek flows intermittently throughout the year, it is typically

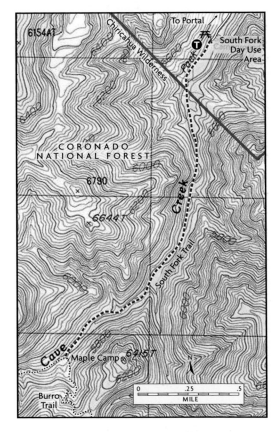

not deep enough to impede crossing, which the trail does on a few occasions. Not far from the trailhead, the route crosses a fence that marks the Chiricahua Wilderness boundary, and at 1.6

Prodigious ferns in the South Fork Cave Creek

miles it reaches Maple Camp, the turnaround point for this hike.

More of a spot on the map than an actual camp, Maple Camp is marked by a trail sign and junction. Branching south is the Burro Trail, which climbs steeply to Horseshoe Pass 3.2 miles away. The South Fork Trail continues up its namesake canyon, which at this point becomes a bit rougher. In 5.2 miles this route reaches the Crest Trail in the vicinity of Sentinel Peak. The Crest Trail runs the length of the Chiricahua Mountains.

**Be prepared:** Watch for poison ivy along this route. The canyon is for day use only. Serious bird-watchers should keep in mind that the use of audio recordings (for calling birds) is prohibited.

## 88 *Rucker Canyon*

*Distance:* 9.2 miles roundtrip
*Difficulty:* strenuous
*Hiking time:* 6 hours
*Elevation:* 6150 to 7600 feet
*Management:* Coronado NF

*Wilderness status:* Chiricahua WA
*Season:* May to November
*USGS map:* Chiricahua Peak
*GPS coordinates:* 31.784154 N, 109.304190 W

*Getting there:* To reach the Rucker Canyon trailhead, drive about 29 miles south from Interstate 10 on US Highway 191, then turn left on graveled Rucker Canyon Road. Follow this route (it becomes Forest Road 74 at the national forest boundary) a little more than 23 miles to where Forest Road 74E turns left. Follow FR 74E to its end at Rucker Forest Camp. The Rucker Trail leaves from the west end of this small campground.

Located in the southernmost corner of the state, the Chiricahua Mountains are home to a number of plants and animals not normally found in the United States. Fauna usually associated with Mexico's Sierra Madre, such as the Apache fox squirrel and the Mexican chickadee, are often spotted in the Chiricahuas. Tree species such as the Chihuahua pine grow here as well. A good place to enjoy these semi-exotic species is in Rucker Canyon, which is in the southern end of the range.

For the first few miles, the Rucker Trail climbs a gentle grade as it follows the canyon bottom. Although flow in portions of the creek is intermittent at times, various riparian trees grow along the route, including Arizona sycamore and Arizona cypress. Some impressive stands of ponderosa, Apache, and Chihuahua pine can also be enjoyed. The trail may be faded in spots due to flooding as it follows the creekside.

About 3 miles in, the Rucker Trail begins a steep ascent of the south canyon wall. Climbing through a series of switchbacks, the route gains much of its 2000 feet of elevation in this last portion. As you climb, however, the rugged stature of the canyon becomes more obvious as colorful cliffs define the opposite canyon wall. Manzanita and yucca plants are found growing along portions of this segment of the trail, where the steep slopes are much drier than the canyon floor below.

A pool of still water along the Rucker Trail

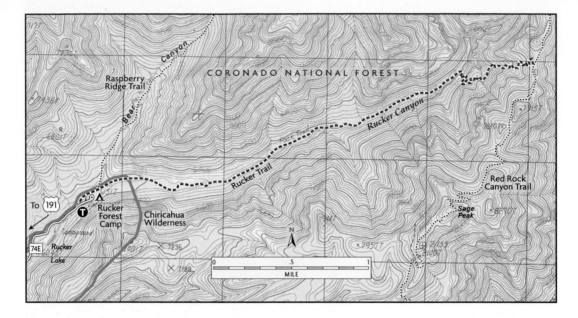

Eventually, 4.6 miles from the trailhead, the Rucker Trail reaches a ridgetop where it intersects with the 4.9-mile Red Rock Canyon Trail and the turnaround point for this hike. Having climbed up from its namesake drainage, the Red Rock Canyon route continues north up the ridge before ending at the Price Canyon Trail. The Price Canyon Trail then meets up with the Crest Trail, which can take you up and over Chiricahua Peak.

**Be prepared:** Although water is usually found along parts of Rucker Canyon, it should be treated before drinking. Watch for lightning in higher terrain.

## 89 *Pole Bridge Canyon*

*Distance:* 4.8 miles roundtrip
*Difficulty:* strenuous
*Hiking time:* 3 hours
*Elevation:* 6200 to 8000 feet
*Management:* Coronado NF

*Wilderness status:* Chiricahua WA
*Season:* May to November
*USGS map:* Chiricahua Peak
*GPS coordinates:* 31.861442 N, 109.338150 W

*Getting there:* From Willcox, drive approximately 32 miles southeast on Arizona Highway 186 to where it intersects Arizona Highway 181. Continue south on Highway 181 for another 10 miles to where Turkey Creek Road (Forest Road 41) turns east. Follow this good gravel road 9.6 miles to the signed start of the Pole Bridge Trail.

The Chiricahua Mountains are home to a number of plants and animals that are not normally found in the United States. Fauna such as the Apache fox squirrel and the Mexican chickadee are often spotted in the Chiricahuas. Tree species such as the Chihuahua pine are

A flowing stream adds to the allure of Pole Bridge Canyon.

also found in these mountains. The Pole Bridge Research Natural Area was designated to protect a sampling of the Chiricahuas' unusual collection of flora and fauna. Encompassing a short yet steep drainage, the area is accessed by the Pole Bridge Trail.

For the first 0.75 mile the trail climbs up the canyon bottom along a mostly easy grade. Unfortunately, this portion of the route was greatly affected by the 223,000-acre Horseshoe II Fire in 2011. Although formerly forested with a mix of oaks (Emory and silverleaf), ponderosa pine, and Chihuahua pine, this stretch of trail now includes many torched tree trunks. In addition, post-burn flooding has rearranged the canyon bottom in places with rocks, mud, and other debris. Because undergrowth is thick in places, the trail may be hard to spot.

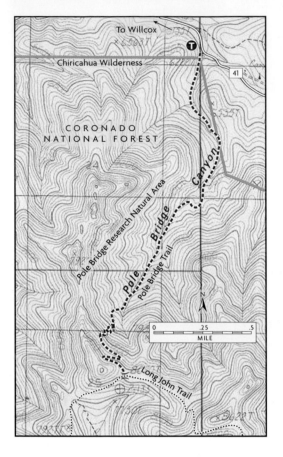

Nearing the 1-mile mark, the trail enters forest that was only marginally affected by the fire. It also becomes steeper as the first of several switchbacks is reached. Beyond this point the route ascends a moderate to strenuous grade as it climbs 1400 feet in the next 1.5 miles. During this gain in elevation, the forest type begins to change. Although pines are still plentiful, Douglas firs are now more common. Gambel oak becomes the prominent species of deciduous tree, although silverleaf oak is still present. Ferns find suitable habitat on the open forest floor.

As the trail nears a saddle on the ridge that separates Pole Bridge Canyon from Long John Canyon to the south, the terrain becomes sufficiently steep to allow for limited vistas through the upper branches of trees growing below. In a few places you can glimpse the overall ruggedness of the west side of the Chiricahua Mountains. On the saddle, the Pole Bridge Trail connects with the Long John Trail, which runs in both directions along the ridgetop. A right turn eventually leads south to Long John Canyon, and a left turn continues 1.4 miles east to Johnson Peak. Although this hike turns around at the saddle, be sure to walk a short distance east for a nice view into the southwestern quarter of the Chiricahua Mountains.

**Be prepared:** Because water is not always available in Pole Bridge Canyon, be sure to bring all that you will require. Watch for falling timber and unstable trail conditions in the burn areas.

## 90 Fort Bowie

| | |
|---|---|
| **Distance:** 3 miles roundtrip | **Wilderness status:** none |
| **Difficulty:** easy | **Season:** year-round |
| **Hiking time:** 2 hours | **USGS map:** Cochise Head |
| **Elevation:** 4700 to 5152 feet | **GPS coordinates:** 32.150280 N, |
| **Management:** Fort Bowie NHS | 109.447225 W |

**Getting there:** The hike to Fort Bowie begins along graveled Apache Pass Road, which runs south from the town of Bowie on Interstate 10 to Arizona Highway 186. The well developed trailhead is 13 miles from Bowie and 7.9 miles from Arizona Highway 186.

Situated in the Apache Pass area, Fort Bowie played an integral role in the conquest and settlement of the American Southwest. A visit to this national historic site today will reveal the complete story. To better protect the delicate antiquities of the site, the facility is accessed by a 3-mile roundtrip interpretive trail.

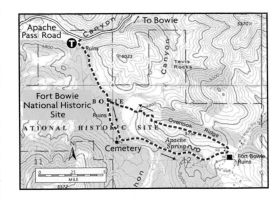

Before starting out, be sure to read the interpretive signs at the trailhead. One describes how the Apache Pass area lies on the border of two distinct biomes—the Sonoran and Chihuahuan Deserts—and how plant and animal species of both are represented here. This lesson in natural history is continued all along the hike in the form of small signs that identify numerous plants, including ocotillo, cane cholla, Palmer agave, soaptree yucca, saltbush, desert sumac, alligator juniper, scrub live oak, and Arizona walnut. Other plants that are plentiful along the trail are mesquite, sotol, and prickly pear cactus.

A second sign begins an interesting historical narrative that is continued along the entire hike. Originally the domain of the Chiricahua Apache Indians, Apache Pass proved to be of strategic interest to settlers because of Apache Spring— the only reliable source of water for dozens of miles. In 1854, a survey party explored the pass in search of a route for the Southern Pacific Railroad; the line was eventually built to the north. In 1858 the famous Butterfield Overland Trail, a stage route between St. Louis and San Francisco, crossed the pass for three years before a conflict between the Apache chief Cochise and the US Army arose. This disagreement shut down the stage line and led to a decade of warfare and the establishment of Fort Bowie.

In the years that followed, conditions on the reservation deteriorated and discontent grew. In 1876, two years after Cochise's death, the Chiricahua Reservation was closed and its occupants were moved north to the San Carlos Reservation.

The stabilized remains of Fort Bowie

After fleeing to Mexico, breakaway bands renewed fighting with the army. Best known of these factions was a group led by Geronimo. Fort Bowie became headquarters for the lengthy campaign to quash Geronimo's resistance, and it was not until 1886 that he finally succumbed. His surrender brought an end to the nation's Indian Wars and opened up settlement of the region. Eight years later, Fort Bowie was officially closed.

Today, the hike to Fort Bowie reveals many reminders of this chapter in American history. A stone foundation recalls a station along the Butterfield Overland Trail. The post cemetery reflects the ferocity of the times. Some grave markers read "killed by Indians," and one gravesite is that of Little Robe, the son of Geronimo. The adobe foundation of the Chiricahua Indian Agency hints at the spirit of cooperation that existed during the first years of the Chiricahua Reservation. A re-created Apache wickiup nearby offers a glimpse of what life was like for these mostly nomadic people. The much-coveted Apache Spring still gurgles at trailside near the fort itself.

About 0.5 mile from the trailhead, this hike reaches an intersection. The trail to the left is the return segment of this loop, and the right-hand route winds easily through the desert hills before reaching Fort Bowie, 1.5 miles from the start. The ruins of the original Fort Bowie are located on a hill just south of the spring, and the second, much larger fort is situated on the flats east of the spring. Included in the complex were corrals and stables, a general store, a hospital and school, officers' quarters, infantry barracks, a mess hall, and more. As part of the national historic site, a visitor center at the fort site offers an interesting display of old photos and relics. Books are for sale, and a ranger is on hand to answer questions. Drinking water is also available.

From the fort site this hike returns to the trailhead via a different, more scenic route that climbs a ridge behind the visitor center. From this high point it is possible to look down on Fort Bowie and much of the rest of the hike. Dropping through some switchbacks off the north end of the ridge, the route soon rejoins the incoming trail shortly after crossing a dry wash. Turn right to return to the trailhead.

**Be prepared:** Although water is available at the ranger station, it is wise to bring along a canteen. Watch for rattlesnakes (they have the right-of-way here), and be prepared for temperatures above 100 degrees Fahrenheit in summer. Removal of any historic or natural items within a unit of the National Park Service is strictly prohibited. Metal detectors, shovels, and guns are also prohibited. Sitting or climbing on any walls or mounds is prohibited.

## 91 *Arcadia National Recreation Trail*

**Distance:** 10.2 miles roundtrip
**Difficulty:** strenuous
**Hiking time:** 7 hours
**Elevation:** 6700 to 9500 feet
**Management:** Coronado NF

**Wilderness status:** none
**Season:** May to October
**USGS map:** Mount Graham
**GPS coordinates:** 32.648534 N, 109.820285 W

**Getting there:** From Safford, drive 8 miles south on US Highway 191 to the turnoff for Arizona Highway 366. Follow Arizona Highway 366 west for 11.7 miles to the Upper Arcadia Group Site, just past the Arcadia Campground. The trail takes off from the back end of the facility. The upper end of the trail is found at Shannon Park Campground, which is another 10 miles up Arizona Highway 366.

Hiking along the Arcadia Trail in autumn

Topped by 10,720-foot Mount Graham, the Pinaleño Mountains are the highest of southeastern Arizona's sky islands. Surrounded by arid basins, this mountain range rises decisively near the town of Safford. In so doing it provides a dramatic shift in climatic conditions, which in turn supports flora remarkably different from that of the desert below. A hike along the Arcadia National Recreation Trail reveals much about the range's ecology.

Because this roundtrip route description includes the return hike to your car, it begins at the trail's lower end at the Arcadia Campground. Within the first 0.5 mile, the Arcadia Trail climbs moderately up a few switchbacks before leveling off to cross a drainage bottom. In contrast to the open ponderosa pine forest that first shades the trail, this ravine features a relatively lush collection of bigtooth maple, Arizona walnut, Gambel oak, limber pine, and several large Douglas firs. Upon crossing the normally dry streambed, the

trail begins to climb again as it bends around an east-facing slope. For the next 3.5 miles the route encounters a generally arid mix of scattered ponderosa pine and desert oak.

Climbing over 1000 feet in the next 1.5 miles, the Arcadia National Recreation Trail follows a long series of switchbacks before connecting with the upper end of the Noon Creek Ridge Trail. At this point you are 2 miles into the hike. After keeping left at the junction, the route continues to climb up a moderate to steep grade through additional switchbacks as it heads toward Heliograph Peak. Some nice views to the north and east come into play all along this leg of the hike.

About 4 miles from the trailhead, the Arcadia Trail connects with a 1-mile spur trail that leads to the summit of Heliograph Peak (elevation 10,022 feet). It then tops out on a small saddle that serves as the high point of the hike. Some nice vistas are possible from a rock outcropping

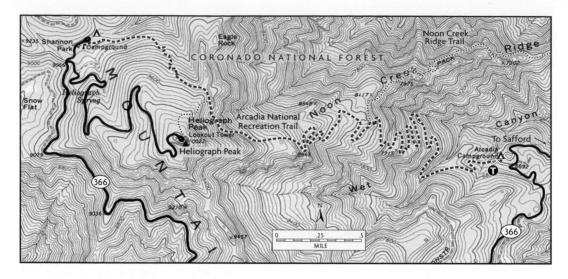

to the right. Beyond the saddle the trail drops down a few easy switchbacks beneath a mix of quaking aspen and Engelmann spruce. Engelmann spruce are a rarity in southern Arizona because only a few mountains are high enough in elevation to support them.

In the last 0.5 mile the Arcadia Trail is mostly level as it heads west through stands of Douglas fir and Engelmann spruce. After 5.1 miles the trail ends at the Shannon Park Campground

(elevation 9100 feet). The return to your car is easier, as you now descend the same 2800 vertical feet just climbed. With a vehicle shuttle, it is possible to follow the Arcadia National Recreation Trail in only one direction. If you choose this option, keep in mind that it is easier to follow the route downhill, in the opposite direction of this description. The Shannon Park Campground lies 10 miles beyond the Arcadia Campground via a good paved road.

**Be prepared:** Bring drinking water on this hike as none is found along the way. Watch for lightning and changing weather conditions.

# 92 *Powers Garden*

| | |
|---|---|
| **Distance:** 17 miles roundtrip | **Wilderness status:** Galiuro WA |
| **Difficulty:** strenuous | **Season:** year-round |
| **Hiking time:** 2 days | **USGS map:** Kennedy Peak |
| **Elevation:** 5000 to 6200 feet | **GPS coordinates:** 32.668982 N, |
| **Management:** Coronado NF | 110.276678 W |

**Getting there:** From Safford, drive 17 miles south on US Highway 191 to Arizona Highway 266. Turn right and drive 19 miles to Bonita. Continue north on Aravaipa Road and drive 19 miles to Forest Road 253. Turn left and drive 6.7 miles to the Deer Creek trailhead, where this hike begins. The last few miles of the drive may be rough but still passable in most carefully driven vehicles.

Located in a remote area of southeastern Arizona, the Galiuro Wilderness is a real treat for backcountry hikers intent on escaping the crowds found in more accessible wilderness areas. A good choice for exploring this 76,317-acre tract of wildland is the 8.5-mile hike to Powers Garden in the heart of the wilderness.

Climbing west from the trailhead along easy to moderate grades, the East Divide Trail traverses some beautiful grasslands which typify the eastern slopes of the Galiuro Mountains. Some reports suggest that the trail may be hard to find in this portion of the hike as the tall grass is overgrown in places but rock cairns occasionally mark the way. After 1.5 miles the route takes up the Tortilla Trail, which is indicated by a sign at the trail intersection. Cross through a fence and continue west for another 1.25 miles to Mud Spring. This is probably the most reliable water source along this entire hike.

From a signed intersection near Mud Spring, the Sycamore Trail turns right and eventually reaches the end of Forest Road 96 north of the wilderness area. This hike bears left, however, to continue along the Tortilla Trail. Shortly, the route begins to climb more strenuously, and it eventually tops out on a ridge a mile or so

beyond the spring. All along this section great vistas to the east and north reveal the neighboring Pinaleño and Santa Teresa Mountain Ranges. You may also note that the grasslands below have slowly given way to forests of live oaks, alligator juniper, pinyon pine, and manzanita. At the ridgetop the hike has reached its high point of 6200 feet. Over a distance of nearly 4 miles, it has climbed about 1200 feet.

Beyond the ridgetop the Tortilla Trail drops a few hundred feet into the head of Sycamore Creek where it intersects a spur of the above-mentioned Sycamore Trail. Whereas older maps show the Tortilla Trail climbing quickly back out of the Sycamore Creek drainage to continue west over Topout Divide and into upper Horse Canyon, the trail now follows the normally dry drainage bottom downstream for about 0.5 mile to a stock tank. From the tank the Tortilla Trail leaves the drainage by contouring easily along its southwest slope. Eventually, after a mile or so, the route tops out again on a second saddle, which overlooks the mouth of Horse Canyon. It then drops some 900 feet in a little over 1 mile (keep in mind that this will make for a strenuous climb on the return trip) to reach the bottom of Horse Canyon near its junction with Rattlesnake

A hiker among the cabins at Powers Garden

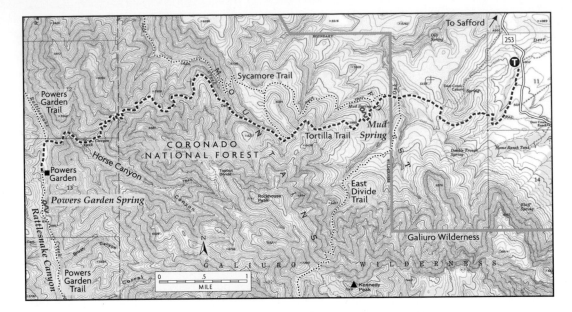

Canyon. Once there, keep right to follow Horse Canyon 0.5 mile to where it intersects the larger Rattlesnake Canyon. Here, the Tortilla Trail ends along the 8.9-mile Powers Garden Trail, which mostly follows Rattlesnake Canyon north and south. Turn left and continue south for a short distance along the Powers Garden Trail to Powers Garden itself. Whereas the bottom of Horse Canyon hosts some tangled riparian stands of maple, Arizona walnut, and Arizona sycamore, the much broader and more orderly Rattlesnake Canyon bottom is characterized by tall ponderosa pines and open meadows.

Named for the Powers family, which settled in Rattlesnake Canyon in 1909, Powers Garden and its collection of a cabin, sheds, corrals, and other antiquated structures are reminders of one of the more colorful events in Arizona history. In February 1918 federal marshals came to arrest Tom and John Powers for draft evasion. A shootout erupted, which left four dead. The Powers brothers escaped and fled to Mexico. After one of Arizona's largest manhunts ever, they were captured by the US Army south of the border. Today, because the main cabin is well maintained and even stocked with supplies by hikers and equestrians, it serves as an ideal place to spend the night. Because bears are plentiful in these mountains, be sure to secure the cabin's door behind you. Water is sometimes found at Powers Garden Spring a short distance south.

To return to the trailhead, you can retrace your route. With more time, you can return along the Powers Garden, Rattlesnake, and East Divide Trails. This second option would add some miles to the hike but would make for a nice multiday loop.

**Be prepared:** Water is usually available at Mud and Powers Garden Springs, but it should be treated before drinking. In drier times of the year, you should check in advance about the availability of water. Expect to find rugged conditions in places and sections where the trail may be hard to find. Watch for lightning in the higher reaches of this hike, and be wary of rattlesnakes.

Opposite, top: Prickly pear cactus along the hike up Vulture Peak

Opposite, below: Along the rugged and scenic White Rock Canyon

# Western Deserts

93. Vulture Peak . . . . . . . . . . . . . . . . .228

94. Margies Cove . . . . . . . . . . . . . . . .230

95. Harquahala Peak . . . . . . . . . . . . .232

96. Ben Avery Trail . . . . . . . . . . . . . .234

97. Bull Pasture . . . . . . . . . . . . . . . . .236

98. Palm Canyon . . . . . . . . . . . . . . . .238

99. Hualapai Mountain Park . . . . . .240

100. Arizona Hot Spring . . . . . . . . . .242

*Arizona's western deserts comprise some of North America's most arid and* desolate topography. Yet, interspersed with several incredibly rugged mountain ranges, it is a land of grand vistas and a handful of great hikes. This landscape is unique in many respects, and hikers may find the region's unusual array of plant life fascinating. In addition to saguaro cactus, cholla, century plants, and ocotillo, the western deserts are also home to errant stands of palm trees. Because of the desolate and remote nature of this region, established trails are few and far between. On the plus side, however, visitors may find that they have the whole place to themselves. Because of extreme heat in the summer, hiking in this region should be reserved for late fall, winter, and early spring. Bring plenty of water, and watch for venomous creatures of various persuasions.

## 93  *Vulture Peak*

*Distance:* 5 miles roundtrip
*Difficulty:* strenuous
*Hiking time:* 3 hours
*Elevation:* 2500 to 3420 feet
*Management:* BLM

*Wilderness status:* none
*Season:* October to May
*USGS maps:* Vulture Peak, Vulture Mine
*GPS coordinates:* 33.877223 N, 112.817526 W

*Getting there:* From downtown Wickenburg, drive west on US Highway 60 to the paved Vulture Mine Road. Turn south there and drive nearly 7 miles to a signed left turn. The trailhead is found 0.4 mile down this good gravel road.

Vulture Peak is one of those nice little surprises that dot southwestern Arizona. Jutting skyward a few miles south of Wickenburg, this rugged and rocky summit is a visibly alluring target for hikers. Just 2.5 miles in length, the Vulture Peak Trail climbs to a saddle just below the summit. From there experienced hikers can attempt the top by way of a short but rugged scramble.

Taking advantage of the many old mining roads in the area, access to the base of Vulture Peak and the final leg of the Vulture Peak Trail are possible in a four-wheel-drive vehicle or on foot. From the trailhead, a jeep road continues east for a short distance before entering a shallow arroyo. In all, this road runs 1.4 miles to a secondary four-wheel-drive trailhead at the base of the peak. Conversely, a foot trail (also about 1.4 miles in length) heads south from the main trailhead for a short distance before crossing the same arroyo. It then continues eastward to eventually reach the secondary trailhead. This description forgoes the four-wheel-drive route in favor of a memorable meander through a nice example of Sonoran Desert.

The entire Vulture Peak Trail is well established and easy to follow. Along the first 1.4 miles hikers will enjoy a relatively lush mix of saguaro and cholla cactus, palo verde, and creosote bush. This desert land is especially beautiful in the early morning. The four-wheel-drive approach to the second trailhead similarly winds through the same cactus-studded foothills, but the terrain is best experienced in quiet solitude. At one point

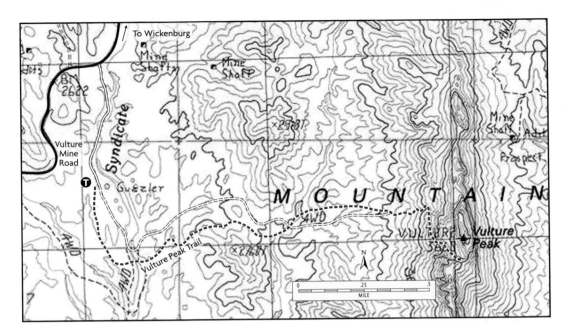

the two routes cross paths, then meet up again at the secondary trailhead. In most spots where routefinding might be a problem, the BLM has posted small brown trail signs to mark the way.

From the second trailhead the Vulture Peak Trail begins a steep, nearly 1000-foot climb to the saddle above. This last segment of the trail switchbacks a few times before following a boulder-strewn gully directly below the saddle. At the saddle, the views are outstanding as you can see east into the often hazy Valley of the Sun or south and west across more of the Vulture Mountain Range. Although this trail description turns back here, more adventurous hikers may

Saguaro cactus at the saddle below Vulture Peak

want to attempt the summit, which rises directly north. From the saddle, a scramble route follows a rugged couloir where you must pick your way through the best hand and toe holds. Because of the exposure to falling along this 200-foot climb, use extreme caution and don't attempt it alone. From the summit you can considerably extend your vistas in all directions.

**Be prepared:** In addition to heeding the warnings in the hike description if you opt to scramble to the summit, watch for lightning storms everywhere on the mountain. Be wary of rattlesnakes, and bring plenty of water. Do not attempt this hike during hotter months.

## 94  Margies Cove

*Distance:* 11.5 miles roundtrip
*Difficulty:* easy
*Hiking time:* 7 hours
*Elevation:* 1100 to 1800 feet
*Management:* BLM, Sonoran Desert NM
*Wilderness status:* North Maricopa Mountains WA

*Season:* October to May
*USGS maps:* Butterfield Pass, Cottonwood Center SE
*GPS coordinates:* 33.125786 N, 112.582047 W

*Getting there:* The trailhead for the Margies Cove Trail is reached by driving about 21 miles south from Interstate 10 on Arizona Highway 85 to Woods Road (which is near mile marker 134). Turn east and drive 0.1 mile to a cattle guard. Turn left after the cattle guard and drive about 1 mile north along the right-of-way fence. Turn east onto BLM Road 8001 and drive 3.8 miles to a right-hand turn. Turn right (south) and drive 1.2 miles to the trailhead at road's end. This road requires a high-clearance two-wheel-drive vehicle.

In January 2001, President Bill Clinton designated the 496,337-acre Sonoran Desert National Monument. Encompassing a vast stretch of its namesake, this national monument incorporated three desert mountain ranges and the interceding basins into a single unit that typifies the seemingly sparse yet ecologically diverse desert lands west of Phoenix. Because much of this preserve is often overlooked by hikers, few actual hiking trails enter the expansive monument. One that does is the Margies Cove Trail, which penetrates the northern third of the monument.

From the trailhead, the Margies Cove Trail heads south for a bit before reaching the fenced boundary of the North Maricopa Mountains Wilderness. Shortly after this the trail turns east and then southeast. Because the Margies Cove Trail is following the gently sloping bottom of

Detail of hedgehog cactus along the Margies Cove Trail

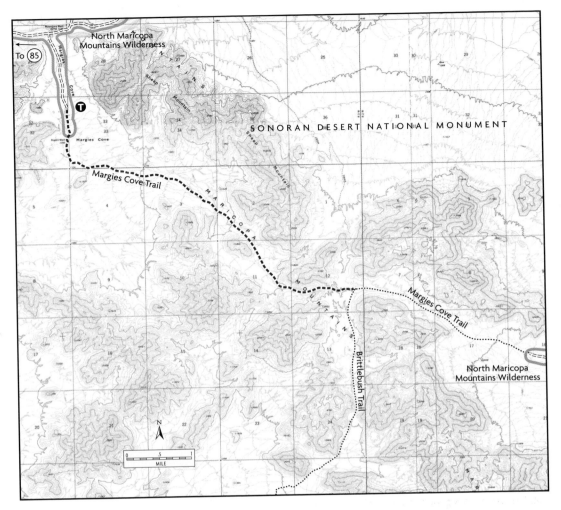

a broad basin, the hiking is particularly easy. In addition, because the first few miles follow an old jeep trail, the route is easy to find. Eventually, however, the former four-wheel-drive route ends and the trail begins following a heavily braided wash. Here the best strategy is to watch for widely spaced rock cairns and to follow the footprints of previous hikers. Up to this point the desert vegetation includes some nice stands of saguaro cactus, along with ocotillo, palo verde, and cholla cactus.

About 3.5 miles into the hike, the route enters a more defined wash complete with small rock walls. The scenery is limited, but the routefinding

is easy as the trail simply follows the sandy bottom of the wash. After following this shallow canyon for a ways, the Margies Cove Trail reaches its intersection with the Brittlebush Trail, which branches right to climb out of the wash; it eventually ends at the Brittlebush trailhead 6 miles south. From this intersection, the Margies Cove Trail continues for another 3.25 miles before reaching the east Margies Cove trailhead, which is reached via an 8.4-mile four-wheel-drive route that turns north from Maricopa Road.

Although this description turns around at the Margies Cove–Brittlebush Trail intersection, an interesting one-way hike would follow the

Margies Cove Trail for its entire length. Keep in mind that the shuttle drive around to the east end of the Margies Cove Trail is long and requires a four-wheel-drive vehicle.

**Be prepared:** Be sure to pack plenty of water because this is some of the most arid and desolate terrain in the state. Watch for rattlesnakes and flash flooding.

## 95 *Harquahala Peak*

*Distance:* 11 miles roundtrip
*Difficulty:* strenuous
*Hiking time:* 7 hours
*Elevation:* 2300 to 5681 feet
*Management:* BLM

*Wilderness status:* Harquahala WA
*Season:* October to May
*USGS map:* Harquahala Mountain
*GPS coordinates:* 33.858572 N, 113.355711 W

*Getting there:* To reach the trailhead for the Harquahala Pack Trail, drive west on US Highway 60 from Wickenburg (or east from Interstate 10) to between mile markers 70 and 71. Turn south on a dirt road (be sure to close the gate behind you) and drive 2.2 miles to the trailhead at road's end. This road requires a high-clearance two-wheel-drive vehicle.

Saguaro cactus along the Harquahala Pack Trail

At 5681 feet, Harquahala Peak is the tallest mountain in southwestern Arizona, and indeed its hulk strikes an impressive profile from miles around. Its geographical stature also made it the ideal spot to locate an early-day observatory. Completed in 1920, the Smithsonian Astrophysical Observatory provided scientists the opportunity to study solar activity. Today the observatory is just a cluster of abandoned buildings, but they nevertheless grace a visit to the summit. Although the top is accessed by a four-wheel-drive road, the 5.5-mile Harquahala Pack Trail—the primary nonmotorized access route to the observatory—offers hikers a highly scenic alternative to bouncing up the steep, rugged road.

Well maintained the entire way, the Harquahala Pack Trail is easy to follow. Within the first 0.5 mile, the trail ascends gently sloping bajada (alluvial deposits) that feature some nice saguaro cactus stands as well as cholla cactus, ocotillo, and creosote bush. As the trail nears steeper terrain, it reaches the site of a base camp built to supply the observatory. Except for a sign, some rusted barrels, and an old foundation, little marks that spot today. During the

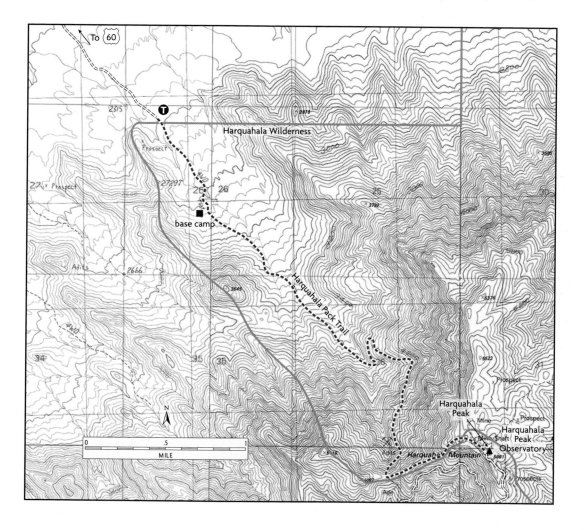

observatory's years of operation, however, it was a drop-off point for supplies to be carried up the pack trail by mule.

About 1.5 miles into the hike, the Harquahala Pack Trail reaches the toe of the steep mountainside, at which point it begins climbing in earnest. Through several switchbacks, the route rarely relents in its goal of gaining more than 3500 feet to reach the top. As you climb, you may note a change in vegetation. Eventually no saguaro cactus are to be found, and grasses, Mormon tea, and mountain mahogany are more commonplace. You will also pass the remains of some old mining camps that preceded the observatory by several years. These prospectors were in search of gold and silver, but their efforts went mostly unrewarded.

Nearly 5 miles in, the trail reaches a saddle that lies just west of the summit. From this point you look both north and south across several rugged ranges and broad basins. You can also see the summit above. From the saddle to the top it is a little less than a mile and 600 additional feet of climbing. Because a four-wheel-drive road reaches the summit from the south, there is a chance you may have to share your time on top with less hardy visitors.

The observatory was in use from 1920 to 1925 and, although it never had a telescope, equipment used there included a theodolite that measured the sun's height above the horizon, as well as other items used to study the sun. Data collected here were then compared with that collected at other sites.

**Be prepared:** When hiking up Harquahala Peak, bring plenty of water, as none is available along the way. Watch for poisonous snakes, and be especially mindful of lightning during stormy periods on the upper reaches of this highly exposed mountain. In addition, keep in mind that all antiquities—be they prehistoric or historic—are protected by law.

## 96 Ben Avery Trail

*Distance:* 4 miles roundtrip
*Difficulty:* easy
*Hiking time:* 3 hours
*Elevation:* 1700 to 1820 feet
*Management:* BLM
*Wilderness status:* Eagletail Mountains WA

*Season:* October to April
*USGS maps:* Eagletail Mountains East, Eagletail Mountains West
*GPS coordinates:* 33.461382 N, 113.371792 W

*Getting there:* To reach the northern trailhead for the Ben Avery Trail, drive west from Phoenix on Interstate 10 to Exit 81 and the turnoff for Harquahala Valley. Drive 5 miles south to Courthouse Rock Road and then turn west. Follow this good road for about 7 miles to where a natural gas pipeline road angles right. From this gravel route, several side roads turn left to lead a short way into the desert. After driving 10.8 miles from the turn onto Courthouse Rock Road, turn left and follow a high-clearance road 1.5 miles to its end and the trailhead.

Forming a rugged and scenic line of crags, buttes, and mountains in the desert between Phoenix and the California border, the Eagletail Mountains offer intrepid hikers a wonderful opportunity to explore some desolate yet interesting terrain. The best route for entering the area is the Ben Avery Trail. Named for a noted Arizona outdoor writer, this established trail cuts through the heart of the 100,600-acre Eagletail Mountains Wilderness.

Cholla cactus in early morning along the Ben Avery Trail

Following an old jeep route, the Ben Avery Trail heads south from the trailhead into the Eagletail Mountains Wilderness. Crossing open and gently rolling terrain, the route is easy to follow and a real pleasure. The surrounding plant life includes an array of Sonoran Desert species including saguaro cactus, ocotillo, cholla, palo verde trees, and creosote bush. You might also keep your eyes open for resident mule deer, desert bighorn sheep, bobcats, mountain lions, Gila monsters, and desert tortoises. Complementing the ecological interest of the area is some fine scenery. Passing just west of Courthouse Rock, the trail provides up-close views of the rugged Eagletail Mountains to the south and far-off views of the Bighorn Mountains to the east.

Approximately 1 mile from the trailhead, the route tops a low ridge before dropping into a wash. After following this dry streambed for another mile, the route then reaches the turnaround point for this hike, Indian Spring. Although no permanent source of water is found here, some interesting prehistoric petroglyphs can be spotted among the rocks along the wash. To protect natural resources, camping is prohibited within 0.25 mile of the spring.

To extend this hike, it is possible to continue south on the Ben Avery Trail. Over 12 miles in

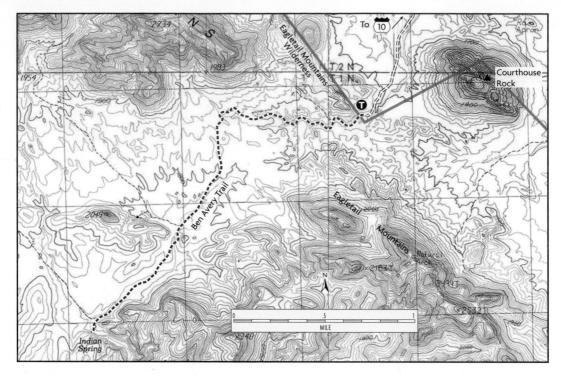

length, this trail continues into the central portion of the wilderness before reaching a second trailhead in the southeastern corner of the wilderness area. This access point can be reached by driving southwest on Arlington–Clanton Well Road.

**Be prepared:** Although summers can be quite hot in the Eagletail Mountains Wilderness, weather during late fall, winter, and early spring can be pleasant. Do not expect to find any water along this hike, and be wary of rattlesnakes and other venomous creatures.

## 97 *Bull Pasture*

**Distance:** 3.7 miles roundtrip
**Difficulty:** moderate
**Hiking time:** 3 hours
**Elevation:** 2360 to 3250 feet
**Management:** Organ Pipe Cactus NM

**Wilderness status:** Organ Pipe WA
**Season:** October to April
**USGS map:** Mount Ajo
**GPS coordinates:** 32.016028 N, 112.711924 W

**Getting there:** After making the drive to Organ Pipe Cactus National Monument from either Phoenix (drive south on Arizona Highway 85) or Tucson (drive west on Arizona Highway 86 to Arizona Highway 85 and turn south), stop at the visitor center and get up-to-date information on road conditions to the trailhead. From the visitor center, cross Arizona Highway 85 onto Ajo Mountain Drive, heading north. Be advised that this dirt road, although passable to cars, crosses washes that may become flooded during rainstorms, thereby closing it. The trailhead is located about 10.5 miles in, at the Estes Canyon Picnic Area.

Situated along a remote stretch of the Arizona–Mexico border, Organ Pipe Cactus National Monument encompasses a vast parcel of pristine desert country. Included among the twenty-eight species of cactus that grow here is the organ pipe cactus. Although common in Mexico, this strangely beautiful succulent is rare in the United States. The hike to Bull Pasture passes some fine specimens as it climbs into the monument's primary mountain range, the Ajos.

Roughly 0.1 mile beyond the trail's start, the route splits. The left-hand fork, the Estes Canyon Trail, winds gently up the bottom of Estes Canyon for 1.3 miles before ascending the canyon's south wall and reaching Bull Pasture 2.1 miles from the start. The right-hand fork climbs more directly to Bull Pasture—this route, known as the Bull Pasture Trail, makes the 850-foot climb in 1.5 miles. The two trails join 0.5 mile from the top, making for a nice loop hike. Whichever way you decide to go, there are steep grades to contend with, especially in the last 0.5 mile. The trail is often rough and rocky, so be sure to watch your footing. Bull Pasture, a broad, V-shaped basin surrounded by the rugged Ajo Mountains, is quite scenic.

The Ajos resulted from volcanic eruptions 14 million to 22 million years ago, and the alternating deposits of ash and lava left behind a range of color from ochre to deep red. Lichen adds a tint of yellow and green to many rock faces. Ranchers

In the spring Mexican poppies carpet the desert floor in Organ Pipe Cactus National Monument.

Bill and Birdie Miller once utilized this natural enclosure to winter their cattle. Today, grasslands interspersed with saguaro cactus and ocotillo cover much of the basin. Wildlife species found here include coyote, javelina, desert bighorn sheep, mountain lion, and a variety of birds.

Once at Bull Pasture, be sure to scramble up the rocky ridge a short distance to the west. From here you get excellent views of the basin-and-range topography that typifies southern Arizona and neighboring Mexico. From the summit of 4808-foot Mount Ajo (the high point of the monument) about 1 mile northeast of Bull Pasture, a clear day will provide a glimpse of the Gulf of California, some 70 miles to the southwest. Although no established trail climbs Mount Ajo, it is possible to pick your way for 2 miles or so up

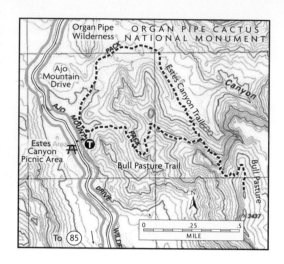

a ridge leading north to the peak. Check with the visitor center for more information.

**Be prepared:** Bring plenty of drinking water because temperatures can get quite hot along this trail. Do not attempt the hike in summer. Watch for rattlesnakes throughout the hike, and be wary of lightning during thunderstorms. Be sure to get a monument entrance permit from the visitor center. This trail is only open during daylight hours.

## 98 *Palm Canyon*

**Distance:** 1 mile roundtrip
**Difficulty:** easy
**Hiking time:** 1 hour
**Elevation:** 2100 to 2500 feet
**Management:** Kofa NWR

**Wilderness status:** Kofa Refuge WA
**Season:** October to April
**USGS map:** Palm Canyon
**GPS coordinates:** 33.360529 N, 114.106205 W

**Getting there:** Located off US Highway 95 between Yuma and Quartzsite in the southwestern corner of the state, Palm Canyon is part of the sprawling Kofa National Wildlife Refuge. Drive either 18 miles south from Quartzsite or 63 miles north from Yuma to the signed turnoff for the canyon. Follow this dirt road 7 miles east to the base of the imposing Kofa Mountains. This road is usually passable to all vehicles.

The short hike into Palm Canyon reveals one of nature's more alluring surprises. Tucked into a narrow abyss of the Kofa Mountains is a grove of naturally occurring palm trees. These, along with a few more in other secretive canyons of the Kofa Range, are thought to be one of the few places where you can find palms native to

Arizona. The name Kofa is an acronym adopted from the King of Arizona Mine in the southern end of the range.

From the parking area at road's end, an established trail leads into the high-walled canyon before you. It is only 0.5 mile to a sign that points north into a narrow side canyon. Growing in the upper reaches of this canyon are forty or so California fan palms and several seedlings. It is possible to scramble up to the trees for a closer look. Sitting among the palms and listening to their fronds rustle in the cool breeze imparts a marvelous appreciation of these venerable trees.

Two different theories explain the presence of these palms. One says that they were left over from the last ice age, when the environment was not so hot and dry. The other suggests that their seeds were transported via the digestive tracts of birds or coyotes. In either case, protected from direct sun and supplied with adequate moisture, these palms have been able to survive for many years. As precarious as their existence is, a fire in 1954 and thoughtless people etching their initials into the bark have not deterred them to any great degree.

Other plants found in Palm Canyon include the green-barked palo verde, ironwood, the rare Kofa Mountain barberry bush, and nolina—a plant that is sometimes mistaken for young palm trees. Desert bighorn sheep are frequently spotted in Palm Canyon. The entire 665,400-acre refuge, in fact, is home to several hundred desert bighorn sheep. Coyotes are common. Desert kit fox also live here, as do desert tortoises.

After enjoying the palm trees, you may want to venture farther up the main canyon and to the basin above. Although no trail exists, it is not too difficult to scramble among the boulders and scree slopes that litter the canyon bottom. Look back down the canyon to gain a good feel for the ruggedness of these mountains. The Kofas consist mostly of rhyolite, a volcanic rock.

**Be prepared:** Bring drinking water as none is found along the way. Because this is one of the hottest regions of the state, hiking Palm Canyon should be restricted to the cooler times of the year. Watch out for rattlesnakes and flash floods.

Among the stately native palms of Palm Canyon

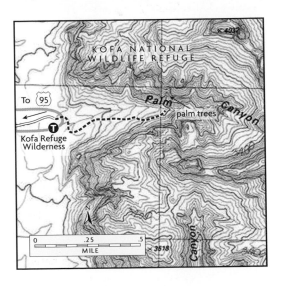

# 99 *Hualapai Mountain Park*

*Distance:* 4.3-mile loop
*Difficulty:* moderate
*Hiking time:* 3 hours
*Elevation:* 6814 to 7600 feet
*Management:* Mohave County Parks

*Wilderness status:* none
*Season:* May to October
*USGS map:* Hualapai Park
*GPS coordinates:* 35.096660 N, 113.889589 W

*Getting there:* From Kingman, turn south from Andy Devine Drive onto Hualapai Mountain Road and continue 12 miles to the park entrance. Drive another 0.7 mile to the Hualapai trailhead. Keep right at each of the several forks in the road between the park entrance and the trailhead to a small parking area.

Rising rather abruptly above Kingman, the Hualapai Mountains offer a welcome contrast to the arid desert basins below. Topping the 8000-foot level, the upper reaches of this range feature cool forests and a variety of wildlife. A pleasurable hike across this mountain terrain follows the Potato Patch Loop Trail in Hualapai Mountain Park, which is owned and operated by Mohave County.

Originally constructed in 1937 by the CCC and rebuilt in 1981 by the Youth Conservation Corps, the Hualapai Mountain Park trail system is well established and easy to follow. From the trailhead this hike first follows the Aspen Springs Trail for nearly a mile to where it connects with the northern end of the Potato Patch Loop Trail. Climbing along a mostly moderate grade, the Aspen Springs Trail switchbacks among stands of ponderosa pine and Gambel oak. As it nears the junction, however, Douglas fir and white fir become common. Some interesting outcrops of granite are encountered along the way as well.

Upon reaching the Aspen Springs/Potato Patch Loop Trail junction, this hike turns right to follow the loop counterclockwise. Shortly beyond, vistas to the north open up as the trail continues to gain in elevation. The rocky summit of Aspen Peak also comes into view directly

Granite boulders along the Potato Patch Loop Trail

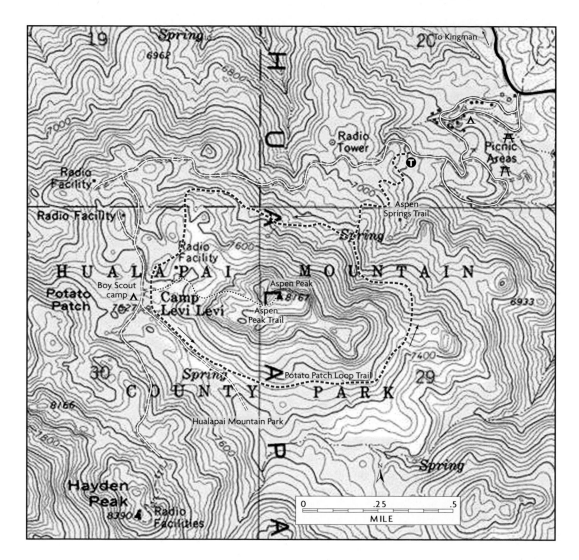

south. Near an interesting rock formation known as the Three Gossips, the trail encounters the first of several stands of aspen along the way. After passing beneath a powerline about 0.5 mile from the junction, the Potato Patch Loop Trail levels off and reaches its highest point. In the 1.5 miles from the trailhead to here, the hike gains about 800 feet.

The trail then drops slightly into a broad and scenic basin characterized by ponderosa pine and scattered aspens. The summit of Hayden

Peak (elevation 8390 feet) with its array of radio towers rises to the south, and Aspen Peak (elevation 8239 feet) lies directly east. Within a short distance the trail joins a dirt road, which it follows to the left for 100 yards or so. At a signed left turn the route takes up a foot trail again as it enters a rustic Boy Scout camp. The Aspen Peak Trail branches off nearby to access the summit, 0.6 mile away. Shortly after, the route reaches a second road and turns left to follow it for 25 yards or so before turning left again onto another road. Although this turn is not signed, you will know the way because it passes a large concrete block building. The trail follows this road through a string of established campsites (still part of the Scout camp) for 0.3 mile to where a foot trail turns left into the brush. This turn is signed.

Beyond this point, the Potato Patch Loop Trail climbs briefly as it skirts around Aspen Peak's south-facing slope. Drier than the opposite side of the mountain, this section of trail encounters open ponderosa pine and Gambel oak forests, along with some manzanita. This is a good area to spot mule deer or elk, both of which inhabit the Hualapai Mountains. You will also get an unobstructed view of nearby Hualapai Peak. At 8417 feet, this is the highest summit in the range. As with Hayden and Aspen Peaks, pine, fir, and aspen grow on Hualapai Peak's rocky and jagged façade.

Eventually, the Potato Patch Loop Trail rounds the eastern side of Aspen Peak to complete the circle. Along this section of trail several vistas take in the broad valley to the east and the Aquarius Mountains beyond. Return to the trailhead via the Aspen Springs Trail.

**Be prepared:** Although water may be available at the Boy Scout camp, there are no other reliable sources along the Potato Patch Loop Trail. Watch for lightning in exposed areas, especially during summer thunderstorms.

# 100 *Arizona Hot Spring*

| | |
|---|---|
| **Distance:** 6.4 miles roundtrip | **Wilderness status:** none |
| **Difficulty:** moderate | **Season:** October to May |
| **Hiking time:** 4 hours | **USGS map:** Ringbolt Rapids |
| **Elevation:** 1600 to 700 feet | **GPS coordinates:** 35.980171 N, |
| **Management:** Lake Mead NRA | 114.697441 W |

**Getting there:** From Kingman, drive north on US Highway 93 for about 67 miles to mile marker 4. Turn right onto a paved road, and follow it a short distance to the signed trailhead. If you are approaching from the north, the trailhead turnoff is just before mile marker 4, south of Hoover Dam. Turn left and cross the divided highway to reach the trailhead.

Though quite rugged and inhospitable (for hikers) during the warmer months of the year, Lake Mead National Recreation Area is not without its interesting backcountry excursions. One such hike leads down White Rock Canyon to the Colorado River and then on to Arizona Hot Spring.

From the trailhead the route drops into White Rock Canyon wash, which passes beneath the highway before heading west towards the Colorado River. Although no actual trail tread exists here, finding the way is easy in that you simply follow the wash bottom downstream.

About 0.4 mile from the trailhead the White Rock Canyon Route intersects the Hot Spring Canyon Route, which similarly leads to the hot spring but via more mountainous terrain to the south. (The Park Service brochure refers to these trails as Routes.) Because the Hot Spring Canyon Route approaches the spring from upstream, it bypasses a 20-foot-high ladder that must be climbed if you approach the spring from the Colorado River. This hike continues west along the White Rock Canyon Route to explore some interesting canyon narrows and to reveal a nice stretch of the Colorado River before reaching the spring.

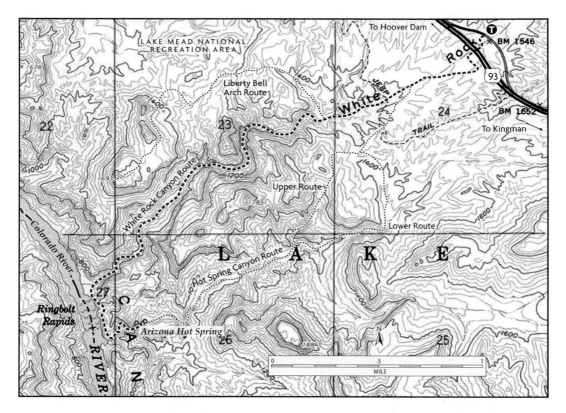

Just under a mile from the trailhead the White Rock Canyon Route connects with a second side trail known as the Liberty Bell Arch Route. This 1.5-mile trail accesses a scenic viewpoint that looks out over Black Canyon and the Colorado River. It does not, however, access the river or the hot spring. From this unmarked intersection the White Rock Canyon Route continues to follow its namesake as it becomes more defined by tall canyon walls. Interestingly, although this canyon cuts through dark red and even black volcanic rock, the canyon's name originated with many large boulders of white granite that washed down from nearby Mount Wilson during flash floods. Once inside White Rock Canyon the trail follows the canyon floor the rest of the way to the Colorado River. Some deep and narrow sections in the canyon add to the allure of this portion of the hike, but expect to find stretches of loose sand and occasional rocky areas that must be scrambled over along the way.

Despite the extreme climate of this desert environment, a variety of plants do manage to survive here. A partial list includes brittlebush, creosote bush, arrowweed, indigobush, globe mallow, mesquite, acacia, barrel cactus, and beavertail cactus. Some animals have adapted to living here as well. Most impressive are desert bighorn sheep, which favor the rugged walls of White Rock and other nearby canyons.

A little more than 2 miles from the trailhead the White Rock Canyon Route reaches a scenic bend in the Colorado River and Ringbolt Rapids. From the mouth of White Rock Canyon the trail continues downstream for another 0.5 mile or so before reaching the next side canyon to the south. This section of the hike passes among thickets of tamarisk as it climbs up and over outcrops of rock. Watch your footing along the way.

Upon reaching the mouth of the next side canyon south, turn left and follow the narrow drainage upstream. Although the hot spring is

The Colorado River near the mouth of White Rock Canyon

located less than 0.25 mile up the canyon, getting to it involves scrambling up some small drop-offs and climbing the 20-foot ladder. Use caution when climbing the ladder as it may be wet. Producing between 30 and 50 gallons of water per minute, the hot spring ranges in temperature from 85 to 120 degrees. Heated deep below the ground, this water contains a variety of minerals. According to the Park Service, it also contains *Naegleria fowleri,* a microorganism that can cause infection and even death. They suggest that you avoid splashing or submerging your head in the water because it can enter the body through the nasal passages.

**Be prepared:** Because temperatures can reach 120 degrees Fahrenheit in summer, do not attempt this hike between May and September. During the rest of the year, you still need to bring plenty of drinking water. A hat is also a good idea. Watch for rattlesnakes, and be aware of the possibility of flash floods during periods of storm activity.

# Appendix A:
# Land Management Agencies

## NATIONAL FORESTS

*Apache–Sitgreaves National Forest*
www.fs.usda.gov/main/asnf/home

**Alpine Ranger District**
P.O. Box 469
Alpine, AZ 85920
(928) 339-5000

**Clifton Ranger District**
397240 Arizona Highway 75
Duncan, AZ 85534
(928) 687-8600

**Springerville Ranger District**
P.O. Box 760
Springerville, AZ 85938
(928) 333-6200

*Coconino National Forest*
www.fs.usda.gov/main/coconino/home

**Flagstaff Ranger District**
5075 North Highway 89
Flagstaff, AZ 86004
(928) 526-0866

**Red Rock Ranger District**
P.O. Box 20429
Sedona, AZ 86341-0429
(928) 203-7500

*Coronado National Forest*
www.fs.usda.gov/main/coronado/home

**Douglas Ranger District**
1192 West Saddleview Road
Douglas, AZ 85607
(520) 364-3468

**Nogales Ranger District**
303 Old Tucson Road
Nogales, AZ 85621
(520) 281-2296

**Safford Ranger District**
711 14thAvenue, Suite D
Safford, AZ 85546
(928) 428-4150

**Santa Catalina Ranger District**
5700 North Sabino Canyon Road
Tucson, AZ 85750
(520) 749-8700

*Kaibab National Forest*
www.fs.usda.gov/kaibab

**Williams Ranger District**
742 South Clover Road
Williams, AZ 86046
(928) 635-5600

*Prescott National Forest*
www.fs.usda.gov/main/prescott/home

**Bradshaw Ranger District**
344 South Cortez Street
Prescott, AZ 86303
(928) 443-8000

**Chino Valley Ranger District**
735 North Highway 89
Chino Valley, AZ 86323
(928) 777-2200

**Verde Ranger District**
300 East Highway 260
Camp Verde, AZ 86322
(928) 567-4121

*Tonto National Forest*
www.fs.usda.gov/main/tonto/home

**Cave Creek Ranger District**
40202 North Cave Creek Road
Scottsdale, AZ 85262
(480) 595-3300

**Globe Ranger District**
7680 South Six Shooter Canyon Road
Globe, AZ 85501
(928) 402-6200

**Mesa Ranger District**
5140 East Ingram Street
Mesa, AZ 85205
(480) 610-3300

**Payson Ranger District**
1009 East Highway 260
Payson, AZ 85541
(928) 474-7900

## NATIONAL PARKS AND MONUMENTS
**Agua Fria National Monument**
21605 N. 7th Avenue
Phoenix, AZ 85027-2929
(623) 580-5500
www.blm.gov/az/st/en/prog/blm_special
_areas/natmon/afria.html

**Canyon de Chelly National Monument**
P.O. Box 588
Chinle, AZ 86503
(928) 674-5500
www.nps.gov/cach/index.htm

**Chiricahua National Monument**
12856 East Rhyolite Creek Road
Willcox, AZ 85643
(520) 824-3560
www.nps.gov/chir/index.htm

**Fort Bowie National Historic Site**
3327 Old Fort Bowie Road
Bowie, AZ 85605
(520) 847-2500
www.nps.gov/fobo/index.htm

**Glen Canyon National Recreation Area**
P.O. Box 1507
Page, AZ 86040
(928) 608-6200
www.nps.gov/glca/index.htm

**Grand Canyon National Park**
P.O. Box 129
Grand Canyon, AZ 86023
(928) 638-7888
www.nps.gov/grca/index.htm

**Grand Canyon–Parashant National Monument**
Interagency Information Center
345 East Riverside Drive
St. George, UT 84790
(435) 688-3200
www.nps.gov/para/index.htm

**Kofa National Wildlife Refuge**
9300 East 28th Street
Yuma, AZ 85365
(928) 783-7861
www.fws.gov/refuge/kofa

**Lake Mead National Recreation Area**
601 Nevada Way
Boulder City, NV 89005
(702) 293-8906
www.nps.gov/lake/index.htm

**Navajo National Monument**
P.O. Box 7717
Shonto, AZ 86045
(928) 672-2700
www.nps.gov/nava/index.htm

**Organ Pipe Cactus National Monument**
10 Organ Pipe Drive
Ajo, AZ 85321
(520) 387-6849
www.nps.gov/orpi/index.htm

**Petrified Forest National Park**
P.O. Box 2217
Petrified Forest National Park, AZ 86028
(928) 524-6228
www.nps.gov/Pefo/index.htm

## Saguaro National Park East
3693 South Old Spanish Trail
Tucson, AZ 85730-5601
(520) 733-5153
www.nps.gov/sagu/index.htm

## Saguaro National Park West
2700 North Kinney Road
Tucson, AZ 85743
(520) 733-5158
www.nps.gov/sagu/index.htm

## Sunset Crater Volcano National Monument
6400 North Highway 89
Flagstaff, AZ 86004
(928) 526-0502
www.nps.gov/sucr/index.htm

## Tonto National Monument
26260 North Arizona Highway 188 #2
Roosevelt, AZ 85545
(928) 467-2241 (ext. 8450 to make a reservation
  for ranger-led tours)
www.nps.gov/tont/index.htm

# BUREAU OF LAND MANAGEMENT

## Arizona Strip Field Office
345 East Riverside Drive
St. George, UT 84790-6714
(435) 688-3200
www.blm.gov/az/st/en/fo/arizona_strip
  _field.html

## Hassayampa Field Office
21605 North Seventh Avenue
Phoenix, AZ 85027-2929
(623) 580-5500
www.blm.gov/az/st/en/fo/hassayampa
  _field_office.html

## Lower Sonoran Field Office
21605 North Seventh Avenue
Phoenix, AZ 85027-2929
(623) 580-5500
www.blm.gov/az/st/en/fo/lower_sonoran
  _field.html

## Yuma Field Office
2555 East Gila Ridge Road
Yuma, AZ 85365-2240
(928) 317-3200
www.blm.gov/az/st/en/fo/yuma_field
  _office.html

# STATE PARKS

## Lost Dutchman State Park
6109 N. Apache Trail
Apache Junction, AZ 85219
(480) 982-4485
www.azstateparks.com/Parks/loDU
  /index.html

## Picacho Peak State Park
P.O. Box 907
Eloy, AZ 85131
(520) 466-3183
www.azstateparks.com/Parks/PIPE

# COUNTY AND MUNICIPAL PARKS

## City of Phoenix Parks and Recreation (Phoenix Mountains Park)
17642 North 40th Street
Phoenix, AZ 85032
(602) 262-6696
www.phoenix.gov/parks/trails/locations
  /piestewapeak

## City of Phoenix Parks and Recreation (South Mountain Park)
1346 East South Mountain Avenue
Phoenix, AZ 85040
(602) 262-6111
www.phoenix.gov/parks/trails/locations
  /south-mountain

## McDowell Mountain Regional Park
16300 McDowell Mountain Park Drive
MMRP, AZ 85255
(480) 471-0173
www.maricopa.gov/parks/mcdowell

**Mohave County Parks**
6250 Hualapai Mountain Road
Kingman, AZ 86401
(928) 681-5700
www.mcparks.com/parks/hualapai-mtn-park

**Tucson Mountain Park**
8451 West McCain Loop
Tucson, AZ 85735
(520) 877-6000
webcms.pima.gov/cms/one.aspx
   ?portalId=169&pageId=1539

**OTHER AGENCIES**
**Havasupai Tourist Enterprise**
P.O. Box 160
Supai, AZ 86435
(928) 448-2121
www.havasupaifalls.net

# Appendix B:
# Further Reading

## BOOKS ON BACKCOUNTRY SAFETY

Anderson, Kristi. *Wilderness Basics,* 4th ed. Seattle: Mountaineers Books, 2013.

Eng, Ron, ed. *Mountaineering: The Freedom of the Hills,* 8th ed. Seattle: Mountaineers Books, 2010.

Grubbs, Bruce. *Desert Sense: Camping, Hiking & Biking in Hot, Dry Climates.* Seattle: Mountaineers Books, 2005.

Johnson, Mark. *The Ultimate Desert Handbook: A Manual for Desert Hikers, Campers and Travelers.* Camden, ME: International Marine/Ragged Mountain Press, 2003.

## BOOKS ON HIKING IN ARIZONA

Grubbs, Bruce. *Hiking Arizona: A Guide to Arizona's Greatest Hiking Adventures,* 3rd ed. Guilford, CT: Globe Pequot Press, 2007.

Laine, Don, Barbara Laine, and Lawrence Letham. *Best Short Hikes in Arizona.* Seattle: Mountaineers Books, 2006.

Stieve, Robert. *Arizona Highways Hiking Guide.* Phoenix, AZ: Arizona Highways, 2011.

Warren, Scott S. *Exploring Arizona's Wild Areas,* 2nd ed. Seattle: Mountaineers Books, 2002.

# Index

Abineau/Bear Jaw Loop   62–63, 69
Africanized bees   19
Agassiz Peak   65, 67, 69
Agua Fria River National Monument   141, 142, 143
Airport Loop   89–90
Ajo Mountains   12, 237
Alpine Zone   13, 65
Amethyst Trail   160
Ancestral Puebloans   24, 49, 57, 59, 60
Apache Pass   21, 221
Apache trout   132
Arcadia National Recreation Trail   222–24
Arizona Hot Spring   242–44
Arizona Trail   14–15, 71, 73, 162
Aspen Loop   15, 198–200
Aspen Springs   Trail 240

Baboquivari Peak   205
Badger Springs Trail   141–43
Ballantine Trail   157, 158
Barnhardt Trail   161
Basin and Range   11, 12, 180
Bear Creek   187, 189
Bear Wallow   132–34
Bell Rock   93, 94
Bell Trail   101, 102
Ben Avery Trail   11, 234–36
Betatakin Cliff Dwelling   56
Big Lake   120, 122
Bill Williams Mountain   65, 75, 77–78, 106
Black Canyon Trail   144–46
Blue Mountains   82, 127
Blue Range Primitive Area   127, 129
Blue River   131
Bluff Spring Trail   172
Bluff Trail   156
Bog Springs   200–03
Bonanza Bill-Tige Rim Loop   128–32
Boulders, The   157–59
Boynton Canyon   91–92
Bridal Wreath Falls   185–87
Bright Angel Creek   36
Bright Angel Trail   24–27, 35, 38
Brittlebush Trail   231
Brown Mountain   179, 182–84

Browns Saddle   159–60
Buckskin Gulch   48, 49
Bull Pasture   236–38
Butcher Jones   153–55
Butterfield Overland Trail   221, 222

Canadian Zone   13
Canyon de Chelly National Monument   58–60
Catalina State Park   193
Cave Creek Trail   146–48
Cave Trail   169
Cheyava Falls   32
Chihuahuan Desert   221
Chiricahua Apache Indians   221, 222
Chiricahua Mountains   12, 180, 205, 212, 215, 216, 217, 218, 220
Chiricahua National Monument   207, 210, 212
Chiricahua Peak   212–14
Clear Creek Trail   15, 32–34
Cochise Stronghold   18, 206, 207
Cochise Trail   206–07
Coconino Plateau   60, 71, 76
Colorado Plateau   24, 42, 47, 82
Colorado River   24, 32, 41, 42, 45, 47, 50, 52, 54, 242, 243
Courthouse Butte Loop   93–94
Crest Trail   205, 212, 213, 214, 216

Derrick Trail   118, 120
Dripping Springs   30–31
Dutchmans Trail   20, 169–72

Eagletail Mountains   234, 236
East Baldy Trail   124, 125
Echo Canyon   210–12
Engelmann spruce   13, 213
Escalante, Silvestre Velez de   50
Escudilla Mountain   125–26
Esperanza Trail   180, 182
Estes Canyon Trail   237

Fat Mans Pass   140
Finger Rock Canyon   191–93
Flagstaff   11, 60, 61, 68, 71, 73
flash floods   19

Flys Peak  213
Fort Apache Indian Reservation  123, 124
Fort Bowie  21, 220–22
Fossil Springs  115–17
Four Peaks  158, 159
Fremont Peak  65, 67
Fremont Saddle  168, 169

Galiuro Wilderness  225
Geronimo  222
giardia  20
Glen Canyon  50
Grand Canyon  12, 24, 35, 37, 38, 44, 45, 52, 54, 65, 75
Grand Canyon–Parashant National
     Monument  43–44
Grandview Trail  27
Granite Mountain  107–09, 110, 112
Green Mountain  196–98
Groom Creek Loop  111–12

Hack Canyon  41
hantavirus  19
Harquahala Peak  232–34
Havasu Canyon  44–47
Havasu Falls  47
Havasupai Indians  45
Hayden Peak  242
Heart of Rocks  207–10
heat exhaustion  18
Heliograph Peak  223
Hermit Trail  30, 31
Hidden Valley  140–41
Hieroglyphic Canyon  14, 17, 165–66
Highline Trail  118, 120
Horse Canyon  226
Horseshoe Mesa  27, 28
Horton Creek Trail  118–20
Hot Spring Canyon  242
Huachuca Mountains  240
Hualapai Mountain Park  240–42
Hualapai Peak  242
Hudsonian Zone  13
Hugh Norris Trail  181
Humphreys Peak  24, 62, 64–65, 69
Hunter Trail  177
Hutchs Pool  190, 191
hypothermia  19

Icehouse Canyon  174–77

Indian Garden  24
Indian Spring  120–22
Inner Basin Trail  16, 68–69
Inner Gorge  24, 29, 32

Jacks Canyon  97–98

Kachina Trail  66–67
Kanab Creek  40–43
Keet Seel  56–58
Kendrick Mountain  65, 75–76, 77, 106
Kent Spring  201, 203
Kitt Peak  181, 184, 205
Kofa Mountains  238
Kofa National Wildlife Refuge  238

Lake Mead National Recreation Area  242
Lake Powell  52
Lees Ferry  49, 50
Lenox Crater  70–71
Leopold, Aldo  125
lightning  19
Little Colorado River  124
Lost Dutchman State Park  151, 169
Lost Dutchman's Mine  167, 169
Lower Sonoran Zone  13
Loy Canyon  95, 96

Madera Canyon  201, 203, 204, 215
Maple Camp  216
Marble Canyon  52, 53, 54
Margies Cove  230–32
Marshall Gulch Trail  198, 199
Mazatzal Divide Trail  162, 163
Mazatzal Mountains  12, 114, 158, 159
Mazatzal Peak  15, 161, 163
Mazatzal Peak Loop  161–63
McDowell Mountain Park  155–57
Mexican gray wolf  82, 121, 132
Mexico  205, 222, 226, 238
Mogollon Rim  12, 13, 65, 82, 95, 96, 101, 103, 105, 106,
     112, 115, 118
Montrose Canyon  194
Mooney Falls  46, 47
Mount Ajo  238
Mount Baldy  122–25
Mount Elden Lookout  60–61
Mount Graham  223
Mount Kimball  191, 193

Mount Lemmon   196, 205
Mount Trumbull   43–44
Mount Wrightson   203–05
Munds Mountain   97, 98

Narrows, The   48, 49
National Trail   140, 141
Navajo Indian Nation   56
Navajo National Monument   56–58, 59
Navajos   56, 57, 58, 59
Nelson Trail   113, 114, 115
North Kaibab Trail   15, 35–37, 40
North Rim   32, 35, 37, 39, 41

Oak Creek Canyon   65, 75, 82, 86, 98
Oak Flat   172–74
Old Apache Railroad   121
Old Baldy Trail   203, 204, 205
Onyx Bridge   54–56
Organ Pipe Cactus National Monument   236, 237

P-Bar Lake   127–29
Painted Bluff   134–36
Painted Desert   54, 65
Palm Canyon   238–39
Paria River Canyon   47–50
Parsons Spring   99–100
Pass Mountain Loop   148–51
Peralta Trail   167–69, 172
Petrified Forest National Park   54–56
Phantom Ranch   26, 32, 36
Phoenix   138, 139, 140, 142, 144, 146, 155, 160, 177, 234
Picacho Peak   177–78
Piestewa Peak   138–39
Pinal Peak   175
Pinaleno Mountains   12, 223
Pine Mountain   113–15
Pole Bridge Canyon   218–20
Pole Bridge Research Natural Area   218–19
Pomeroy Tanks   80
Potato Patch Loop Trail   240, 242
Powell, John Wesley   42
Powers Garden   179, 224–26
Prescott   107, 109, 110, 111
Pusch Ridge   194

rattlesnakes   19

Red Mountain   73–74
Red Rock Canyon Trail   218
Ribbon Falls   36
Rim Trail   78–80
Rincon Mountains   178, 181, 185, 205
riparian ecosystem   13, 14
Roaring Springs   35, 36
Romero Canyon   193–96
Rucker Canyon   216–18

Sabino Basin   191
Sabino Canyon   15, 189–91, 200
Saguaro National Park   180, 183, 185
San Carlos Apache Indian Reservation   134, 135
San Francisco Peaks   11, 12, 24, 61, 62, 64, 66, 68, 70, 75, 80, 106, 110, 112
Santa Catalina Mountains   12, 178, 180, 181, 187, 190, 191, 194, 198, 200
Santa Rita Mountains   180, 201, 203
Secret Mountain   95–97
Sedona   82, 85, 87, 89, 91, 94, 95, 97, 101
Seven Falls   187–89
Sky Islands   180
Smithsonian Astrophysical Observatory   205, 233
Soap Creek   52–54
Sonoran Desert   82, 221
Sonoran Desert National Monument   230
South Fork Cave Creek   215–16
South Kaibab Trail   27, 35
South Mountain Park   140
South Rim   27, 30
Spencer Trail   50–52
Spruce Mountain   110, 111, 112
Summit Trail   138, 139
sunburn   18
Sunset Crater National Monument   70–71
Super Trail   203, 204
Superstition Mountains   137, 138, 160, 166, 167, 169, 172, 173, 174
Sycamore Canyon   79–80, 99, 106
Sycamore Rim Trail   78–80

Thumb Butte Loop   109–10
Tonto National Monument   163–65
Tonto Plateau   27, 29, 32
Tonto Trail   15, 27–29, 31, 32
Tortilla Trail   225
Transition Zone   13

Treasure Loop    151–53
Tucson    12, 180, 182, 183, 185, 187, 193, 196, 200, 205
Tucson Mountain Park    182, 183, 187

Uncle Jim Trail    38–40
Upper Cliff Dwelling    163–65
Upper Sonoran Zone    13
Usery Mountain Regional Park    148

Verde Rim Trail    113, 114, 115
Verde River    99, 114
Vermilion Cliffs National Monument    47–50
Vultee Arch    87–88
Vulture Peak    227, 228–30

Walnut Canyon    15, 71–73
Wasson Peak    180–82
Weavers Needle    168, 169, 170, 172

West Baldy Trail    124
West Clear Creek    103–05
West Fork Oak Creek    82–84
Wet Beaver Creek    101–02
White House Ruin    58–60
White Mountains    11, 82, 122, 125
White Rock Canyon    227, 242, 243
Wickenburg    228, 232
Widforss Trail    37–38, 39
Wilderness Act    16
Wilderness of Rocks Trail    199
Willow Spring Trail    114
Wilson Mountain    84–87
Woodchute Mountain    105–06

Y Bar Basin Trail    163

Dark Vishnu schist rises along Inner Gorge along the Tonto Trail.

# About the Author

Scott S. Warren has lived in the American Southwest for over forty years. He has spent part of that time in Arizona exploring its many different natural areas. "What I really love about hiking in Arizona is the incredible variety of terrain and plant life," Warren says. "From cactus forests and canyon bottoms to lush forests and high alpine summits, Arizona has it all." In addition to writing about the outdoors, Warren is also a photographer. He holds a bachelor of fine arts degree in photography from Utah State University, and his images have appeared in *Audubon, Nature Conservancy, Outside, Sierra, Travel & Leisure, Time, Smithsonian,* and various *National Geographic* publications, as well as many books.

**MOUNTAINEERS BOOKS** is a leading publisher of mountaineering literature and guides—including our flagship title, *Mountaineering: The Freedom of the Hills*—as well as adventure narratives, natural history, and general outdoor recreation. Through our two imprints, Skipstone and Braided River, we also publish titles on sustainability and conservation. We are committed to supporting the environmental and educational goals of our organization by providing expert information on human-powered adventure, sustainable practices at home and on the trail, and preservation of wilderness.

The Mountaineers, founded in 1906, is a 501(c)(3) nonprofit outdoor activity and conservation organization whose mission is "to explore, study, preserve, and enjoy the natural beauty of the outdoors." One of the largest such organizations in the United States, it sponsors classes and year-round outdoor activities throughout the Pacific Northwest, including climbing, hiking, backcountry skiing, snowshoeing, bicycling, camping, paddling, and more. The Mountaineers also supports its mission through its publishing division, Mountaineers Books, and promotes environmental education and citizen engagement. For more information, visit The Mountaineers Program Center, 7700 Sand Point Way NE, Seattle, WA 98115-3996; phone 206-521-6001; www.mountaineers.org; or email info@mountaineers.org.

Our publications are made possible through the generosity of donors and through sales of more than 600 titles on outdoor recreation, sustainable lifestyle, and conservation. To donate, purchase books, or learn more, visit us online:

MOUNTAINEERS BOOKS

1001 SW Klickitat Way, Suite 201 • Seattle, WA 98134

800-553-4453 • mbooks@mountaineersbooks.org • www.mountaineersbooks.org

 Mountaineers Books is proud to be a corporate sponsor of the Leave No Trace Center for Outdoor Ethics, whose mission is to promote and inspire responsible outdoor recreation through education, research, and partnerships. • The Leave No Trace program is focused specifically on human-powered (nonmotorized) recreation. • Leave No Trace strives to educate visitors about the nature of their recreational impacts and offers techniques to prevent and minimize such impacts. • Leave No Trace is best understood as an educational and ethical program, not as a set of rules and regulations. • For more information, visit www.lnt.org or call 800-332-4100.

## OTHER TITLES YOU MIGHT ENJOY FROM MOUNTAINEERS BOOKS

**Best Hikes with Dogs Arizona**
Renée Guillory
More than 70 dog-legal and dog-fun hikes
to enjoy with your four-legged partner

**Weekend Rock Arizona**
Lon Abbott
Trad and sport routes from 5.0 to 5.10a with
no long approaches and close to urban areas;
ideal for busy people who need to climb

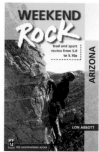

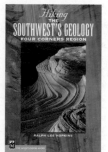

**Hiking the Southwest's Geology**
Ralph Lee Hopkins
Fifty diverse hikes explore
the Four Corners Region

**Red Rock Canyon: A Climbing Guide**
Roxanna Brock and Jared McMillen
More than 1500 trad and sport routes, all in
Red Rock Canyon National Conservation Area

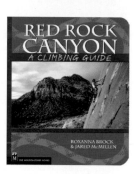

**Resurrection: Glen Canyon and a
New Vision for the American West**
Annette McGivney, photography by James Kay
"Through insightful narrative and stunning
photographs, Annette McGivney and James Kay
introduce us to an ecological miracle that
is occurring in the American Southwest:
the reemergence of the Glen Canyon."
— Robert Redford

**The Last Voyageur**
Vince Welch
The definitive biography of Amos Burg,
the only person to have paddled the
great Western rivers from source
to mouth prior to their damming

www.mountaineersbooks.org